Goth Culture

Gender, Sexuality and Style

D0223572

Dunja Brill

Oxford • New York

First published in 2008 by
Berg
Editorial offices:
1st Floor, Angel Court, 81 St Clements Street, Oxford, OX4 1AW, UK
175 Fifth Avenue, New York, NY 10010, USA

Berg is the imprint of Oxford International Publishers Ltd.

Library of Congress Cataloguing-in-Publication Data
Brill, Dunja.
   Goth culture : gender, sexuality and style / Dunja Brill.
     p. cm.
   Includes bibliographical references and index.
   ISBN-13: 978-1-84520-767-0 (cloth)
   ISBN-10: 1-84520-767-X (cloth)
   ISBN-13: 978-1-84520-768-7 (pbk.)
   ISBN-10: 1-84520-768-8 (pbk.)
   1. Goth culture (Subculture)—Great Britain. 2. Goth culture (Subculture)—
United States. 3. Goth culture (Subculture)—Germany. 4. Sex role. I. Title.

   HQ796.B6887 2008
   306'.10941—dc22   2008032686

British Library Cataloguing-in-Publication Data
A catalogue record for this book is available from the British Library.

ISBN 978 184520 767 0 (Cloth)

ISBN 978 184520 768 7 (Paper)

Typeset by Avocet Typeset, Chilton, Aylesbury, Bucks
Printed by the MPG Books Group in the UK

www.bergpublishers.com

ulture

A
[

Dress, Body, Culture

Series Editor: **Joanne B. Eicher,** *Regents' Professor, University of Minnesota*

Advisory Board:
Ruth Barnes, *Ashmolean Museum, University of Oxford*
James Hall, *University of Illinois at Chicago*
Ted Polhemus, *Curator, 'Street Style' Exhibition, Victoria and Albert Museum*
Griselda Pollock, *University of Leeds*
Valerie Steele, *The Museum at the Fashion Institute of Technology*
Lou Taylor, *University of Brighton*
John Wright, *University of Minnesota*

Books in this provocative series seek to articulate the connections between culture and dress which is defined here in its broadest possible sense as any modification or supplement to the body. Interdisciplinary in approach, the series highlights the dialogue between identity and dress, cosmetics, coiffure and body alternations as manifested in practices as varied as plastic surgery, tattooing, and ritual scarification. The series aims, in particular, to analyze the meaning of dress in relation to popular culture and gender issues and will include works grounded in anthropology, sociology, history, art history, literature and folklore.

ISSN: 1360-466X

Recently published titles in the series

Brian J. McVeigh, *Wearing Ideology: The Uniformity of Self-Presentation in Japan*
Shaun Cole, *Don We Now Our Gay Apparel: Gay Men's Dress in the Twentieth Century*
Kate Ince, *Orlan: Millennial Female*
Nicola White and Ian Griffiths, *The Fashion Business: Theory, Practice, Image*
Ali Guy, Eileen Green and Maura Banim, *Through the Wardrobe: Women's Relationships with their Clothes*
Linda B. Arthur, *Undressing Religion: Commitment and Conversion from a Cross-Cultural Perspective*
William J.F. Keenan, *Dressed to Impress: Looking the Part*
Joanne Entwistle and Elizabeth Wilson, *Body Dressing*
Leigh Summers, *Bound to Please: A History of the Victorian Corset*
Paul Hodkinson, *Goth: Identity, Style and Subculture*
Michael Carter, *Fashion Classics from Carlyle to Barthes*
Sandra Niessen, Ann Marie Leshkowich and Carla Jones, *Re-Orienting Fashion: The Globalization of Asian Dress*
Kim K. P. Johnson, Susan J. Torntore and Joanne B. Eicher, *Fashion Foundations: Early Writings on Fashion and Dress*
Helen Bradley Foster and Donald Clay Johnson, *Wedding Dress Across Cultures*
Eugenia Paulicelli, *Fashion under Fascism: Beyond the Black Shirt*
Charlotte Suthrell, *Unzipping Gender: Sex, Cross-Dressing and Culture*
Yuniya Kawamura, *The Japanese Revolution in Paris Fashion*
Ruth Barcan, *Nudity: A Cultural Anatomy*
Samantha Holland, *Alternative Femininities: Body, Age and Identity*
Alexandra Palmer and Hazel Clark, *Old Clothes, New Looks: Second Hand Fashion*
Yuniya Kawamura, *Fashion-ology: An Introduction to Fashion Studies*
Regina A. Root, *The Latin American Fashion Reader*
Linda Welters and Patricia A. Cunningham, *Twentieth-Century American Fashion*
Jennifer Craik, *Uniforms Exposed: From Conformity to Transgression*
Alison L. Goodrum, *The National Fabric: Fashion, Britishness, Globalization*
Annette Lynch and Mitchell D. Strauss, *Changing Fashion: A Critical Introduction to Trend Analysis and Meaning*
Marybeth C. Stalp, *Quilting: The Fabric of Everyday Life*
Jonathan S. Marion, *Ballroom: Culture and Costume in Competitive Dance*

Contents

List of Illustrations

Acknowledgements

The completion of this book would not have been possible without the kind help and support of various people and institutions. My sincere thanks go to: the DAAD (German Academic Exchange Service) and the former Research Centre for Culture and Communication of Sussex University for funding my research; Dr Caroline Bassett and Dr Michael Bull for their encouragement and competent supervision throughout the research process; Prof. Barbara Einhorn, Prof. Liesbet van Zoonen and Prof. Martina Claus-Bachmann for invaluable critical comments and suggestions regarding my approach and argumentation; Hannah Shakespeare for helpful guidance throughout the publication process; Dr Paul Hodkinson for an extremely useful and perceptive review of the manuscript, and for generous advice on various matters regarding the publication; SaRn Satino and Synara for proofreading the text and many enlightening discussions about my findings; and – last but not least – the numerous Goths in Brighton, Edinburgh, Cologne/Bonn and Berlin who agreed to be interviewed, and who shared valuable information and sometimes very personal views and feelings with me.

Very special thanks go to: Amanda Michl for encouragement during the writing process, and for patient help with typing and formatting the manuscript; Dieter and Karin Brill for their continuing support throughout my educational career, and for always believing in me.

Setting the Scene

Spring 1992, the Ballhaus, an underground venue in the centre of Bonn (Germany). Eerie, wailing guitar sounds, deep husky vocals and pounding drumbeats fill the foggy air of the small club. On the dance floor I see theatrical, mysterious figures and shapes slowly moving in the fog. Most wear flowing velvet dresses or capes, elaborate make-up and long black hair, and even when the fog lifts for a moment it is often hard to tell whether these strange, beautiful, black-clad creatures elegantly swaying their bodies are male or female. In fascination, I watch a girl with pale make-up, dark lipstick and heavy black eyeliner, wearing a hooded velvet cape around her frail body. Only when my eyes are caught by the waving movements of the rather large, bony hands sticking out of the wide black sleeves do I realise that 'she' is actually a boy. In my plain black jeans and shirt, I feel slightly out of place among all these meticulously styled, arcane beings, but still I am instantly hooked. A rather inconspicuous, bookish girl of eighteen, I have just discovered Alternative music for myself, and this is my first encounter with the Gothic subculture.

A Researcher between Two Worlds – or: My Life as a Transnational Part-time Goth

Spring 2003, Lowlife, a Goth clubnight in Brighton (England). More than a decade later I am again sitting in the corner of a smoke-filled club, watching people dance. The eerie guitar sounds have become rare over the years; the rhythms have got faster and harsher, and so have the dance styles. I spot a man with a crew cut, combat fatigues and a muscle shirt, stomping back and forth in a martial manner to the sound of distorted electronic beats. Next to him there is a girl dressed in a tight black PVC corset, miniskirt and high-heeled platform boots, whose tiny-stepped, wriggly dancing somehow calls to mind a dark, lascivious nightclub sequence from a David Lynch movie. A woman in a luxurious medieval dress is sitting in the corner opposite me, obviously waiting for more mellow sounds to resume the gentle, fairylike dancing she displayed earlier.

All these people have long lost their mysterious, untouchable air to me; in fact many of these 'strange creatures' are now my friends or acquaintances. However, I again feel a certain distance as I am watching with a critical eye, jotting down field notes. Today I am here mainly as an academic researcher, gathering data in order to answer some questions which have formed in my head during my long years of active participation in the Gothic subculture. Over these years, I have moved from the initial uncritical fascination of someone who has just discovered a new world for herself, into a phase of disillusionment at encountering all too familiar flaws in this world, and finally to a realistic, almost mundane perspective on the once so arcane subculture. Now twenty-nine, I have gradually turned into what the subculture jokingly calls a 'sad old Goth'. I have spent countless nights in Goth clubs in Cologne and Bonn where I originally hail from, in Edinburgh and Brighton where I spent some years studying, and I am just about to head off to Berlin for another year of fieldwork experience. Hence it has always seemed a perfectly natural idea to combine my passion for Goth with my equally strong passion for sound academic research.

Balancing the 'Goth' and the 'researcher' part of me did not always come quite as naturally. Yet the fact that my long-standing relationship with the subculture has always been somewhat conflicted may have made it a bit easier for me to look at Goth from a relatively detached perspective. Never having been a very dressy person, my first visit to a Goth club was actually not the only time I felt slightly out of place on the dimly lit yet highly scrutinised catwalks of Gothic style to which many of the scene's spaces amount. Goth certainly offered many facets of subcultural engagement, enabling me to participate as an avid reader and active contributor to various fanzines, as a music connoisseur and even as a singer. As a woman who was never too keen on performing the routines of femininity, however, I experienced subtle yet insistent pressure to perform subcultural rituals of dress and beauty which, in part, were simply not for me.

Starting my fieldwork in a city and country which were foreign to me – namely Brighton – also helped me a great deal in developing a necessary sense of distance from my object of study. Goths are a friendly yet pretty reserved bunch, especially when it comes to a stranger turning up alone at a local Goth club, trying to ask people strange questions. So in spite of my own Gothic leanings, my thorough insider knowledge of the German scene and my moderate yet suitably dark styling, I basically had to start from scratch. It took some time and effort for me to become familiar with the 'field', to gain the trust and sometimes friendship of my 'informants', and to establish an overall understanding of the 'social milieu' under scrutiny.

Later, jetting back and forth between the different regions and the two nations where I carried out my fieldwork, I more and more developed the skill of using differing degrees of 'distance' and 'closeness' strategically, managing to frame my field experiences accordingly. In fairly new research settings (e.g. the thriving scene in Berlin when I first arrived there), I found ways to make the strange more familiar, drawing on my vast experiences of other local settings. In all too familiar settings (e.g. the small scene in my former home town of Bonn), I employed strategies to make the routine seem strange, consciously recreating the mindset which had accompanied my first fieldwork experiences in Brighton. In short, I took on the subjectivity of a transnational part-time Goth, somewhere in the middle between native and foreign, between indulgent participant and relentless researcher – and that is, I hope, what has made my vision of a poignantly critical insider study work.

Throughout my personal involvement in Goth, I have always been intrigued by one particular aspect of the subculture; namely, its generous use of ambiguously gendered imagery. I have long wondered what really lies behind the seemingly 'genderless' but at the same time heavily gender-saturated styles, practices and images of Goth. From this general paradox, three central questions can be distilled. How are masculinity, femininity and sexuality represented in Gothic style (dress, body stylisation) and media (music, magazines, Internet forums)? How do the gendered style practices of Goths and the gendered representations in Gothic media relate to the subjectivities of male and female Goths? And finally, how do these gendered practices and representations relate to subcultural status hierarchies? The present ethnographic study of gender, sexuality, dress and representation in the Gothic subculture explores these questions and comes up with some quite surprising insights into the obscure world of Goth.

A Brief Cross-cultural History of Goth

The Gothic subculture emerged in Britain in the early 1980s, in the wake of a musical genre originally referred to as Post-punk (Gunn, 1999). The characteristic features of this genre – whose early protagonists included bands like Bauhaus and Siouxsie and the Banshees – were echoing guitars, slow, repetitive drums and wailing vocals fused into an eerie, hazy sound. Song lyrics revolved around the dark recesses of the human soul: death, suffering and destruction as well as unfulfilled romance and isolation, but also the more arcane, taboo aspects of magic and mythology (e.g. ancient rituals, vampires). The presentation of this music involved elements of theatrical performance, most notably pale make-up, black clothes and melodramatic gestures. Adopted and further developed by the fans of the genre, these performative features came to constitute the mainstays of what is called *Goth*, *Gothic* or simply *Black* style.[1]

It is impossible to identify the exact point in time when the term Gothic was associated with this particular kind of underground music and style. However, the links between the two historical meanings of the term – a form of medieval architecture and a genre of nineteenth-century Romantic horror novels – and its present incarnation as a subculture are easily discernible. Goth in its modern form draws liberally on these epochs of cultural history (Baddeley, 2002), and its disciples revel in tracing back its lineage to sources in the distant past. Consequently, medieval music, Romantic poetry and the fine arts in general are revered as ardently as the current stars of the scene.

Goths' predilection for all things ancient and Romantic is also reflected in their dress style. Traditional Goth chic is, above all, black clothing, along with a penchant for precious fabrics like velvet, lace or leather and stylistic inspirations from Victorian era dress (e.g. corsets, lace-up dresses, pirate shirts). Other traditional features of Gothic style include elaborately modelled, long, black-dyed hair, thick black eye make-up with white grounding, and lots of silver jewellery (e.g. crosses, magical symbols, skulls, bats). However, Goth music and style have evolved and diversified considerably over the last two decades. The 1990s saw a rise in electronic music and Fetish style (e.g. PVC, rubber, piercings) in Goth clubs. These elements have been widely adopted and have partly relegated the more traditional Gothic style of flowing velvet garments to the margins of the scene.

While still displaying significant levels of cultural substance (see Hodkinson, 2002, 2004) in sharing distinct spaces and tastes, the Gothic subculture has spawned a host of internal factions, ranging from 'Cyber' to 'Middle Ages'. The internal structure of the scene today presents itself more as a conglomerate of overlapping subgroups, which differ considerably in style and music despite displaying a relatively strong collective distinctiveness vis-à-vis general culture. Moreover, the changes and diversifications within the subculture have taken different shapes in different countries. Since its inception in Britain Goth has spread throughout the world, with different countries and regions generating or adopting new subcultural trends to varying degrees at varying points in time.

In the early 1990s the second wave of Goth shifted its impetus from Britain to Germany, which has since been the unrivalled epicentre of the scene. While the subculture lay dormant in large parts of the world, in Germany a thriving network of independent record labels, magazines, clothing companies and event promoters specialising in Goth developed throughout the 1990s (Matzke and Seeliger, 2000). In Britain and other countries, by contrast, Goth has remained largely 'underground' in the last decade. The following sections give an overview of recent developments in the national scenes in Germany, Britain, the rest of Europe, the US and Asia.

Germany

The most striking feature of the German Gothic scene is the fact that it has grown much larger than in any other country,[2] making inroads into the cultural mainstream even in commercial terms. With a good selection of news-stand Goth magazines (e.g. *Orkus*, *Sonic Seducer*), various 'Black' summer festivals (e.g. Wave-Gotik-Treffen, M'Era Luna) which routinely draw audiences of 15,000 to 20,000 people, and a plethora of professional bands and record labels (e.g. Trisol, Out of Line), German Goths today are spoiled for choice. The German scene has spawned a number of financially successful individuals who can earn a good living through their subcultural activities. Many people who started fanzines, bands or labels in the early or mid-1990s have become what Duncombe (1997, p. 163) calls 'subcultural entrepreneurs'; they have managed 'to launch themselves or their zines into the commercial media world'.

Because of its sheer size and growing commercial success, the German scene also attracts many 'hangers-on' or peripheral members. As Goth has become more and more accessible and less arcane in Germany, with its magazines and commercially successful bands, it draws quite a few people who entertain a liking for Goth music, clubs and styling without necessarily going the whole way in terms of adopting the style and centring their social life around the subculture. Furthermore, the expanding German scene is a lot more fractured than the smaller scenes of other countries, harbouring a number of sometimes conflicting subgroups under its wide-ranging 'Black' umbrella.

Despite the bustling cross-fertilisation between national scenes in the age of the Internet, German Goths have developed some distinctive and fairly idiosyncratic musical and sartorial styles. A prime example is German Goths' widespread obsession with the Middle Ages, which has spawned a phenomenon dubbed *Middle Ages Goth*. So-called 'Middle Ages Rock', a crossover between secular medieval music and Rock, has become extremely popular on the German scene over the last few years but is almost unheard of in Britain, for example. Through mingling with the Role-playing scene, a whole Middle Ages faction has developed within the German 'Black' subculture. This faction listens to medieval or quasi-medieval music and tries to emulate medieval costume, while enjoying Middle Ages enactments or markets and often displaying a strong interest in the customs of the times.

An even bigger but less nationally restricted substream is the *EBM/Electro/Industrial* faction, whose origins lie in Germany and Belgium. Its mostly male devotees listen to harsh, beat-driven electronic music and dress in muscle shirts or band T-shirts, combat trousers, army boots and crew cuts for men and less specific Fetish-inspired dress (e.g. PVC trousers, hot pants or miniskirts) for women. While many of the more traditional Goths do not regard EBM with its militant, macho style as a proper part of the Gothic subculture, the fact remains that self-declared Goths and Electroheads hare the same spaces and events, and often the same music. Today most of the music played at Goth clubs is of the electronic, beat-driven variety, and Electro, EBM and its various subgenres are among the most popular musical styles in the Gothic subculture in general. This trend towards harsher electronic music first took off and is still strongest on the German scene, but has also gained prominence in many other national scenes (e.g. Britain and the US).

A smaller yet much more controversial current in the German Gothic scene, which has been growing over the last few years, is the *Neo-folk* faction. This faction centres around a dark style of folk-inspired music and a strong interest in German and European history. Customising pieces of military uniforms for – especially male – Goth style is a particularly widespread practice among Neo-folk fans, who have gained a certain notoriety for their flirting with military or even totalitarian chic. Some of the biggest bands in Neo-folk hail from Britain (e.g. Death in June, Sol Invictus). Yet over the last decade a thriving scene of

German bands has developed, and Neo-folk is now much more popular among German Goths than among British ones.

Great Britain

As the Neo-folk example indicates, it is impossible to draw a rigid dividing line between German and British Goth despite the existence of certain idiosyncratic factions, especially as far as music and its media representation are concerned. Apart from a few subgenres and substyles which are popular in one country but not in the other, there has always been a strong cross-fertilisation between the two scenes. Many German Goths still listen to the early British cult bands (e.g. Sisters of Mercy, Bauhaus), and many British Goths – among them a lot of DJs – now look to Germany for new bands and styles. Triggered by and also further triggering this cross-national interest in new music, Gothic magazines from any country regularly report on bands from abroad.

However, there is a crucial difference between the media and music-related infrastructures of British and German Goth in terms of their political economy. In Britain, involvement in subcultural production and organisation has remained largely a labour of love, with a relatively low degree of financial gain. There are a number of small record labels (e.g. Nightbreed, Wasp) and specialised fanzines (e.g. *Meltdown, Kaleidoscope*), yet even the longest-running titles have never gone monthly, let alone made it to the news-stand. Although cities like London, Edinburgh and Manchester have a good Gothic club scene, the biggest British festival (the Whitby Gothic Weekend) only draws around 2,000 people.[3] With this 'underground' status comes a high level of commitment to the Gothic lifestyle among British Goths. As Hodkinson (2002) shows, they generally display a strong and fairly exclusive investment in the subculture in their identities and going-out habits.

The most prominent idiosyncratic faction on the British scene is *Cyber Goth*, a style characterised by brightly coloured hair extensions in dreadlock shapes, UV-reflective materials and other futuristic gadgets and high, clumpy platform boots. Cyber – which is linked to a melodic, fairly upbeat style of electronic music – emerged in the London area and has become particularly widespread in south-east England. While it used to be a distinctly British phenomenon in the 1990s, the new millennium has seen Cyber Goth enclaves springing up in bigger cities throughout Germany and the Netherlands.

Other European Countries

While Germany and Britain undoubtedly host the leading and most thriving Goth scenes in Europe, other European countries have also nourished quite substantial scenes and generated their own brand of innovations in music and style. Foremost are the Scandinavian countries, which have always harboured strong Metal scenes and around the mid-1990s contributed a new facet to the international face of Goth in the form of a hybrid genre named *Gothic Metal*. This genre has become enormously popular among Goths throughout continental Europe, and some of its early protagonists (e.g. Nightwish from Finland) have managed to rise to chart-breaking fame. The musical crossover between Gothic and Metal has led to an influx into the Gothic scene of people with a (Black or Death) Metal background – who prefer a dark version of Metal style with black leather trousers and coats, heavy boots, band T-shirts and unstyled long hair – not only in Scandinavia but also in Germany.

The south of Europe has also spawned a couple of internationally renowned Goth bands, for instance Ataraxia (Italy) and Moonspell (Portugal). France, Italy and Spain boast a small yet lively Gothic club scene in cities like Paris, Rome and Barcelona. Eastern Europe has made up for its late start in terms of subcultural developments after the fall of the Iron Curtain, with Poland and Hungary in particular establishing a viable network of bands, gigs and underground clubs across their bigger cities.

Most Goths from the south or east of Europe orient themselves towards the vast and well-organised Goth music and festival landscapes of Germany, and to a much lesser extent Britain, travelling to big events like the Wave-Gotik-Treffen if they can afford it. This is all the more true of Germany's smaller neighbouring countries, although some of the biggest names in German-language Gothic Rock (e.g. Lacrimosa from Switzerland and L'Ame Immortelle from Austria) hail from there. The Netherlands represent something of an exception here, in that Dutch Goths seem far more inspired by the British scene and have even taken on the 'Cyber' current of Goth.

The US

In the US, Goth took off only a bit later than in Britain, with bands like Christian Death popularising a slightly rougher style of Gothic Rock referred to as *Death Rock* from the early 1980s onwards. In the early 1990s US Goth received a new lease of life through the rise to fame of bands like Marilyn Manson and Nine Inch Nails. These bands are not usually regarded as producers of Goth music proper but still share many of the genre's dominant themes and atmospheres in the form of mixing dystopian electronics with heavy guitar riffs – a mix now dubbed *Industrial Metal*.

Apart from the millions of Manson fans, who tend to be seen as 'Spooky Kids' rather than Goths, the US Gothic scene has remained pretty much an underground phenomenon. The vast size of the United States, in terms of both territory and population, means that it harbours a considerable number of Goths, but also that these are dispersed across huge distances. Apart from big cities like New York or Los Angeles, which have a well-developed club and gig infrastructure, US Goth happens mostly online. With a plethora of news-groups, chatrooms and websites catering for Goths, in the US – even more than in other countries – a virtual Gothic community has established itself alongside the actual network of clubs and venues.

The biggest Goth festival is Convergence, an annual event organised through the *alt.gothic* newsgroup. Besides the growing popularity of electronic styles of music on the US scene, there has been a Death Rock revival of sorts over the last couple of years, which has been associated mainly with the thriving music scene of Los Angeles. This Death Rock revival and its prominent bands (e.g. London After Midnight, Cinema Strange) have also been taken up enthusiasti-cally abroad, in particular on the German Gothic scene. Alternatively called *Batcave* after an early London cult club, modern Death Rock harks back to the origins of Goth in Post-punk music and style, with mohawks and ragged yet feminine black clothes – e.g. ripped tights and mesh, Punk-style miniskirts or tight trousers – for both genders.

Asia

Asia used to be a blank spot on the map of international Goth for the first two decades after its inception, especially through the eyes of the self-consciously Western-oriented European and US-American scenes. The Western monopoly over Goth has ended in the new millennium, though, with fresh bands and styles hailing from Japan gaining worldwide recognition among Goths, espe-cially in Germany. There the biggest Gothic magazine, *Orkus*, has started promoting 'exotic' bands like Moi Dix Mois and Dir En Grey with several cover stories.

These Japanese bands largely play a mix of 1980s Goth influences, dark Metal and so-called *Visual Kei*, a Japan-bred style of Rock/pop music which has traditionally hinged on the use of pompous stage costume, make-up and styling that bears a strong resemblance to Western Gothic styles. This crossover between Japanese Visual Kei and Western Goth influences has also partly trig-gered the popularisation of a dress style dubbed *Gothic Lolita* among young Japanese females and to a lesser extent males with or without Goth leanings. Gothic Lolita fashion can be described as a frilly, playful and sometimes darkly twisted mixture of 'French maid' and Manga-style, girly school uniform attire, and is also popular among German fans of Japanese Goth Rock and Visual Kei.

It should be said that the more 'serious' Goth fans in Japan generally insist on distancing their musical and sartorial tastes from Visual Kei, which tends to be seen as a rather shallow fad by proponents of a classic Western-style Gothic sensibility. In recent years some regular Goth clubnights have sprung up in Tokyo, where sweetish Gothic Lolitas with their frills and bonnets happily mingle with Goths in more traditional or Fetish dress, dancing mostly to European and US varieties of guitar-based or electronic Goth music but also enjoying home-grown bands.

Lifestyles, Values, Practices

The Gothic subculture displays some characteristic lifestyles, values and practices, some of which are closely related to issues of gender and sexuality. One conspicuous feature of the Gothic scene is its broad age range, from mid-teens well into adulthood. In comparison with other long-lived subcultures (e.g. Punk), Goth boasts an unusually high proportion of adults with steady professions, especially in science and academia, art and design, social work and computer programming. Many older Goths lead a fairly normal life and have well-paid jobs, their own car and flat, and a steady relationship or even family. This makes for typical scene biographies where an increasing separation between subcultural and everyday life is practised.

A demographic factor closely related to the typical lifestyle arrangement of Goths as a mixture of extraordinary cultural practices and well-integrated social and professional lives is class. Nearly all authors analysing Goth (e.g. Farin, 2001; Hodkinson, 2002) have pointed out that it is primarily a middle-class subculture. Of course there are some Goths with working-class backgrounds, yet the values the scene propagates (see below) represent typically middle-class ideals. Many of its collectively shared fields of interest – e.g. literature, poetry, fine art, history – mark Goth as an unusually educated and literate subculture. The racial make-up of the scene is predominantly white.

Goths also display a strong interest in religious or spiritual questions, especially the taboo areas of magic and Satanism; yet, contrary to popular opinion, practising Satanists are rare in the subculture (Brill, 2007). Religious motifs from various sources – e.g. occultism, paganism, ancient cults, Christianity – are sometimes appropriated through critical intellectual engagement, which leads to a highly eclectic and individual 'private religion' or 'occult-religious-philosophical bricolage' (Helsper, 1992, pp. 288/295). Goths lack a collective political orientation, although there is a general tendency towards liberal or moderate left-wing stances. While mainstream media coverage often picks on alleged right-wing tendencies in Goth,[4] such tendencies are marginal. Customising pieces of military uniforms is not uncommon on the scene, but this provocative toying with military or totalitarian chic only sometimes spills over into a fascination with the history and ideology of totalitarianism in the Neo-folk and Industrial factions (see Speit, 2002). An outright embracing of such ideology is rare among Goths.

Another interesting aspect of Gothic lifestyle is Goths' very open-minded attitude towards eroticism, sexuality and gender play. The subculture shows a strong interest in Fetish, S&M and other taboo modes of eroticism. While the majority of Goths do not actively engage in Fetish or S&M practices, there is a significant overlap between the Gothic and Fetish/S&M scenes in terms of style codes and imagery. Moreover, Goths display acceptance towards same-sex flirtation and mingle in some of their spaces with sexual minorities such as Fetish/S&M enthusiasts, transvestites or gays. Playful or eroticised gender performances are widely accepted in the subculture, and some Goths regularly or occasionally engage in stylised gender bending in their practices of dress and eroticism.

As to Gothic values, the subculture's juxtaposition of retrospective, traditional, conservative tendencies and postmodern, individualistic, emancipatory ideals is particularly characteristic. On the one hand, Goths harbour a strong affinity to certain historical periods. They cherish the Romantic era, with its cult of emotionalism, and delve into ancient notions of mysticism and spirituality, such as paganism. On the other hand, they cultivate a – decidedly post-modern – individualism, which manifests itself in 'a radicalised claim to self-realisation' (Schmidt and Neumann-Braun, 2004, p. 316) and the endorsing of an extreme pluralism of values.

A second fundamental characteristic of Goth is the subculture's self-reflexive, introspective, subjectivist rather than activist, confrontational stance. Its form of protest or opposition vis-à-vis general society is one of withdrawal and refusal rather than open rebellion. One central Gothic value flowing from this attitude is the seemingly paradoxical ideal of 'demonstrating strength through weakness, through tolerance, endurance and suffering' (Schmidt and Neumann-Braun, 2004, p. 75). Through a conscious confrontation of the self with topics commonly regarded as demanding, taboo or terrifying – e.g. death, perversion, the occult, psychological extremes – Goths aim to realise a specific form of intellectual difference and profundity. Another central Gothic value, critical reflection on philosophical and transcendental questions and the search for alternative perspectives on life, is closely related to this stance. Of course such a reflexive, intellectual stance is often as much a pose as an attitude, which leads some Goths to reject or ironise it as a cliché.

The self-reflexive, passive nature of Goths' subcultural opposition also informs two further central values of the subculture; namely, an exceptional peacefulness and almost complete absence of violence, and a high degree of tolerance and acceptance of different lifestyles (e.g. in terms of sexuality, relationships, and religious or philosophical worldviews). Another important Gothic value lies in romanticising, aestheticising and re-mystifying modern life (Richard, 1995). The aesthetic appropriation of everyday life and surroundings – e.g. through decorating one's body, flat, car and favourite hangouts as elements of a sacred 'dark microcosm' – is set against the pragmatic and functional profanity of the modern world.

As in many other subcultures, the constitutive practices of Goth are its distinctive dress style and music. Style-related practices like the creation, selection, combination and display of clothes, hairstyles and accessories are among the most important activities in the subculture. In such practices, aspects of dress Eicher and Roach-Higgins (1993) class as 'body modifications' (e.g. tattoos, piercings, make-up, haircuts) play just as prominent a role as the 'body supplements' (e.g. clothes, jewellery, other accessories like handbags and fans) which are commonly thought of as constituting dress. While most Goths make a special effort with their style when going out, they also wear a toned-down version of this style in their everyday life as far as social pressures permit. Apart from its dark, twisted air, Gothic style's most striking feature is the generous adoption in both male and female dress of elements traditionally coded as feminine; this feature will form a central point of enquiry in my analysis of gender in Goth.

Like the subculture as a whole, Goth as a musical genre is a mix of various coexisting styles. Gothic music covers a wide spectrum of sounds and atmospheres, ranging from gentle, introverted styles inspired by folk or classical music (Neo-classicism or Neo-folk), across Rock or Metal-inspired styles (Gothic Rock or Gothic Metal), to harsh, martial styles of electronic music (Electro and Industrial). The roots of Goth music lie in guitar-based (Post-punk, Gothic Rock) as well as electronic (New Wave, Dark Wave) genres. *Gothic Rock* (e.g. Sisters of Mercy) combines melancholic guitar melodies in minor keys with dominant bass lines and static mid-tempo drums, usually accompanied by a deep, husky male voice. A more recent development is *Gothic Metal* (e.g. Tristania), which combines the heavy, slow riffs of Death or Doom Metal with orchestral sounds and melodies. Vocal duties are often shared between a female soprano voice and low-pitched male 'growls'.

Electronic subgenres of dark music created with samplers and synthesizers are much in demand at Goth clubs, and have also become very popular for home-listening among Goths over the last two decades. More melodious varieties are *Wave* or *Dark Wave* (e.g. Deine Lakaien), with sounds and structures resembling a dark, sombre version of Synth Pop and clear, emotional vocals. A more beat-driven, much harder genre is *EBM = Electronic Body Music* (e.g. Front 242), whose newer variants are commonly referred to as *Electro* (e.g. Wumpscut). EBM/Electro is a harsh, repetitive, pounding type of electronic music with distorted male vocals, often displaying strong militaristic overtones. Even harsher and more aggressive is the subgenre of *Rhythm/Noise Industrial* (e.g. Sonar), with distorted staccato beats, sounds reminiscent of machine noise, and samples evoking an atmosphere of war and destruction.

Almost diametrically opposed are the genres *Neo-classicism* (e.g. Dead Can Dance) and *Neo-folk* (e.g. Death in June). Neo-classical music is often produced with electronic equipment but aims for an organic, orchestral sound resembling a dark, simpler and more song-oriented version of classical music, sometimes with medieval, ethnic or folk influences. Most singers in this genre, which is also referred to as 'Heavenly Voices', are females with angelic soprano voices. Neo-folk consists in sparsely arranged songs dominated by simple acoustic guitar lines and other folk instruments, often with clear male vocals.

Goth music is surrounded by other relevant practices, most importantly media use and dance as an expressive club ritual. Gothic dance has been described as a 'dance of mourning' (Helsper, 1992) or an 'anti-dance' (Schmidt and Neumann-Braun, 2004). While the dance styles of Goths vary according to the type of music played and are sometimes markedly gendered (see chapter 6), the prototypical Gothic dance consists in a monotonous, self-absorbed walking back and forth to the beat of the music. Most Goths are avid consumers of specialist music magazines or fanzines and Internet sites. Goth magazines have their roots in non-commercial fanzines, and even though some of them have developed into full-fledged news-stand titles, they still embody the doctrine of being written by insiders for insiders (Brill, 2008). In Germany five Goth-related news-stand titles – *Orkus*, *Sonic Seducer*, *Zillo*, *Gothic*, *Astan* – with a total monthly circulation of about 250,000 (Farin, 2001) were competing for readership at the time of my research, with the most popular ones being *Orkus* and *Sonic Seducer*. In Britain there were two regular, nationally distributed titles, *Kaleidoscope* and *Meltdown*, both much smaller than their German counterparts and issued quarterly at most.

The Internet is another important medium for the exchange of information, ideas and opinions among Goths (Hodkinson, 2002, 2003); apart from band or club websites, subcultural newsgroups and other participatory forums are very popular. In Britain at the time of my research there was one newsgroup (*uk.people.gothic*) and one major Web forum (*slashgoth.org*) geared toward Goths nationwide. Germany hosts a plethora of Gothic Internet newsgroups or forums (e.g. *de.soc.subkultur.gothic*, *Nachtwelten.de*, *Gothiccommunity.de*), along with sites catering to various niches within the scene (e.g. *gothicgays.de*).

Staking out the 'Field'

Given the importance of subcultural media use to Goth, my study of gender in the Gothic subculture adopts a dual methodological strategy. It combines a media-centred approach (i.e. analysing textual and visual elements of Goth magazines and Internet forums) with the people-focused approach offered by ethnography (i.e. observing social agents and asking them for their own meanings and interpretations). Following Willis (2000), I understand ethnography as a broad array of qualitative methods of data collection and analysis – chiefly observation, interviews and informal interaction – with the objective of providing a close interpretation of everyday cultural practices. Crucially, this interpretation aims to combine structural theoretical assumptions with a heightened sensitivity to the subjective meanings and experiences of the people studied.

Based on a combination of Willis's (2000) notion of socio-symbolic analysis, Stanley Cohen's (1997) critique of traditional approaches to studying subcultures and Turner's (1967) useful distinction between three basic levels of field data,[5] I have settled for a research strategy resting on three main pillars: in-depth interviews with members of the subculture, flanked by participant observation at Goth clubs and festivals; a textual analysis of selected Goth Internet newsgroups and forums; a textual and visual analysis of selected Goth magazines. I staked out the 'field' – i.e. the material and virtual loci of observation – for my ethnographic study as follows.

From July 2002 to December 2003, I conducted forty in-depth interviews with Goths, twenty in Britain and twenty in Germany, with interviewees roughly balanced for gender (twenty males, twenty females) and age (ranging from fourteen to forty-five). To cover regional varieties in both countries, I made observations and recruited interviewees at Goth festivals or clubs in four different areas: Brighton (south-east England), Edinburgh (Scotland), Cologne/Bonn (West Germany) and Berlin/Leipzig (East Germany). In the selection of interviewees I took care that people representing the different factions of the Gothic scene were included. My interviewees either identified themselves as Goths or were chosen on the grounds of their involvement in the subculture in terms of style, going-out habits, music and other cultural preferences.

As to Gothic media, I chose two magazines and two Internet forums in each country for analysis. In Germany I monitored the big monthly titles *Orkus* and *Sonic Seducer* from April 2002 to June 2003; in Britain I monitored the quarterly magazines *Kaleidoscope* and *Meltdown* from summer 2000 to summer 2003. Data gathered in Internet forums have particular qualities, as they occur 'naturally' instead of being prompted by the researcher (Clandinin and Connelly, 1998) and represent the voices of a broad population of contributors.[6] I decided to monitor one Goth newsgroup and one Web forum in each country, crucially without active participation so as to keep intact the uninfluenced status of the data gathered. In Britain I monitored *uk.people.gothic* from September 2002 to February 2003 and *slashgoth.org* from January 2002 to November 2002; in Germany I opted for *de.soc.subkultur.gothic* (January 2003 to June 2003) and *Gothiccommunity.de* (September 2002 to June 2003).

A Sense of Place

In the following I introduce the four regions where I carried out my research, describing the local Goth scenes there and highlighting their particularities.

Brighton is a fairly small city (about 120,000 inhabitants) yet boasts a colourful subcultural history, with many shops, bars and clubs catering to various scenes. In addition to a strong gay scene, which has earned the city its nickname 'Britain's Gay Capital', Brighton also harbours a vibrant Goth underground with quite a few bands (e.g. Synthetic, Psychophile). Along with London, Brighton is the UK's Cyber Goth stronghold. At the beginning of my fieldwork in late 2001, there was only one monthly Goth club called Lowlife, with mixed dark music; in 2002 another monthly club called Nightshade was launched. Local Goths also frequented other events and places, for instance an Alternative pub called the Hobgoblin, an Alternative/Rock venue called the Gloucester, and the weekly 1980s night at the gay pub the Harlequin. Many local Goths occasionally travelled to London on weekends to visit Britain's biggest Goth club, Slimelight, which offers a main floor with hard electronic music and a smaller floor with more traditional tunes.

I travelled to Edinburgh (about 500,000 inhabitants) – whose Gothic scene I was already familiar with – for two weeks in February 2002, when the first Edinburgh Goth Weekend festival took place, making observations and conducting interviews. In comparison with south-east England, Scotland harbours a more traditional scene, with many Gothic Rock fans. At the time of my research, Edinburgh offered more and bigger club events than Brighton; there were the main monthly clubs Ascension (more Gothic Rock) and Vain (mixed Goth music), the small monthly club Finsternis (Medieval, Industrial) and the fortnightly club the Mission with an Alternative/Rock floor and a smaller Goth floor.

From May to July 2003 I spent six weeks in the Cologne/Bonn area – where I had regularly gone out to Gothic clubs before moving to Britain – to get an impression of the current scene there and conduct some interviews. Bonn (about 350,000 inhabitants) still hosted its mixed weekly Goth night at the N8Schicht, and another one at a venue called Atlantis. The main clubs in Cologne (over a million inhabitants) were the long-running venue LaLic with different Goth-oriented clubnights, the newer Rose Club, and occasional big club events at the Live Music Hall. Quite a few Goths from the Cologne/Bonn area travel to the densely populated Ruhr Region at weekends to visit the big, very electronic clubs in Bochum (the Matrix) or Essen (Zeche Carl). The Ruhr Region has traditionally been one of West Germany's Goth strongholds and has become extremely Electro-dominated over the last decade.

Another Goth stronghold with more traditional and diverse musical inclinations has developed in East Germany since unification, most notably in Berlin (about 3.4 million inhabitants) and Leipzig (about 500,000 inhabitants). I conducted research in Berlin from July 2003 onwards, entering one of the most vibrant Gothic scenes currently existing, with a plethora of weekly and monthly club events catering to various tastes. In Berlin one can go out on the scene nearly every night, as there are some venues – the relatively big K17 and Kato, the smaller Lime Club and Duncker – holding Goth events on different days of the week. Moreover, the city offers a Gothic pub called Last Cathedral, and many additional monthly clubs like Blüthenrausch (Medieval, Batcave, Neo-folk) or Factory (1980s–90s Goth). Leipzig hosts the biggest annual Gothic festival in the world, the Wave-Gotik-Treffen, which I visited in June 2003 for observations and interviews. The Treffen attracts many German Goths and quite a few from abroad, offering a wealth of gigs, clubnights and events ranging from Fetish shows to poetry readings.

Outlook

My study presents a cross-cultural analysis of gender representations and identities in the Gothic subculture and its media.[7] It explores gendered images and attitudes within the subculture in relation to dominant cultural values of femininity and masculinity. The central question is to what extent Goth and its media incorporate and reflect common gender stereotypes, and to what extent they offer alternative or even subversive images and roles.

Chapter 2 clarifies the central theoretical concepts guiding my study, namely gender, style and subculture. I outline a conception of gender as a fragmented, contested and continually negotiated discourse, discuss dress style as a medium of gender subversion, and develop a modern definition of subculture based on the works of Hodkinson (2002), McRobbie (1994) and Thornton (1995). This definition focuses on subjective identification, individual investment and the notion of *subcultural capital*. In addition, I present a critical overview of existing academic studies of gender issues in subcultures.

The next three chapters of my analysis examine Gothic style practices through the lens of gender, with a special focus on dress. Chapter 3 discusses two central forms of Gothic style which directly relate to gender, namely *male androgyny* and *female hyperfemininity*. These typical dress styles are analysed in relation to the 'fantasy of genderlessness' espoused by Goths and to subcultural capital. Chapter 4 focuses exclusively on the style practices of female Goths, examining the subjective meanings and functions these practices hold for women. Drawing on the concept of *femininity as masquerade* (Doane, 1982) and the 'stories' of Goth women, I unearth the reasons why many female Goths experience their style as empowering. Chapter 5 looks at the style practices of Goth men. It highlights the liberating potential of androgynous style as well as the tensions between androgyny and masculinity which often surface in the stylistic and discursive practices of male Goths. I also take up the issue of cultural differences in the construction and negotiation of Gothic masculinities.

In chapter 6 the focus turns from issues of style to the seemingly more mundane sphere of everyday gender relations. I present the Goth scene as a deeply heterosexual space, whose 'fantasy of genderlessness' is not really borne out in the actual relations between men and women, but also point to the progressive nature of some Gothic renegotiations of gender. Chapter 7 approaches the issue of sexual relations from a different angle, examining Goths' attitudes and practices with a view to queer sexualities and same-sex eroticism.

Chapter 8 highlights the role Goth music and other subcultural media play in the discursive construction of gender and eroticism. In the various strands of Goth music, in Goth photography and especially in the media texts surrounding these art forms, I trace gendered meanings in the sounds, words and images of the subculture. In chapter 9, the conclusion, I attempt to bring together the findings of all six analysis chapters to highlight common threads as well as apparent tensions. I argue that to fully understand the social relevance of subcultural practices one has to pay attention to both their micropolitical (i.e. individual or internal) and their macropolitical (i.e. larger cultural) effects.

2

Subverting Gender, Gendering Subculture

November 2001, Brighton, the University of Sussex library. I am sitting at a reading desk in the short loan section, close to the shelves storing key works on gender and sexualities. This place has become something of a second home for me over the last few weeks, as I am in the process of reading into the three main fields of study relevant to my planned research – gender, dress and subcultural theory – in order to develop a sound theoretical groundwork for my analysis. While I was already familiar with the classic readings on subculture, the field of gender theory is alien territory for me. Having been trained in the 'hard science' discipline of experimental psychology before venturing into the terrain of cultural studies, I knew gender mainly as a binary variable taken to explain observable differences between men and women. Heavily influenced by postmodern philosophy and poststructuralist linguistics, however, the conceptions of gender offered by cultural studies seem to turn this rationale right upside down. Here gender features as a second-order construction, itself constituted and performed through the very cultural acts and structures it is supposed to explain.

Looking up from the tall stack of books I have assembled on my desk, I notice a black-clad figure standing in front of the anthropology shelf – a girl with dark eyeshadow and deep-red lipstick, sporting long hair dyed black and purple and a flowing satin skirt. How is this Goth woman's gender constructed?, I ask myself. Exactly how does she 'perform' her femininity? The text on gender performance I have just read still seems rather abstract to me. But as the girl walks past me with small, soft steps in her clumpy Rangers boots, I begin to sense how the sometimes contradictory workings of gender performance might be explored on living, breathing bodies and their dress.

Constructing Gender

Academic definitions of subculture have shifted considerably over the last four decades, with gender turning from a factor which used to be completely passed over into a central element of subcultural research. Likewise, since the feminist movement placed gender on the cultural and academic agenda in the 1970s, the meanings assigned to this concept and the ways it is applied to humanities research in particular have changed markedly.

Postmodern conceptions of gender (e.g. Butler, 1990, 1993; van Zoonen, 1994) have discarded the notion of a unified sex–gender system in favour of a

17

more fluid understanding. Characteristic of such conceptions is the deconstruction of the traditional binary categories 'masculine' and 'feminine' as
rooted in social discourse instead of human nature. One of the most influential
gender theories in this vein has been Judith Butler's conception of gender as
performative. In her seminal text *Gender Trouble* (1990), Butler seeks to reveal
the notion of gender identity, construed as a stable core of the human subject
from which behaviour originates, as a regulatory fiction. This fiction is
produced by the 'heterosexual matrix', a normative set of discourses
prescribing a congruence between sex, gender and (heterosexual) desire. Butler
conceptualises gender as produced '*on the surface* of the body' as 'a *stylised
repetition of acts*' (ibid., pp. 136/140, original emphasis). This position goes
beyond the traditional sex/gender dichotomy in placing both concepts in the
domain of discourse, more precisely as two facets of the same regulatory
discourse of binary sexual difference.

In *Bodies That Matter* (1993) Butler reworks the concept of gender performativity as citationality. While *Gender Trouble* posits performativity as inten-
tional, though involved in power relations which cannot be transcended but
only redeployed, Butler's later formulations restrict the agency of the subject
even further. Citationality 'consists in the reiterating of norms which precede,
constrain, and exceed the performer' (ibid., p. 234). Thus, we do not act or
articulate our assigned sex through discourse, but the discourse of sex – i.e. the
law of binary heterosexuality – acts and articulates itself through us.

Butler's approach has been instrumental in radically deconstructing common
ideas of gendered identity and subjectivity. Her notion of the hegemonic
power of the heterosexual matrix and its binary gender discourse is problematic,
however, as it poses this discourse as seemingly all-encompassing and monolithic.
Although Butler's position does not completely exclude the possibility of subversive acts within the gender system, the agency of the subject to challenge the
dominant discourse is bounded by strict limits. The idea of a compulsory reiter-
ation of signifying practices and meanings defined, even if not fully determined,
by the discursive power of the heterosexual matrix stands at odds with current
conceptions of human agency in media and cultural studies.

To accommodate the view of human beings as active and critical subjects
who construct their own meanings (see Fiske, 1987, 1989; Jenkins, 1992), a
notion of discourse as multiform and fragmented seems more adequate. Such
a notion of gender discourse as 'a set of overlapping and often contradictory
cultural descriptions and prescriptions referring to sexual difference' is
advanced by van Zoonen (1994, p. 33). Here discourse is not seen as univocal
or total, but as ambiguous and continually contested. It follows that 'the disci-
plinary power of discourse, prescribing and restricting identities and experiences, can always be resisted and subverted' (ibid., p. 34). Moreover, gender is
not the only powerful discourse inscribed in the subject; sexual difference is
just one factor constituting the subject as a cultural being, along with race,
class, sexuality, ability and various others.

Gender should thus be conceived, not as a fixed property of individuals, but as part of an ongoing process by which subjects are constituted, often in paradoxical ways. The identity that emerges is therefore fragmented and dynamic; gender does not determine or exhaust identity. ... Defined as such, gender is an intrinsic part of culture – loosely defined as the production of meaning – and is subject to continuous discursive struggle and negotiation. (ibid., p. 33)

Treating gender as a contested discourse enables the researcher to ask what part representations of femininity and masculinity in the media – and in cultural signifying practices generally – play in the ongoing construction and negotiation of gender. As Pollock (1991, 1992) points out, representation is a (re)productive instead of merely reflective process; orders of sexual difference are actively constructed, modified, resisted and reconstituted in and through representations.

With reference to de Lauretis (1987), who sees gender as produced, among other discursive and social practices, by various 'social technologies' like the cinema, van Zoonen (1994, p. 41) suggests an understanding of the media consistent with this view of representation: 'Media can thus be seen as (social) technologies of gender, accommodating, modifying, reconstructing and producing disciplining and contradictory cultural outlooks of sexual difference.' In addition to mass media and niche media (e.g. subcultural music magazines), various other cultural signifying practices play a role in producing meaning and constituting gender as a fragmented and shifting discourse – for instance, the dress styles, utterances and behaviour codes of Goths that I am going to explore in my analysis.

Queer Crossings

The idea of cultural signifying practices as productive of meaning opens up a crucial set of questions: to what extent can representations and other cultural practices work to subvert common gender discourse, and which specific shapes would such subversive practices have to take? As already mentioned, Butler's conception of performativity or citationality concedes the subject only a very limited agency, an agency located within the realm of discursive power and hence itself constructed through discourse. However, Butler's theory still leaves some room for subversive acts from *within* the power matrix constituted by the law of binary heterosexuality: 'there might be produced the refusal of the law in the form of the parodic inhabiting of conformity ..., a repetition of the law into hyperbole, a rearticulation of the law against the authority of the one who delivers it' (Butler, 1993, p. 122).

Subversive potential is thus located in appropriating dominant discourse, in resignifying hegemonic definitions through their repetition – i.e. their citation – in contexts not intended by the law. This concept of gender subversion leads

Butler (1990) to cite cross-dressing practices like gay male drag or lesbian butch and femme styles as a prime example of subversive signifying practices. In the parodic imitation of binary heterosexual gender models within 'queer' (i.e. gay, lesbian, bisexual or transsexual) contexts, she sees a means to denaturalise and deconstruct dominant definitions of gender identity by revealing their contingent and constructed nature.

In response to critiques of her seemingly uncritical celebration of cross-dressing, Butler (1993, p. 125) revised her notion of the subversive potential of drag, conceding that drag 'may well be used in the service of both the denaturalisation and reidealisation of hyperbolic heterosexual gender norms'. The problem is that Butler fails to specify the conditions in which drag is supposed to have either subversive or reactionary qualities. Her critique (ibid., p. 129ff.) of the film *Paris Is Burning* offers some hints, though, in that it construes the wish to 'pass as straight' as stripping drag of its subversive edge. This touches on a question I deem crucial, but which cannot be thought through within Butler's framework of a radically deconstructed subjectivity: what role do the *subjective intentions* of the 'performers' engaging in cross-dressing practices and the *subjective perceptions* of the 'audiences' watching such practices play for their subversive potential?

In erasing the active volition of the subject from her theory by viewing agency 'as the inherent indeterminacy of symbolic structures rather than as the result of social practice' (McNay, 2000, p. 45), Butler fails to consider the motivations and interpretations of the people practising or perceiving drag. Another problem is that while Butler aims to break up the traditional binaries of sex and gender, her notion of gender subversion – particularly evident in her examples – remains trapped within these very binaries. As she holds there are no subversive acts thinkable outside the heterosexual matrix, it seems consistent to cite male drag queens and lesbian butch and femme styles as prototypical examples of such acts; these are practices which stay well within the confines of the binary gender code, typically presenting hyperbolic versions of its stereotypes. Such practices leave the masculine and feminine sign systems of that code intact, instead of deconstructing them by taking their various elements as discrete signs which can be recombined freely in modes which transcend binary notions of gender.

Here Garber's (1992) thoughts on cross-dressing, which highlight distinct gender signs, offer a more flexible way of looking at gender subversion that may be better suited to illuminate the style practices of Goths. In an essay programmatically titled 'Breaking the Code', she delineates the subversive potential of drag as follows: 'If transvestism offers a critique of binary sex and gender distinctions, it is not because it simply makes such distinctions reversible but because it denaturalises, destabilises, and defamiliarises sex and gender *signs*.' (ibid., p. 147, original emphasis) Consequently, she champions cross-dressing practices in which 'sex role referents within the sartorial system may be deliberately mixed or self-contradictory' (ibid., p. 152) as a model of gender subversion.

A central feature theories of cross-dressing share is the emphasis they place on queer identities; the protagonists in their transgressive play of gender signifyers are supposed to be lesbian, gay, bisexual or transgender people. The term 'queer' has become a buzzword in gender-related sections of cultural theory over the last decade. Under this umbrella, bisexuals in particular have been hailed as a culturally progressive and subversive sexual minority. Theorists of bisexuality (e.g. Eadie, 1999; Garber, 1999; Rust, 1992) typically stress the radical liberatory potential of bisexual practices and subjectivities. Bisexuality is hailed as a sphere of fluid desires, as 'a practice that refuses the restrictive formulas that define gender according to binary categories' (Pramaggiore, 1996, p. 3). A prime example of such bi-affirmative academic discourses is Garber (1999, p. 138), who celebrates bisexuality as a disruptive and progressive force which 'defies and defeats categorisation' – not only in disrupting traditional sexual and gender categories, but further in displacing the social mechanism of categorising and stereotyping in general.

However, bisexual feminist theorists (e.g. Baker, 1992; Kaplan, 1992; Udis-Kessler, 1992) have cautioned that simply setting up bisexual identity as such as a panacea supposed to eradicate sexism and restrictive gender norms is misguided. In a culture where gender categorisation and sexist discrimination are social realities, a gender-blind bisexual politics based on the illusory ideal of genderless love – i.e. 'one that pretends it is presently possible to "go beyond gender"' (Baker, 1992, p. 260) – can actually work to perpetuate those realities through ignoring and thus masking them. Bisexuality as an effective strategy for disrupting or transcending sexual and gender oppression must be grounded in a critical analysis of these and other forms of oppression (Bennett, 1992). Crucially, it also needs to be aware of its own ambivalent status with a view to the social institutions of compulsory heterosexuality and heterosexual privilege (Kaplan, 1992). These characteristics of a culturally progressive notion of bisexual identity will form an important benchmark for assessing the Gothic subculture's affinity to queer sexualities in my analysis.

Subversion through Style?

Gender subversion through cross-dressing, as proposed by Butler and Garber, hinges on style practices and their potential for signifying resistant meanings.[1] The relationship between style, power and resistance is an intricate and often contradictory one. Wilson (1992, p. 14) stakes out the field of dress codes as a site of struggle around cultural definitions and identities by understanding dress as 'a powerful weapon of control and dominance' with '*simultaneously* subversive qualities' (original emphasis). Theorists of dress differ widely regarding which of these two sides of the power struggle – control or subversion – they emphasise. On the one side, there are Marxist critics like Ewen and Ewen (1982) or Emberley (1988) who maintain that stylistic dissent actually stabilises the dominant capitalist order by displacing concerted political protest onto the sphere of mere consumerism. On the other side, there are advocates of popular culture who see subversive potential in dress (e.g. O'Neal, 1999; Silverman, 1986; E. Wilson, 1985).

Hebdige (1979) has put forward a classic account of the subversive power of subcultural style and its co-optation by the dominant order. He sees the dress practices of subcultures as a form of semiotic guerrilla warfare, 'a symbolic violation of the social order' (ibid., p. 19). However, the resistant meanings communicated through original subcultural styles are eventually incorporated and stripped of their subversive edge by the dominant culture, in the form of commercial exploitation by the media and fashion industries. Evans and Thornton (1989) deliver a discussion of subcultural style from an explicitly feminine perspective. The relation between feminism and style has been an uneasy one ever since Simone de Beauvoir's (1953) *The Second Sex* set the scene with its negative view of female narcissism and adornment. Evans and Thornton point out that the early feminist rejection of self-adornment was based on refusing the sexual stereotype of female narcissism. According to this line of argument, narcissism is a 'false consciousness' which prevents women from emancipating themselves, and the concern for dress and appearance is to be shunned as a tool of oppression.

If it is fashion and artificially created beauty which set out the terms of control for female appearance, however, these rationales of self-adornment could also be used to break or subvert that control. Evans and Thornton (ibid., p. 18) cite the example of Punk women, who are highly 'confected' yet outside the cultural norms of femininity, to illustrate how dress and style can be used in a strategy of resistance: 'By using the body itself as a site of signification punk women turned around the way in which the age-old identification of women with the body ... serves to silence them.' Hebdige (1988) puts forward a similar argument about women in Punk and Post-punk – which notably includes Goth – subcultures, who play with style and their bodies in public, thereby refusing their traditional silencing in the cultural sphere. Through their style practices, these women 'flirt with masculine curiosity but refuse to submit to the masterful gaze. These girls turn being looked at into an aggressive act' (ibid., pp. 28/29).

In this connection, Kaplan's (1983) thoughts on the *male gaze* can provide a useful framework. Kaplan argues that although the objectifying gaze – in contrast to Mulvey's (1992) classic postulate – is not necessarily male, to activate it is to adopt a masculine position. An effective challenge to this dominant structure, in which people assume masculine (the active 'onlooker') and feminine (the passive 'to-be-looked-at') positions, requires that the common dichotomies on which culture and language are based (e.g. male/female, active/passive) be transcended. From this perspective, to 'turn being looked at into an aggressive act', that is to transcend the passivity traditionally associated with the female position in visual discourse, is a practice holding a high subversive potential.

However, rebellion through style is fraught with specific difficulties for women. In particular, dress practices which aim to subvert or challenge stereotypes of female sexiness by means of parody or excess run the risk of affirming those very stereotypes through the backdoor. The identification of women with visual eroticism in our culture means that very quickly 'the vocabulary of sexual rebellion may be returned to that of sexual conformity' (Evans and Thornton, 1989, p. 31).

The relation between style and gender is a complex one not only for women but also for men. On the one hand, Silverman (1986, p. 139) points out that the history of Western dress with its phases of indulgent self-decoration and display for (upper-class) men 'poses a serious challenge both to the automatic equation of spectacular display with female subjectivity, and to the assumption that exhibitionism always implies woman's subjugation to a controlling male gaze'. On the other hand, the influence of what Flügel (1950) dubbed the 'Great Masculine Renunciation' of narcissism and decorative dress – brought about by the Industrial Revolution with its emphasis on work and sobriety – can be felt to the present day in a 'continuing strong male gender barrier towards all paraphernalia evocative of femininity' (Davis, 1992, p. 37). While female fashion has always borrowed features of traditionally male dress (e.g. trousers), a crossing in the opposite direction seems hampered by cultural taboos.

Regarding mainstream dress practices, this means greater freedom of stylistic expression for women, who have a wider choice of different cuts, colours and fabrics deemed proper both for formal (e.g. work) and social (e.g. dining out) occasions. In subculture, however, where provocation is actively sought and hailed, the lack of transgressive potential in the female adoption of male attire (except for extreme butchness) has certain drawbacks for women. As 'dressing up' is firmly associated with 'woman' in our society and hence transgressive only for men, Evans and Thornton (1989) argue, girls in subcultures centring on narcissism and excessive adornment (like the New Romantics, a precursor of Goth) can again only play a second-class – because less conspicuously transgressive – part: that of 'camp followers' displaying their femininity in excess of conventional codes.

To conclude, one problem with many classic readings of subcultural style is that they treat features of dress as language-like signs to be decoded within a semiological framework. The model of (post)structuralist semiotics, introduced into cultural studies by Barthes (1972, 1983), has led the majority of existing interpretations of dress to reduce it to a medium of quasi-linguistic communication (e.g. Barnard, 1996; Hebdige, 1979; Rubinstein, 1995). If one acknowledges the essential ambiguity of dress and other cultural codes (Davis, 1992; Hebdige, 1997; Sawchuk, 1988), and the grounding of material cultural practices in the sensuous experience of the people who perform them (Willis, 2000; Wilson, 1992), semiotic decoding does not seem sufficient for understanding such practices. Without considering the views and interpretations of the people who create and don a style, readings of subcultural dress can easily slip from the wittily imaginative to the wilfully imaginary.

Moreover, apart from Evans and Thornton's (1989) less prominent analysis, the leading conceptions of subcultural resistance through style discussed here (Butler, 1990, 1993; Garber, 1992; Hebdige, 1979) share one fundamental blind spot. All these approaches proceed from the explicit or implicit assumption that 'subculture' as oppositional culture and 'mainstream' as dominant culture are somehow positioned as starkly opposed forces in the cultural power field. Within subculture, by contrast, they assume something like a power-neutral zone. Relations of domination and oppression only seem to exist between 'ruling' and 'subordinate' social groups, regardless of tensions and inequalities within them.

Subcultures have traditionally been interpreted in terms of 'resistance' towards hegemonic powers (Hall and Jefferson, 1976; Hebdige, 1979), a viewpoint which ignores what Thornton (1997, p. 208) calls the 'microstructures of power' at play within all forms of social groups. If (postmodern) culture is defined as a 'multi-dimensional social space' (ibid., p. 208) rather than a monolithic system of hegemony, and it is further assumed that the idea of any collectivity – including subcultures – is grounded in discourse, which 'by definition has the effect of excluding, annihilating and delegitimizing certain views and positions, while including others' (van Zoonen, 1994, p. 40), this points to the necessity of critically analysing even seemingly oppositional cultural practices. In addition to tracing the relations of subcultural practices to hegemonic cultural definitions and values, it seems crucial to analyse the *interior logic* of such practices within their subcultural context. Only an analysis which takes account of the micro- as well as the macrostructures of power regulating social systems can reveal the intricate patterns of inclusion and exclusion structuring the 'multi-dimensional social space' of contemporary culture.[2]

Subculture and Identity

The main academic tradition of analysing subcultures and their styles originated in the Centre for Contemporary Cultural Studies (CCCS) at Birmingham University during the 1970s.[3] A seminal edited volume, *Resistance through Rituals* (Hall and Jefferson, 1976), which was followed by other influential works, was devoted to unearthing the meanings behind the styles of the conspicuous subcultures springing up in post-war Britain: Mods, Hippies, Bikers, Skinheads, Teds and Punks. Proceeding from a neo-Marxist conflict model of society and semiotic techniques of close reading, the approach interpreted subcultural style along the lines of two themes: *resistance* to subordinate class status and *symbolic communication* of marginalised ideas.

The CCCS concept has been criticised and modified from various perspectives, most prominently from feminist (McRobbie, 2000), discourse analytical

(Widdicombe and Wooffitt, 1995) and postmodernist (Muggleton, 2000) positions. This has eventually led to a plethora of alternative concepts designed to
do justice to the fluidity and diversity of subcultural formations: 'neo-tribes'
(Maffesoli, 1996), 'lifestyles' (Chaney, 2004), 'youth cultures' (Baacke, 1993),
'post-subcultures' (Muggleton, 1997) and the ubiquitous 'scenes' (Blum,
2001).[4] Members of contemporary subcultures themselves most frequently
refer to their social groupings as scenes, which is why this term is taken up by
many researchers – including myself – as an informal alternative to be used
interchangeably with subculture.

Hodkinson (2002, 2004) evades the arguably impossible task of finding a
concept which describes all forms of social structure and affiliation that
modern society offers, instead suggesting a new definition of subculture. This
definition centres on cultural substance and is hence stripped of its former
connotations of youth, working-classness, collective resistance and deviance.
Moreover, his notion of 'translocal subculture' goes beyond the confines of the
local communities which have traditionally been the focus of subcultural
ethnography, thus being better suited for the study of subcultures in the age of
global networking through the Internet.

From his ethnography of the Gothic subculture in the UK, Hodkinson distils
four criteria of cultural substance marking out his conception of subculture:
identity (a subjective sense of identification with a distinct cultural grouping
held by participants), *commitment* (an intensive and continuous involvement
among participants in group-related activities, e.g. going-out habits and
commodity choices), *consistent distinctiveness* (a set of relatively distinctive
and consistent tastes and values shared by participants, which are used to
demarcate 'insiders' from 'outsiders'), and *autonomy* (a relatively independent
network of small-scale cultural production and organisation generating
specialist consumables, media and events).

While Hodkinson's other criteria are also helpful in pointing to the substan-
tive bases and material expressions of subcultural affiliation, it is his notion of
identity which I find most useful. It indicates a shift in subcultural studies away
from weaving grand narratives of collective social resistance out of the sometimes rather thin threads of flamboyant subcultural styles, and towards a closer
examination of the individual meanings and experiences of actual members.
This shift is evident in the bulk of subcultural analyses from the mid-1990s
onwards. While texts from the early 1990s (e.g. Walser, 1993) usually share
with their 1970s and 1980s counterparts a one-sided focus on the analysis of
cultural artefacts, these newer works (e.g. Muggleton, 2000) highlight the
subjective views and individual motives of participants.

This shift in focus reflects a general change in the conception of subcultures
and broader cultural structures, which surfaced in the late 1980s/early 1990s.
Books like Fiske's *Understanding Popular Culture* (1989) and Willis' *Common
Culture* (1990), while hanging on to romantic notions of working-class resistance and displaying a sometimes overeager populism (McGuigan, 1992),

sparked an overdue debate about the legitimacy of conceptual boundaries between 'subcultures' and other taste-based communities. McRobbie (1994, p. 161) summarises the developments: 'the old model which divided the pure subculture from the contaminated outside world, eager to transform anything it could get its hands on into a sellable item, has collapsed, even though there still remains an ideology of authenticity which provides young people in youth cultures with a way of achieving social subjectivity and therefore identity through the subcultural experience'.

Here the shift from collective, politicised notions of subcultural resistance to questions of *social subjectivity, identity* and *experience* is highlighted, as well as another important concept – *subcultural ideology* and an associated *rhetoric of authenticity* (Widdicombe, 1993). These five elements of McRobbie's notion of subculture, along with Thornton's (1995) concept of *subcultural capital*, will form the basis for my analysis of gender identity and representation in the Gothic subculture.

Subcultural Capital

Thornton's approach to subcultural analysis marks another important shift in cultural studies: a shift away from the uncritical celebration of active con-sumption and popular resistance running through Fiske's (1989), Willis's (1990) and many other texts of the late 1980s/early 1990s to a critical analysis of the micropolitics of power in popular cultural formations. Instead of positing the usual dichotomy of dominant ideology versus subversive subcul-tural practices, her study of club cultures focuses on the subtle hierarchies and social distinctions *within* the subcultural terrain. Thornton's approach proceeds from the observation that existing research on subcultures tends to over-politicise their often hedonistic practices while ignoring the microstruc-tures of power at play within them. To redress this slanted, over-idealistic view of subcultures as havens of tolerance and equality, she formulates a critical agenda:

> this book is not about dominant ideologies and subversive subcultures, but about subcultural ideologies. It treats the discourses of dance cultures ... as ideologies which fulfil the specific cultural agendas of their beholders. ... In this way, I am not simply researching the beliefs of a cluster of communities, but investigating the way they make 'meaning in the service of power' – however modest these powers may be. (Thornton, 1995, pp. 9/10)

This critical approach to ethnographic data, along with a focus on microp-olitical structures, suggests a careful assessment of the necessarily partial accounts of subcultural values and structures given by members. A critical, balanced approach to empirical accounts, taking the views of subcultural agents seriously but also analysing them critically, is a principle I adopt for my own study. I aim to tread a middle ground between a subjectivist mode of analysis revolving around notions of identity and subjectivity, and a form of discourse analysis focusing on the ideological construction of subjects' written and spoken texts. Billig (1997, p. 220) suggests treating both types of texts as utterances containing 'a dialectic of constraint and creativity', of conformism and resistance. The resulting framework of analysis, *Critical Discursive Psychology* (e.g. Edley, 2001), is at the same time psychological (considering utterances as subjectively constructed by people) and ideological (considering the larger discursive formations shaping each utterance), thus combining a focus on subjectivity and discourse.[5]

Thornton sees contemporary culture as structured by multi-dimensional patterns of inclusion and exclusion. With reference to Bourdieu's (1984) notion of 'cultural capital', she introduces the concept of *subcultural capital*, a mark of distinction which can be objectified (e.g. in 'hip' clothes and record collections) or embodied (e.g. in subcultural knowledge and 'coolness') and 'confers status on its owner in the eyes of the relevant beholder' (Thornton, 1995, p. 11). A related concept is that of *subcultural ideology*, a particular way of envisioning social worlds, discriminating between social groups and measuring cultural worth, which is based on drawing distinctions between 'us' and 'them'. Behind the overt rhetoric of equality and inclusiveness typical of subcultural ideologies, Thornton maintains, lurks a thinly veiled elitism and separatism, which serves to reaffirm binary oppositions between 'alternative' and 'straight', 'radical' and 'conformist' and, most importantly, between 'subculture' and 'mainstream'.

Subcultural capital stratifies youth cultures and can be used as a means of power brokering within their social worlds. Consequently, it is not a neutral measure of achievement, but 'a currency which correlates with and legitimizes unequal statuses' (ibid., p. 104). The axes of social difference along which it is most systematically aligned are age and gender. Regarding gender, Thornton points out the masculine bias of subcultural capital, expressed in a 'feminini-sation' of the mainstream. She unpicks the misogynist slant in club cultural representations of the denigrated mainstream of 'Handbag House' against which Ravers define their subculture.

Instead of subverting dominant cultural structures and freeing participants from their shackles, Thornton (ibid., p. 115) concludes, the subcultural ideologies used by clubbers 'offer "alternatives" in the strict sense of the word, namely other social and cultural hierarchies to put in their stead'. The social fantasies of 'classlessness' and 'genderlessness', which are particularly widespread in Rave but also feature prominently in the ideologies of some other contemporary subcultures (including Goth, as we will see), clear the field for establishing alternative – but not necessarily progressive – hierarchies within the subcultural sphere. So while issues of gender are conspicuously absent from the discourses of subcultures like Rave, their gendered stratification often all but mirrors the marginal status of femininity in dominant hierarchies of cultural worth in relegating women to inferior, passive positions.

A Tough Boys' World

Thornton's observation that subcultural hierarchies tend to be structured by masculinist standards harks back to a long-standing link between subcultures and ideologies of masculinity. Even long after the heydays of the traditional Teddy Boy, Rocker and Skinhead subcultures with their open display of machismo, authors like Brake (1985) stressed the masculinist character of subcultures. His assertion that 'subcultures in some form or other explore and celebrate masculinity, and as such eventually relegate girls to a subordinate place within them' (p. 182), may seem exaggerated from a twenty-first-century perspective and fails to take account of subcultures like Glam Rock or indeed Goth, which herald androgyny and traditionally feminine traits. However, the fact remains that many subcultures function mainly as turfs for the construction and display of masculinity. This is particularly true of the contemporary Hip-hop or Graffiti and Metal subcultures.

Macdonald's (2001) ethnographic study of the Graffiti scene in London and New York portrays Graffiti as a tool for adolescent male identity construction and consolidation. The subculture is first and foremost a world of traditional machismo, 'a celebration of masculine supremacy' (ibid., p. 123). Through daring Graffiti actions, playing hit and run with the police, making a name for themselves within the scene, and employing a language of warfare and heroism, young males can build and reaffirm their fragile masculine identities free from the constraints of their social position of relative physical and material powerlessness in general society.

However, there is one point of critique Macdonald's analysis cannot escape, which seems symptomatic of studies addressing masculinity. Masculinity is typically studied in male-centred, masculinist subcultures, e.g. hooligans (Armstrong, 1998; Bohnsack, 1997), gangs (Ferrell, 1993; MacLeod, 1995) and Heavy Metal (Arnett, 1996; Seitz, 1998). Such studies effectively trace the subcultural construction of masculinity according to common cultural values (e.g. bravery, competition, toughness), albeit through means outlawed by larger society (e.g. illegal acts, aggressive music). The standards of hegemonic masculinity on which this construction is based are hence nowhere called into question, which implicitly normalises these standards and ignores the potential for alternative masculinities. The potential for such masculinities – masculine identities which transcend or challenge traditional constructions of maleness – in subculture is one issue I want to trace in my analysis of gender in Goth.

Walser's (1993) study of the construction of masculine identity in Heavy Metal is naturally prone to the same shortcoming. His discussion traces how visual and musical elements work in conjunction with song lyrics to forge certain kinds of powerful masculine images and identities for performers and fans. Walser cites the contrasting images of *hypermasculinity* and *androgyny* as visual enactments of transgression employed by Heavy Metal performers. Moreover, he posits four strategies Metal uses to deal with questions of gender, and to contain what patriarchal culture views as the 'threat' of women: *misogyny, exscription, androgyny* and *romance.* Walser sees the sexual politics of Heavy Metal as a conflicted mixture of affirming and subverting dominant gender norms. This applies to androgyny in particular, which the author defines as 'the adoption by male performers of the elements of appearance that have been associated with women's function as objects of the male gaze – the visual styles that connote … "to-be-looked-at-ness"' (1993, p. 124).

Although Heavy Metal androgyny is typically offset by heavily masculine stage posing, lyrical content and displays of musical prowess, Walser does not simply interpret it as a male co-optation of femininity. On the one hand, androgyny with its transgressive force can be used by young males simultaneously as a way of achieving masculinity by 'expressing control over women' and as a form of 'rebellion against dominant men' (ibid., p. 129). On the other hand, Walser (ibid., p. 133) sees in male performers' adoption of traditionally feminine elements of style (e.g. make-up) in connection with macho stage posing a potential challenge to gender norms: 'Heavy metal's androgyny can be very disturbing, not only because the conventional signs of female passivity and objectification are made dynamic, assertive, and transgressive, but also because hegemonic gender boundaries are blurred and the "natural" exclusiveness of heterosexual male power comes into question.'

This assessment has been questioned by Denski and Sholle (1992), who argue that, despite its apparent play with gender signifiers, Heavy Metal iconography is invested in maintaining binary gender codes. Here the observation that Glam Metal bands stylistically feminise the male body – or masculinise feminine signs – is interpreted as 'a thinly disguised reproduction of traditional masculine roles of power and domination presented in the context of an aggressive heterosexuality' (ibid., p. 59). Of course the question of whether male androgyny can be read as transgressing or as confirming conventional gender roles is also highly pertinent to the feminine style practices of Goth men (see chapter 5).

Masculinism for Girls

The Graffiti subculture has already been introduced as a space for male identity construction – a space where girls have a marginal position. Macdonald's (2001) explanation of this marginal female status is twofold. On the face of it, the risks and gains involved in writing Graffiti simply bolster a typically masculine instead of feminine identity. Moreover, interested girls are actively excluded or downgraded through masculinist double standards, which male

Graffiti writers employ to contain the threat female members pose to the construction of their subcultural activities as 'masculine'.

To be accepted in Graffiti, a girl must reject or disguise her femininity and emulate male-defined behaviour. In terms of sexual relations, however, girls are expected to adhere to traditional notions of feminine appearance and propriety. While male Graffiti writers gain a reputation through their skills and courage, girls are mainly seen as sexual objects whose status hinges on physical beauty and on not being perceived as 'slutty'. Macdonald (p. 139) concludes: 'Conventional sex roles and the pressures of heterosexuality are not escaped ..., they are reproduced and reinforced.' Yet she also acknowledges the challenge female Graffiti writers pose to fixed gender categories: 'By renouncing traditional codes of feminine behaviour, the female writer disrupts the subculture's and society's sexual status quo and rejects her subordinate place within it' (p. 140). Thus, Graffiti girls actively contest male dominance and male-defined notions of conventional femininity in relation to both society at large and their scene.

Weinstein's (1991) portrayal of Heavy Metal is similar to Macdonald's observations in depicting the subculture as a patriarchal space, where traditional masculine values (e.g. toughness, male bonding) are venerated and traits associated with femininity and homosexuality (e.g. softness, 'sissiness') are despised. Consequently, the status of women in Metal is low, and its male-centred iconography and social structure leave women only two options: 'Women, on stage or in the audience, are either sex objects to be used and abused, or must renounce their gender and pretend to be one of the boys' (p. 221). This view is not shared by Walser (1993, p. 131), who reads the androgyny of male Glam Metal performers as a combination of male power and female spectacle: 'At the symbolic level, prestige – male presence, gesture, musical power – is conferred upon "female" signs', which can work to empower women. One problem with Walser's discussion of women in Heavy Metal, however, is that he merely examines their reception of male spectacles, without considering active female participation.

Leblanc's (1999, 2002) ethnographic study of Punk girls traces the contradictory relation between an overt resistance to general social norms and a simultaneous collusion with masculinist subcultural norms by females in a male-dominated scene. She characterises Punk as a 'resolutely heterosexualist' space (2002, p. 167), whose gender roles mirror traditional standards of femininity, masculinity and sexual relations. Male Punks hold the authority to define norms of proper sexual expression for Punk girls, who may look threatening to outsiders but are still expected to present themselves as sexually attractive to insiders. Moreover, the male-defined sexual norms of Punk are both contradictory (girls are supposed to be available for erotic banter and play yet are expected to act like 'one of the boys' and stay monogamous if they want respect) and lopsided (while male Punks can 'play around' without loss of status, females must take care to avoid a 'slutty' reputation).

These points are strikingly similar to those made by Macdonald (2001) in her analysis of gender politics in Graffiti. In contrast to that author's portrayal of female Graffiti writers as challenging the masculinist standards of their subculture, however, Leblanc presents Punk girls as radically subverting general norms of (female) propriety yet colluding with the masculinism of Punk. Interestingly, both analyses suggest that the potential for transgressing hegemonic social norms is greater for women than for men in the masculinist Graffiti and Punk subcultures. Through their adoption of traditionally masculine markers of subcultural deviance, female Graffiti writers and Punks confront norms of female propriety along with more gender-neutral social norms. These observations contrast with Evans and Thornton's (1989) appraisal of women's limited transgressive potential in subcultures celebrating male androgyny – a thought my analysis will trace further in relation to Goth.

From 'Teenie-bopper' to 'Ladette'

Women have traditionally occupied a marginal position in both youth culture and academic studies about it. McRobbie (2000, first published 1980) deplores an exclusion of female presence from subcultures on two levels; firstly, the male domination of subcultures and their leisure spaces, and, secondly, the masculinist bias of early subcultural studies. The second factor is rooted in traditional sociology's focus on public spaces and delinquency, which led to an exscription of girls from youth cultural theory. The first constitutes a typical feature of the classic post-war subcultures up to the early 1980s, to the extent that McRobbie dismisses them as offering no attractions to women.

Consequently, McRobbie and Garber (2000, first published 1976) postulate alternative (sub)cultural structures for girls in the form of a 'bedroom culture' where friends are met, secrets shared and pop music consumed within the safe confines of the family home. This 'Teenie-bopper' culture (Ehrenreich et al., 1997) has important functions for teenage girls in offering them a common space for forging friendships and exercising desire. Although bedroom culture still plays a role for teenage girls today (Lincoln, 2004) and many subcultures are still male-dominated, during the 1990s incisive developments have taken place on the youth cultural front. Along with new, more gender-balanced subcultures like Goth and Rave, and the all-girl 'Riot Grrrl' subculture (see Kearney, 1998; Leonard, 1997), a different view of girlhood and femininity in general has emerged in society.

McRobbie (1994, p. 157) speaks of a dramatic 'unfixing' of young women in Western societies: 'There is now a greater degree of fluidity about what femininity means and how exactly it is anchored in social reality.' Although young women tend to reject the label 'feminism' and to don a highly conventional feminine look, they regularly express 'feminist' values and ideas (e.g. female independence) in their everyday talk and actions. McRobbie (1999) argues that mainstream 'girlie culture' has partly broken with traditional norms of feminine behaviour; female sexual assertiveness, hedonism and adventure are now recognised as entitlements. She cites in particular the 'bold, confident and strongly sexualised images' (1994, p. 166) typical of new girls' magazines and club cultures. Such hypersexual modes of femininity, which McRobbie sees as self-controlled and hence empowering, are also taken up by Pini (2001, p. 10), who hails the rise of the 'post-feminist "ladette"' – a hard-drinking, partying, sexually aggressive young woman.

Femininity Strikes back

Unlike more traditional, overtly masculinist subcultures, Goth tends to be analysed from the perspective of femininity. This is not surprising in view of the prominent status of feminine styling in this subculture. Make-up, jewellery, long hair and traditionally female modes of attire (e.g. tight fishnet tops, skirts) have long been staples of Gothic style for males and females. More recently, elements of Fetish gear (e.g. PVC and rubber clothes) have also been embraced by Goths of both genders. Many authors (e.g. Hodkinson, 2002; Gunn, 2007) stress the theme of androgyny – more precisely, the veneration of a dark and mystical version of *femininity* for both sexes – running through the subculture. Hodkinson's (2002, p. 48) ethnography of the British Gothic scene cites 'femininity and ambiguity' in style, bearing and physical appearance as one of its central values and sources of subcultural capital. For males, a slim, hairless, effeminate body is much in demand; for females, here more consistent with dominant fashion, the same standards apply.

Gunn's (2007, p. 41) analysis of gender dynamics in the US Gothic scene aims to unravel the 'ambivalence of resistance and misogyny' he sees at play within Goth. His study focuses on two key elements of Gothic style used in the construction of gender, *androgyny* and *death chic* – i.e. the cultivation of a skinny, pale and frail body. Gunn argues that, despite their overt opposition to common norms of beauty, androgyny and death chic can be read as symptoms of a misogyny deeply rooted in our culture. Firstly, androgyny in Goth is typically reduced to a one-sided appropriating of feminine style codes by men. Secondly, Gunn interprets the 'death chic' look as indicating a pathologisation of the feminine at the level of the body, a claim which remains rather unconvincing as it rests on a conflation of the material and metaphorical connotations of femininity. The author simply brackets Goth men's adoption of a feminising death chic with that of Goth women as expressing a profound hatred of a metaphorically 'female' body.

Gunn's first line of argument is persuasive, however, and will be taken up in my study. Yet an exclusive focus on such a line of argument effectively restricts the analysis to a female perspective. From this vantage point, male Goths' style practices are simply seen as a co-optation of femininity; the implications of male androgyny for constructions of masculinity are ignored. These implications will form an important area of enquiry in my study. A further problem with Gunn's discussion of gender dynamics in Goth is that the voices of subcultural participants play only a minor, mainly anecdotal part in it instead of forming the basis for a critical, in-depth analysis of field data.

Spooner's (2004, 2006) work on Gothic bodies likewise sees the status of femininity in the scene as ambiguous and partly problematic. What is venerated there seems to be 'men expressing "feminine" traits of dressing up, exploring their sexuality and displaying intense emotion' (2004, p. 178) rather than real women's attributes. Apart from being viewed from the perspective of the elevation of such an abstract ideal of femininity, Goth can also be viewed through the lens of the actual participation of women. In the wake of what McRobbie (1994, p. 155) dubs 'changing modes of femininity', subcultural analyses have emerged which focus on female identity and subjectivity from a liberal feminist perspective. One example is Williamson's (2001, 2005) interview study about the style practices of female Vampire Fans, a subgroup of Goths who enjoy vampiric literature, movies and attire. Her analysis revolves around the notion of an individual, subjectively experienced rebellion as a 'reaffirmation of Self'.

For the female Vampire Fans, the adoption of black, sinister dress is a move towards 'personal emancipation from the paradoxical parameters of femininity and the potential for a more androgynous, less rigidly gendered way of being' (Williamson, 2001, p. 154). Donning vampiric symbols can be a means of handling the paradoxical dictates and experiences of femininity. Through their style practices, the female fans construct their appearance both as subjectively 'more feminine' than contemporary women's fashion and as a rejection of conventional 'pink, frilly' femininity. Moreover, identification with the figure of the vampire, with its ambiguous, non-genital sexuality, leads the women to question the boundaries of gender and heterosexuality. Yet their desire for androgyny remains Utopian because, despite not being totally fixed by the ideology of femininity, the female Vampire Fans cannot construct an identity outside of this context. They continue to hold on to a highly feminine self-definition and at the same time wish for a potential beyond this.

Pini's (2001) study of women in Rave is similar in addressing female subjectivity through experiential accounts of Raving women. Proceeding from the idea that female Ravers experience their practices as sexually liberating, Pini celebrates the space for adventure and discovery Rave offers women, which enables 'explorations of different embodiments of femininity' (2001, p. 171). In Rave, women can party all night, take drugs and go wild without the predatory atmosphere of sexual pick-up pervading mainstream clubs. As they experience Rave as a safe space, they can experiment with formerly tabooed modes of feminine self-expression in 'a "hyper-sexualised" performance of femininity' (p. 121).

However, Pini's study is fraught with the classic problems an insider perspective can entail. Her privileging of subjectivity in effect leads to an uncritical, over-idealistic account, which buys into subcultural ideology by simply taking interviewees' rhetoric at face value instead of critically analysing their statements.[6] Pini's approach illustrates a general problem that insider studies are prone to – researchers may end up uncritically elevating lifestyle choices they are partial to into some form of visionary cultural revolution. This tendency is particularly widespread in discussions of Rave (e.g. Gaillot, 1998; Szostak-Pierce, 1999) and sexual minorities (e.g. Case, 1993; Thompson, 1991). Yet insider studies of subcultures can also produce insightful analyses with a sharp critical edge, as examples like Rose's (1994) work on Rap[7] and DeMello's (2000) study of the Tattoo scene prove.

One of the worst culprits in the uncritical raving about supposed gender subversion in subculture is not even an insider study, namely Siegel's (2005, p. 2) reading of Goth 'as a celebration of S/M practices as liberatory'. Passed off as a study on gender and sexuality in the Gothic subculture, her work seems more concerned with promoting her personal agenda of 'sex radicalism' through a discussion of an arbitrary array of cultural phenomena with a tenuous relation to Goth (e.g. the film *Boys Don't Cry*). Siegel's disregard for a sound methodological rationale leads her to pick random examples as evidence for the idea that Goth enactments of gender and eroticism, especially as steeped in S&M imagery, are inherently subversive – an idea I am going to challenge.

Reality Check

Studies addressing female subjectivity have opened up a new perspective for subcultural analysis, yet this approach entails two problems. Firstly, an exclusive focus on women leads to a view of them largely isolated from the male presence co-structuring their subcultural sphere. Secondly, the spaces girls carve out within subcultures tend to be presented idealistically as havens of female solidarity without hierarchies; struggles for status are seen as a typically male concern, bearing little relevance for girls among themselves. The latter point clearly surfaces in Pini's (2001) critique of studies which highlight the masculinist bias of club cultures (Thornton, 1995; McRobbie, 1994) for writing women out of club cultural history by privileging traditionally male sites of cultural practice (i.e. production and organisation) and marginalising female ones (i.e. dancing and consumption). By focusing on the male-defined stratification of subcultural capital in the allegedly egalitarian dance underground, Pini (2001, p. 7) asserts, Thornton unwittingly 'colludes in reinforcing the very hierarchy she seeks to expose and criticise'.

Pini's criticism is valid insofar as Thornton's analysis one-sidedly centres on male-defined hierarchies and values. In her eagerness to expose the masculine bias of subcultural capital, Thornton (1995) fails to consider gendered economies of capital which might take different forms for males and females, despite citing some observations pointing in that direction. For instance, she mentions clothes – which have traditionally been more closely linked to female status attainment – as an important form of subcultural capital; she names 'the size of a *man's* record collection' (ibid., p. 118, original emphasis) as a classic measure of it; she quotes an author positing clubs as 'classless' spaces where success is the main status criterion and, for girls, physical beauty (ibid., p. 55). But nowhere does she follow up these hints to propose potentially *different* spheres or measures for male and female subcultural distinction.

However, Pini (2001) repeats this omission by completely excluding questions of status and stratification from her analysis. Despite suggesting that 'girls themselves sometimes work to generate *different* hierarchies or economies of subcultural capital' (ibid., p. 33, original emphasis), she analyses these economies only insofar as they challenge male dominance. For instance, she argues that female Ravers define themselves against a 'cattle market' mainstream not mainly for purposes of distinction but as a critique of the sexist gender relations in traditional clubs. Pini's study presents Raving women as generally showing solidarity with each other (e.g. in sharing knowledge about drugs); none of their behaviours is interpreted against the backdrop of subcultural capital. The desire to 'dress up' and 'show off' (ibid., p. 120) and the wish to be admired, particularly by men, is presented as an innocuous form of self-fulfilment – but is there really no competition involved? One interviewee mentions she buys a new outfit for every Rave, for example. If collecting 'hip' CDs is seen as competition for subcultural capital among boys, why should acquiring 'hip' clothes be read as an act of mere self-gratification among girls?

Classically feminine forms of subcultural capital and their hierarchical implications within club cultures are effectively ignored by both Thornton and Pini. I would argue that, without invoking essential gender categories, there can be postulated typically female forms of subcultural capital, forms which are assigned to or chosen by women more often than men for traditional and economic reasons. The currency female capital is made up of, then, is maybe not so much a well-assorted record collection and an impressive CV of subcultural production, but rather an extravagant, sexy wardrobe and a beautiful face and body elaborately styled to meet subcultural standards of femininity. The question of what exactly constitutes male and female subcultural capital in Goth will be a central issue in my analysis.

Conclusion – Some Questions

Existing studies on gender in subcultures usually display at least one of the following two blind spots. Firstly, such studies mostly revolve around the construction of either femininity (e.g. Pini, 2001; Williamson, 2001) or masculinity (e.g. Macdonald, 2001; Walser, 1993). A one-sided approach focusing exclusively on masculinity or femininity fails to consider the relational character of the two sides of the gender binary. As Kimmel (1987, p. 12) points out, 'one cannot understand the social construction of either masculinity or femininity without reference to the other'.

Secondly, studies of subcultures tend to focus either on the 'object' side of cultural practices in the form of a semiotic or discursive reading of subcultural images and artefacts (e.g. Evans and Thornton, 1989; Walser, 1993) or on the 'subject' side in the form of subjective accounts of members gathered through interviews and other ethnographic techniques (e.g. Pini, 2001; Williamson, 2001). There is a lack of studies addressing both femininity and masculinity which systematically analyse the material expressive forms of subcultures (across different media and signifying practices like style) as well as their members' subjective views with regard to gender. My study on gender in Goth attempts such a balanced analysis, revolving around the following questions:

- How do Gothic practices around style, male–female relations and sexualities relate to gendered forms of subcultural capital? What constitutes male and female subcultural capital among Goths?
- To what extent do Gothic practices around style, male–female relations and sexualities challenge the traditional gender binary? Does Goth offer alternative constructions of masculinity, femininity and (hetero)sexuality?
- What are the subjective meanings and functions of Gothic style and other practices for Goth men and women? How do collective ideologies of gender circulating in the subculture relate to individual members' views?
- Is there a relationship between gender-bending style practices (androgyny) and 'queer' sexualities (e.g. bisexuality) in Goth? How are (queer) sexualities conceived and acted out among Goths?
- How do commercial or professional discourses originating from the 'Alternative' music and media industries – which cross-cut the Gothic scene – impact on Goth gender representations? What role does the political economy of the subculture play for such representations?

3

Style and Status

February 2003, the Edinburgh Goth Weekend festival. I have volunteered to help with carrying through the festival, which involves hours of cleaning and decorating before the event. The first gig is just about to start when I enter the ladies' toilet to clean my black clothes of some dust they have picked up during our efforts to prepare the slightly timeworn rooms for their big night. I am not surprised at spotting two men among the five other festival helpers gathering in front of the mirrors to get properly 'gothed up' for the festival. It is one of those funny things about Goth events that, as a rule, the separation between gents' and ladies' toilets tends to be suspended, with males and females happily crowding in front of the ladies' mirrors to do their hair and make-up. Standing at a washbasin, I notice the reflection of a girl who is applying a particularly elaborate eye make-up in the shape of a delicate ornamental pattern. The long-haired man next to her has already finished his make-up, white grounding and a simple dash of eyeliner below the eyes. The way he keeps watching her with a tender yet slightly amused expression makes it easy to guess that he must be her boyfriend. Suddenly, there is a slight slip of the eyeliner on her temple, and half of her creation is ruined. 'Aw, you guys have it so much easier,' she sighs as she carefully starts redoing the piece. 'Just long hair and a bit of eyeliner and you look so damn impressive.'

Transcending Gender?

Conspicuous styles with their high visibility and expressive character form one of the most important markers of subcultural affiliation. In this chapter and the two following ones, I analyse the style practices of the Goth subculture through the lens of gender, here focusing on male androgyny and female hyperfemininity in Gothic dress and the relative value of these style practices in terms of subcultural capital.

The rhetoric of the Gothic scene in relation to gendered style is based on what I call a fantasy or *ideology of genderlessness*, which members of the scene commonly refer to as androgyny. This ideology emphasises the values of equality and self-expression. Its attendant rhetoric is also used to mark out the subculture against what its members see as the ignorant mainstream. The second of the following two statements illustrates this mechanism by juxtaposing the Goth scene as a tolerant, enlightened space for unbridled experimenting with gender and self-expression against an 'ignorant' and intolerant mainstream of 'townies':

The aesthetic of Gothicism isn't really affected by gender. (Lady Lazarus, *slash-goth.org*, 28/02/02)[1]

Androgyny is commonplace and IMHO [in my humble opinion] is to be encouraged. The Goth scene is one place where everyone can be themselves without ridicule – THAT is left for the ignorant townies. (Taoist, *slashgoth.org*, 11/11/02)

Both male and female Goths often stress that gender is not very important – or even completely irrelevant – for their judgement of and relationships with other people, especially other Goths. For instance, a newsgroup thread discussing the fact that Goth men are sometimes mistaken for girls because of their androgynous style contains a fairly typical quote, which hints that certain elements of style considered 'Goth' (e.g. long hair) are far more important than gender in assessing a person:

Would I be the only one from a goth standpoint of thinking, 'long hair, good looking has a pulse' – gender therefore a secondary consideration (Daniel, *uk.people.gothic*, 27/11/02)

This rhetoric of gender being immaterial is not unique to the Gothic subculture but can also be found in other subcultures and even in some sections of so-called mainstream culture. One of the most prominent examples is the Rave scene. Thornton (1995) describes a 'fantasy of genderlessness' pervading the club cultures she researched, and Bradby (1993, p. 166) speaks of a 'Utopian discourse' surrounding Dance or Rave culture, which mainly consists of 'claims about gender equality and the elimination of sexism'. Braidotti (1989, p. 157) goes even further in arguing that 'the fantasy of ... being "beyond sex" ... is one of the most pernicious illusions of our era'. The post-feminist ideological climate of Western culture partly engenders a fantasy of the erasure of gender difference and prejudice among people – a fantasy which can prove dangerous since deceptive.

However, the Gothic scene differs in two crucial respects from most other sections of society entertaining this fantasy. Firstly, in Goth the ideology of genderlessness is expressed not only verbally as a form of rhetoric but also directly in subcultural style practices. Elements of style coded as feminine (e.g. make-up, long hair, delicate fabrics like mesh or lace, skinny-fit clothes, skirts) are popular among both male and female Goths. Secondly, Gothic style and the rhetoric surrounding it promote not so much a 'genderless' aesthetic where masculine and feminine elements are toned down to such an extent that they practically merge – as in the early Rave movement with its stress on comfortable, lose-fitting clothes (Pini, 1997) – as a strongly feminised one for both sexes. Femininity is highly valued in the aesthetic codes of the scene and, rather

Figure 1 Couple at the Edinburgh Goth Weekend. Photograph:
D. Brill, www.dunjabrill.com

than claiming they are 'genderless' creatures, many male and female Goths explicitly align themselves with the feminine:

One of the bands at last year's Whitby [Gothic Weekend] was Beautiful Deadly Children. One of the songs that was called Gothic Sex Machine the guy started off by going: 'Right, so who do you think is more vain, Goth men or Goth women?' My personal point is there's no difference – we're all women. ... All Goths are girls, whether they're born male or not. (Brain Hurts, m, 24, Edinburgh)

Ideals of Beauty

As we have seen, the Gothic scene idealises a highly feminine or feminised style for both sexes. With Goth probably being one of the most conspicuous of the so-called conspicuous subcultures, it is hardly surprising that ideals of beauty and norms of style form major topics of conversation among members of the scene. For instance, all the Gothic Internet forums I monitored contained threads about proper make-up, hairstyles and clothes for Goths. Moreover, although Goths typically argue that being prescriptive about style and appearance would run counter to the ideal of free self-expression at the heart of the subculture's ideology, the personal preferences Goths state regarding male and female style are striking for their conformity, in that they almost unanimously mention long hair, make-up, a feminine dress style and fine facial features as desirable on both men and women. The ideal of androgyny is often invoked in such statements:

I like androgynous males cause I like the imagery. And so any male who has put on make-up, who wears a corset and stockings, but without trying to hide that they're male – we're not talking about being a transvestite for that's something totally different – is a lovely image to see. ... In terms of females I have to confess just like the vast majority of other males, seeing a pretty female in tight clothing, curvacious, hugging her body as she dances is celebratory, it's wonderful, yes. (Veeg, m, 40, Edinburgh)

Regarding appearance, I find women beautiful if they're feminine, delicate and fragile ... and they should have long hair. On men I find androgyny incredibly attractive. I think it's marvellous. The more delicate the better, as with the women... long hair, tall and... well... just an androgynous face. (LadyGiverny, *Gothiccommunity.de*, 14/03/03)

As these quotes show, however, the idealising of androgyny in style and general looks is strictly reserved to male Goths. While different countries and

Figure 2 Male androgynous Gothic style with a Cyber touch. Photograph: D. Brill

regions vary in the extent to which Goth men actually sport androgynous styles (see chapter 5), male androgyny as an ideal is valued by Goths throughout the world. For females, by contrast, the subculture espouses an extremely feminine look, a hyperfemininity which is directly opposed to what the term androgyny would imply for female style. So what the rhetoric of the Gothic scene calls 'androgyny' can more precisely be described as a 'cult of femininity' for both sexes.

Moreover, the consequences of this cult of femininity in Gothic style are very different for male and female Goths. Goths of both genders tend to stress over and over again how 'sexy' and 'beautiful' they think long hair, skirts and make-up are. If sported by a male, such an effeminate look stands in stark opposition to traditional gender stereotypes of style and appearance. This opposition is further highlighted by Goth women often stating that they find traditional markers of male strength and attraction (e.g. bulging muscles) repulsive, and instead prefer ultra-skinny, frail guys – qualities normally deemed improper for a man in our culture. Sported by a female, however, such a look assumes very different meanings, as it is far more in accord with common cultural norms of femininity.

As Gothic style for both sexes prizes femininity, gender-bending as a source of subcultural capital and status works only for male Goths. What is more, the ideal of hyperfemininity the Gothic subculture espouses for women means that female androgyny is strongly discouraged. Even moderate deviations – like wearing less make-up or short hair – from the excessively feminine image which is the norm for Goth women can cause feelings of somehow being out of place on the scene:

> I do wonder if I'm the only goth girlie that doesn't wear a ton of make-up? I usually wear a bit of mascara and some lippy. (mircea, *slashgoth.org*, 04/10/02)

> I used to shave my head until about three years ago. Nobody seemed to have short hair then, especially not girls – I sometimes felt like a Martian amongst all those gorgeous, long-haired creatures. (Glitter Geisha, *slashgoth.org*, 30/07/02)

Of course such feelings of not really belonging are highly subjective and not always directly related to seeing oneself as lacking in terms of certain subcultural standards of female beauty and style. Sometimes they may even reflect a deliberate striving for originality and distinction. However, refusing to conform to the ideal of hyperfemininity (e.g. by wearing no make-up and plain clothes to a Goth club) proves patently ill-suited for gaining status within the scene. Both male and female Goths generally agree that a lack of feminine styling – or, even worse, a conscious adoption of an androgynous look – on the part of women is highly undesirable and unattractive:

> Some women are just dressing in trousers and like in – it just doesn't look nice. I would probably go for my boyfriend like that, but I wouldn't go to a club like that, cause it just looks a bit cheap. (Nin, f, 27, Brighton)

> S: I think androgynous is good, it's a good look for guys. I think it's a look that I prefer on guys than girls.
>
> Me: Really, why?
>
> S: Because I like girls to look as feminine as possible. I like them, you know, to look like strong personalities who are, you know, really expressing themselves, but also very feminine, and obviously if they look sexy then that's a good thing. Whereas if a girl looks androgynous – which is kind of by definition sexually ambiguous – then it's not as attractive as a girl who looks

really feminine, do you see what I mean? Whereas for a guy to look androgynous is a good thing because, I mean, you're accepting a lot of aspects of how to look that are usually sort of taboo for a man, cause you're not going for the sort of short hair, no make-up macho sort of thing, and I think you can look more beautiful and more refined and also more artistic, more like a sort of work of art, more expressive. And also you're kind of neutralising certain preconceptions that people usually have about what it is to be a man in normal Western modern society.

(Synara, m, 33, Brighton)

The first quote expresses a clear dislike for a more casual style on women (e.g. plain trousers, which Goths only deem appropriate if set off by other highly feminine style elements), at the same time implying that this kind of style is much more acceptable on men despite the Gothic ideal of male androgyny. Nin concedes that she would probably go for a man who dresses rather plainly but still maintains that on a woman a plainer style of dress can look 'cheap' when worn to a club.

Synara's statement is more complex and performs a variety of rhetorical functions by drawing on different and sometimes competing discourses. Firstly, he stresses that while he personally likes women to look 'very feminine' and 'sexy', they also should be 'strong' and 'really expressing themselves' – an obvious reference to the ideal of free self-expression which forms a central part of Gothic ideology. However, his statement then juxtaposes a purely aesthetic judgement of female androgynous style against a view of male androgynous style which is mainly based on its supposed social and cultural functions. While female androgyny is simply seen as unattractive, male androgyny is accorded a certain cultural import, namely the power to counteract received ideas about masculinity and to disrupt social norms.

These double standards for judging male and female style – and, more generally, the negative value of female androgyny – seem firmly inscribed in the discourses of modern music-based subcultures. As Reynolds and Press (1995, p. 18) argue, in music scenes it is commonly regarded as a male privilege to experiment with gender-bending glamour: 'Boys putting on eyeliner provides a frisson, but girls boycotting the kohl pencil is merely dowdy.' The following interviewee is obviously aware of these double standards and maintains that, despite the common Goth rhetoric of free self-expression, there is considerable social pressure on girls to conform to subcultural norms of feminine beauty. He further sees a link between this pressure and the fact that the scene also functions as a space for heterosexual courtship:

Well, the question is if as a woman on the Gothic scene you actually have a chance to get experimental when you're just expected to turn up at the club or venue you go to, you know, in a dress, with long hair and beautifully made up to get noticed at all, to be accepted. Well, I think if someone turned up there with short hair and, well, with a rather martial style, then this woman would – unless she's just able to present herself appropriately and to make herself the focus of attention – perhaps also not be met with such great acceptance. Well, obviously there are also ingrained clichés already in place regarding the interest search between the sexes, you know. And within this, these spaces things also still revolve a lot around finding a partner. (Kasch, m, 35, Bonn)

Figure 3 Female hyperfeminine Gothic style. Photograph: Amanda Michl, www.thanisdesign.com

The status of androgyny as a mainly male privilege can be traced back to the very origins of the term in Greek mythology. Writing about the roots of the beauty ideal of androgyny in ancient Greek statues of double-sexed beings, Weil (1992, p. 3) points out that in these statues 'the feminine element served only to soften and complement the masculine, not to challenge its privilege of representing Man'. O'Flaherty (1980, p. 331), discussing the figure of the androgyne – a creature combining male and female physical features – in the myths of different cultures, likewise points out 'the nonequality, the primary maleness, of the androgyne'. Although androgynes are popularly assumed to stand for equality and balance between the sexes, male androgynes by far outnumber female ones in the myths of various cultures and are usually regarded as positive, while female androgynes tend to represent negative meanings and functions.

A masculinist bias in the construction of androgyny also runs through various subcultures preceding or coexisting with Goth, and have often been discussed in relation to Glam Rock and Glam Metal in particular. Weil (1992) sees the same bias operating in contemporary popular culture with its trend towards androgyny in pop music, film and other media representations. Androgyny here largely consists in 'a relaxing of gender stereotypes for men, allowing them to stretch the boundaries of masculinity by appropriating the best of "woman"' (ibid., p. 1), without offering any significantly new role models or aesthetic codes for women. Arguably, this type of androgyny is a kind of lopsided 'gender tourism' (Moore, 1988), where trips into feminine territory enable men to explore or reconstruct their masculinity, in the process effacing the issues of actual women and the power imbalances between the sexes.

From this perspective, gendered Goth style codes could simply be seen as one specific instance of a pervasive and historically grounded tradition of a feminine or effeminate but still strictly male-centred ideal of androgyny. However, this view is complicated by fashion historians generally agreeing that, in our current cultural climate, androgyny in ordinary people's dress mainly consists in the one-sided taking up of traditionally male clothing by women. A prime example is the so-called 'unisex' look – formerly male garments like suits for work or jeans and T-shirts for leisure – adopted by many women from the 1980s onwards. Paoletti and Kidwell (1989, p. 158) even claim that 'the closest we have ever come to androgyny is for women to dress like men'. Consequently, Goths rightly argue that their version of androgyny presents a challenge to the everyday styles commonly worn by men and women. In the Gothic scene, men are allowed to share in the freedom of choice in dress which women are already enjoying to a much larger extent in our society, so the argument goes.

The obvious paradox here is that, on the one hand, Gothic style codes can be seen as sustaining a masculinist ideal of androgyny, while on the other hand presenting a challenge to the ordinary dress codes prevailing in current 'mainstream' culture. This seeming contradiction can be solved, however, if the competing conceptions of androgyny underlying it are examined more closely. In modern Western societies, the female version of androgyny which fashion historians like Paoletti and Kidwell refer to is firmly rooted in the everyday practices of ordinary people, and hence of a rather casual and inconspicuous nature. By contrast, the masculinist ideal of androgyny that Weil and O'Flaherty describe with reference to ancient myths – and also to what could be called the modern myths of our culture (i.e. pop music, film and other media representations) – is an ideal very remote from the mundane sphere of the everyday.

The androgyny of mythical creatures – and this rule applies just as well to pop stars and other media figures whose image partly relies on a self-styled 'mystery' – crucially depends on transcending or transgressing the common and the mundane for its effect. The notion of transgressing common social norms and style codes is certainly one of the core ideals of a conspicuous subculture like Goth, and hence closely linked to the winning of subcultural capital.

Female Beauties, Male Rebels

We have already seen that while the cultural import of male androgyny is generally acknowledged and valued by Goths, female Gothic style tends to be judged merely on aesthetic grounds. Bearing in mind the ideal of hyperfemininity the scene espouses for women, this means that female style is assessed according to fairly traditional criteria of feminine attractiveness and sexiness – even if with a dark edge – by Goths of both genders. So contrary to what the subcultural ideology of genderlessness would have us believe, Gothic style and its relative value on the scene are based on a gendered dichotomy of *female beauty* versus *male rebellion against social norms*.

This dichotomy is not absolute, implying neither that Goth women's dress is devoid of transgressive potential (as we will see in chapter 4, their hypersexy femininity can work as a subjective strategy of defiance), nor that Goth men are not also judged by appearance. In fact aesthetic criteria play a more important role for men on the Gothic scene than for most other straight men. However, their style is not viewed first and foremost through the lens of beauty and attractiveness, and especially they themselves often interpret their style practices in quite different terms, as the following statements by male Goths about their motives for wearing make-up show.

> I'll put on some eyeliner and whatnot if the spirit moves me. I do think it can be attractive, regardless of gender, if done correctly. Part of me likes to spit in the face of social norms by wearing it. (Seth Warren, *slashgoth.org*, 01/08/02)

For me, it's as much about repelling trendies – no I don't want to discuss what happened on pop idol, eastenders or blind date, so f@ck off!! (morbidbloke, *slashgoth.org*, 06/08/02)

Seth Warren invokes the ideology of genderlessness by stressing that make-up can be attractive 'regardless of gender'. Yet the sentence following this rhetorical affirmation of that by now familiar ideology shifts the focus from issues of attractiveness to the arena of social norms, and draws heavily on the tradition of transgressive male androgyny discussed above. According to Seth, make-up can not only look good on a man, but more importantly it can be employed to signal rebellion against and transgression of common social norms. The strong language used by morbidbloke ('f@ck off') and the fact that he sees make-up as a tactic for 'repelling' rather than attracting people – at least those 'trendies' outside the subculture – further suggest that, for male Goths, putting on make-up can be quite an aggressive act. In the eyes of many Goth men, their make-up signals the style-based transgression and rebellion typical of conspicuous subcultures rather than any form of conventional beauty. In the case of females, by contrast, far more prosaic motives for and attitudes towards wearing make-up prevail:

although i tend to wear make-up a lot of the time, i usually only do coz im an ugly cow, and it makes me look better! (DarkFaerie, *slashgoth.org*, 04/08/02)

My younger cousin is more of a traditional Goth, but I'm afraid to ask her for help [with make-up]. We've always been kind of competitive and I don't want her to hold it over me. At the same time I don't want to run into her at clubs with a flaky face and boring eye makeup. (The Empress of Nothin', *slashgoth.org*, 19/08/02)

For Goth women, make-up does not primarily work as a signifier of subcultural transgression, despite it being a specific subcultural style of make-up whose use of strong dark lines and effects sets it apart from fashionable female styles. It rather tends to be employed in a traditionally feminine vein, namely as a way of enhancing the woman's beauty. While male Goths can partly escape the pressures and constraints of hegemonic masculinity through their style practices, female Goths seem to remain locked into fairly traditional norms of feminine beauty and attractiveness on the scene. Obviously, the pressures of conventional femininity still hold powerful sway over their style practices and identities. Make-up is a requisite matter of course in female Gothic style, not a luxury one employs for special effect as in the case of Goth men. Consequently, being caught out with 'boring' or badly done make-up can be humiliating and – as is the case for women in general in a society obsessed with female beauty – can entail loss of status.

Figure 4 Goth woman with elaborate eye make-up. Photograph: Amanda Michl

The double standards of female beauty versus male rebellion according to which Gothic style is commonly judged in the subculture apply not only to make-up but also to other style practices. For instance, long hair on a man is not only regarded as highly desirable and attractive but also confers on the man the air of a romantic rebel precisely because it is normally rather rare. Skilfully styled long hair on females, by contrast, is still the norm for young women in our society and hence nothing special. Among Goths, it is regarded as beautiful and desirable but has none of the transgressive and 'dangerous' air which it can assume on men:

> Like all in black and then nice long hair with it on a bloke *dream* Erm, back to topic... you can do nice things with it. dangerous, romantic... on women it usually looks either nice or boring or over-styled anyway when you do something with the long stuff. (LaLestat, *Gothiccommunity.de*, 03/03/03)

Sexiness and Saleability

The double standards for judging male and female Gothic style seem mainly based on the supposed closeness of female Goth style to conventional femininity. Despite their dark edge and their sometimes confrontational display of female sexuality, subcultural beauty norms for girls (e.g. dresses or skirts, make-up, long hair, sexy outfits) are mostly in accord with current cultural ideals of youthful feminine beauty. In particular, the growing trend towards Fetish wear and very revealing clothes among Goth women – which has relegated the traditional Gothic dress of flowing gowns and velvet dresses to a marginal place in female Goth style over the last decade – parallels a bigger trend towards an increasingly sexualised young women's fashion. The following discussions by two couples I interviewed indicate that Goths themselves are acutely aware of this fairly close relation between Goth and 'mainstream' norms of female style, and obviously struggling to negotiate the sometimes rather subtle differences between the two sets of norms.

> MN: In women I like a good cleavage I have to say – when it's there, when it's exposed that's quite nice; short skirts and tights, sort of a bit slutty, I like that.
>
> V: I mean, most of it, I mean, it has to be explained, that's what most females would wear at traditional straight dance clubs. In Goth clubs it tends to be darker, with a certain edge or darkness to it.
>
> MN: Well, short black skirt and fishnet tights.
>
> V: Yes. And a certain distant attitude.
>
> (Mistress Naté, f, 24, Edinburgh; Veeg, m, 40, Edinburgh)

> PS: Well, like for example if I wear a big corset and I can show my boobs out – I mean, if I was in a normal context I would feel extremely uncomfortable, so

DB: *interrupts* But trendy girls are very exposing themselves.

PS: Yeah, but

DB: But maybe that's more for the purpose of attracting a mate, whereas in the Goth scene it's more

PS: Exactly, because I mean I'm clearly with a boyfriend and I clearly don't want to pull, and

DB: Well, trendy girls do that as well, they're in a couple and they go out very scantily clad, so you can't make that much of a distinction really.

(Petit Scarabee, f, 26, Edinburgh; Deception Boy, m, 24, Edinburgh)

The fact that subcultural beauty norms for girls are pretty much in keeping with common cultural ideals of femininity is also reflected in the gender-specific reactions Goths report they get from other people. As the hyperfeminine style of female Goths is usually deemed attractive even by outsiders, they are seen as less prone to getting abuse than male Goths. Goth men's effeminate, 'sissy' style often makes them a target for homophobic abuse. Conversely, Goth women may even be met with compliments. Both males and females in the subculture generally agree that Goth men take a considerably higher risk of harassment and social censure with their style, while Goth women have it a lot easier because they are still regarded as sexy and pretty in the conventional sense.

Anyone noticed that if you're a girl-goth the population goes "phwoar", yet if you're a bloke they go "poof/queer/batty boy"? (ChromeNewt, *slashgoth.org*, 29/10/02)

B: I think it's worse for men, to get away with it; women tend to be left alone a little bit more. But if you're a guy I think it's harder because, well, I don't know, if you're female I suppose you're prettier, whereas as a guy you're gonna have a lot more abuse I suppose.

Me: What kind of stuff do they get?

B: 'Freak, get your hair cut', 'you transvestite, don't wear make-up', yeah, stuff like that.

(Batty, f, 30, Brighton)

In certain situations, however, female Goths are expressly singled out for abuse by men from outside the subculture. Yet closer analysis reveals that such instances of harassment aimed at Goth women differ in crucial respects from the types of insult Goth men are typically faced with. Firstly, female Goths tend to be hassled by outsiders not because their appearance is at odds with the gendered beauty norms of our culture – as is the case with male Goths – but precisely because their hyperfemininity makes them sexually attractive to ordinary men. The following anecdote about the sometimes unpleasant journey home after a night out illustrates this, suggesting that a certain type of sexually repressed young male may shout abuse at Goth women simply because of his frustration at not having erotic access to them.

> I remember walking home with some Goth friends of mine, I was in my Gothic finery and so were they, and the hassle they got, the aggression they got, sleaziness, comments they got was outstanding. ... It was my female friends who got it most, mostly by young males being completely dorky at seeing – what I imagine they saw in it was this beautiful young woman dressed in very alluring clothing, and they knew they'd never have access to her, so they took it out aggressively. (Veeg, m, 40, Edinburgh)

Secondly, this has direct consequences for the kind of abuse or harassment Goth women get, which is often of an explicitly sexual nature. While female as well as male Goths report they are sometimes insulted in gender-neutral terms by being called names like 'Satan' or 'corpse', the main term of abuse levelled at Goth women is 'slut'. In rural areas in particular, like the small Bavarian village my interviewee Samael originally hails from, sexily styled Goth females risk getting sleazy offers or even outright sexual harassment.

> What I find quite crude most of all is when all the girls get approached, because they often get called sluts then. Well, in our area it's like this, I don't know what it's like elsewhere. But, you know, they often get called sluts, and 'how much do you charge for an hour?' and the like, I've often heard that. ... They did, well, another female friend of mine they even grabbed once, didn't want to let her off again at all, had a real go at her. (Samael, m, 21, Leipzig)

Direct sexual harassment seems a form of abuse only female Goths experience, whereas Goth men are typically faced with mock homophobic insults. Crucially, while both forms of abuse can be disturbing to the individual, on the collective level the Gothic subculture regards the risks and the abuse male Goths have to take for their effeminate style as higher and heavier than the risk of sexual harassment female Goths have to deal with. Certainly there is some truth in the argument that males generally face heavier social restrictions on flamboyant style in our culture. But I think Goth men are regarded as getting more stick partly because women are still tacitly expected to be used to sexual harassment. For a straight man, adopting effeminacy with its attendant risk of homophobic abuse can be seen as a deliberate – and hence courageous – step towards the marginal position which women and gay men have in general society. For a woman, by contrast, at least the milder forms of sexual harassment are a fairly normal experience; they simply come with the territory of the inferior social position women have been assigned in our culture (see Kissling, 1991).

Despite its dark and theatrical slant, the highly feminine ideal of beauty Goth girls aspire to is commonly held to be sexually attractive in conventional terms, not only by ordinary people but also by Goths themselves. Of course this affects Goths' appraisal of how easily male or female Gothic style may be co-opted by mainstream media and fashion. Female Gothic style is seen as fairly easy to exploit commercially, mainly because of its hyperfemininity and sexiness. Conversely, male Gothic style – because of its very effeminacy – is regarded as too much in discord with common cultural norms to be co-optable. In terms of subcultural authenticity and status, androgynous male Goth style is hence accorded a much higher value, whereas the hyperfeminine style of Goth women seems almost too close for comfort to the dreaded spectre of the commercial and inauthentic 'mainstream'. For instance, in 2002 *The Sun* printed a fashionable 'Goth' style guide geared to conventional women, which was hotly discussed among Goths. The following statements illustrate the gender difference in terms of potential co-optation with which Goths view their subcultural style:

> I think it [i.e. Goth style] may just be easier to sell to women and girls by saying how sexy they will look. (Dracos, *slashgoth.org*, 03/10/02)
> Seconded! I doubt the sun would be very successful in selling the He-Goth image to their average male reader by pointing out how wonderfully effeminate they will look. (Glitter Geisha, *slashgoth.org*, 03/10/02)

> the reason that Goth will never be fashionable is because you're not going to get your average trendy putting on the make-up before going out (or dressing extravagantly). So only women will be 'dressing Goth', which is only half of the subculture … . It's just a femme fatale diversion for mainstream culture, and will be forgotten by next year (or until next time they try to push it into the mainstream). (sheridan, *slashgoth.org*, 04/10/02)

Courage and Transgression

While female Gothic style is seen as fairly close to – even if still substantially different from – the 'mainstream' with its bland smack of inauthenticity and sell-out, androgynous male Gothic style is regarded as the crucial purveyor of subcultural authenticity and rebellion. Goths of both genders frequently link male androgyny with qualities like transgression and courage:

i must agree with most of the ladies here – men in skirts are tres gothic and super sexy!!! … i think they are so sexy and wonderous because other than inherent loveliness in skirts, i appreciate any man who is confident and cool enough to wear a traditionally female article of clothing. The same goes for make-up – endearing, adorable and highly encouraged! (scarlett severine, *slashgoth.org*, 15/11/02)

The media seem to have deftly skipped over the issue of male Gothic fashion for some reason. I think they just don't get it, or maybe they think that your average girl is more likely to go Goth than your average guy. Male Goth fashion is, after all, something that takes more "bollocks" to wear than female Goth fashion, IMHO. Probably because of its sexuality-challenging androgyny. (Taoist, *slashgoth.org*, 03/10/02)

Male androgynous style can obviously afford its wearer an air of courage and confidence. Moreover, Taoist's statement reveals the paradoxical nature of the subcultural rhetoric on gender norms. On the one hand, the androgynous style of Goth men is seen as a challenge to the received gender norms of general society; Taoist speaks of its 'sexuality-challenging androgyny'. Yet from the perspective of subcultural norms, Gothic male androgyny works to affirm a traditional masculine status criterion, namely courage. The fact that Taoist uses the word 'bollocks' in this context, a word with a highly masculinist charge, is particularly telling.

The qualities assigned to male androgyny – transgressing and challenging common social norms, displaying courage and confidence towards outsiders – score highly on the subcultural scale of values, and hence are important sources of subcultural capital. The thought that androgynous male style functions as a major status criterion in the Gothic subculture may at first seem odd, considering the dominant academic opinion on the relation between cross-sex dress and social status. Theorists of culture and fashion (e.g. Lurie, 1992; Paoletti and Kidwell, 1989) commonly agree that because masculinity is valued more highly in our culture than femininity, a feminising of the male generally implies loss of status. Elements of male attire on a woman are socially acceptable as long as she remains identifiably feminine; like the female version of the business suit, they can sometimes even bestow traces of masculine status (Ganetz, 1995). By contrast, apart from instances of socially sanctioned play like the drag act or the fancy-dress party, 'men cannot appear in *any* item of women's clothing without immediate loss of the superior status attached to the male and the full imposition of ridicule and censure' (Woodhouse, 1989, p. 6).

Paradoxically, in the Gothic scene exactly the opposite is true. While female androgyny is strongly discouraged and donning a masculine style would incur a loss of social status for a woman rather than a gain, the adoption of feminine style by men is encouraged and forms an important source of subcultural capital. To make sense of this seeming paradox, we have to remember that Goth men draw on a well-established tradition of transgressive male androgyny. This tradition, which harks back to ancient myths, reserves the transgressive or transcendent powers of androgyny to the male. In the subcultural sphere, it can be deployed to turn an apparent 'wilful appropriation of subordinate status' (Amico, 2001, p. 373), that is feminine status, by the androgynous male into a form of courageous masculine defiance. The following exchange between a very effeminate Goth man, who has experienced harassment because of his style, and a Goth woman illuminates this mechanism:

> I've had my fair share of sexist abuse, harassment & "are you looking for business" type comments. But none of that has put me off and I'll continue to cause gender confusion for as long as I feel happy to do it. (Nikki, *slashgoth.org*, 15/11/02)
> YAY! That's the spirit Nikki! Keep giving us goth girls something to admire :) – and be jealous of :P (Princess Thais, *slashgoth.org*, 18/11/02)

As I have argued above, the way androgynous male Goths open themselves up to quasi-sexist and homophobic abuse through their style can be seen as a voluntary embracing of the marginal position assigned to women and gay men in our culture. This deliberate act of stigmatising oneself vis-à-vis general society is seen as courageous and admirable within the subculture. For Goth women, by contrast, the marginal position of femininity with its risk of sexual harassment seems natural and hence not worthy of special admiration, despite their darkly twisted excess of conventional feminine codes being accorded a mildly transgressive edge among Goths (see chapter 4).

Femininity up for Grabs

While the smiley symbols punctuating Princess Thais' above statement indicate a tongue-in-cheek tone, the suggestion that Goth girls have reason to envy the transgressive potential of male androgyny – and the subcultural capital linked to it – does have a serious point. Although Goth women are keen to stress that they love androgynously styled men, discussions about male Goths wearing female clothes regularly contain 'complaints' by females voicing similar feelings:

> I'm so jellous of blokes, they dont have to try too hard at all to look strikingly good, a man wearing a bit of eyeshadow and a dress makes so much more impact than anything females dream to dress up in! (Lvciani, *slashgoth.org*, 11/11/02)

Men can wear women's clothes and look instantly stunning, whereas us women spend hours getting ready and just look the same as every other time we go out. It is just so frustrating. (Witchygoth, *slashgoth.org*, 11/11/02)

Of course these quotes evince that Goth men are also judged according to aesthetics to a notable extent. However, there is a downside to this seeming femininisation of male status criteria. Weil (1992) points out that exalting the feminine as an abstract aesthetic or spiritual principle often goes hand in hand with effacing women as actual people. The fantasy of genderlessness, which is ideologically linked with the transcendent or transgressive tradition of androgyny, in a patriarchal culture where men hold a dominant position and women a marginal one can easily 'lead to a denial of difference – the assimilation of woman as "the feminine" to a male model' (ibid., p. 165). In her study of male transvestites, Woodhouse (1989, p. 87) makes a similar point, speaking of 'the transvestite's enjoyment of the best of both worlds by becoming "better than" a mere woman, because he is a "woman" with a penis'. From this perspective, the apparent transgression of gender boundaries performed by androgynous men seems to do little to subvert the superior status of masculinity and the gender binary on which it is based.

The above quotes indicate that, in the Gothic subculture, androgynous males also tend to be seen as 'better than' actual women with regard to feminine style. In the value system of the scene, femininity on men is accorded more value than on women, a situation which puts female Goths in a double bind. For one thing, they cannot join in Goth men's pose of rebellious gender-bending in their quest for subcultural capital as female androgyny is rejected in Gothic style codes. Moreover, the hyperfemininity these codes prescribe for women is certainly valued in the subculture, but primarily on the aesthetic or erotic level traditionally applied to female style and only secondarily in terms of subcultural capital. It is seen as easily co-optable, and hence not as subversive as Gothic male androgyny.

So for Goth women the main option to gain acceptance and status through subcultural style is capitalising on feminine beauty and attractiveness in a fairly traditional sense – a practice which at the same time defines them as inferior to Goth men in terms of transgression and subcultural capital in the value system of the scene. What is more, some female Goths also seem to see themselves in direct competition with androgynously styled males on the purely aesthetic level of feminine beauty:

I have one problem with men wearing women's clothes and that is that men usually end up looking soooo much better in them. Where's the justice? (Witchygoth, *slashgoth.org*, 11/11/02)

I know androgyny does seem to be a major part, but I get cross when my male friends look better in my "girls" clothes than I do (you know who you are....) ;P (alexx, *slashgoth.org*, 28/01/02)

As the smiley symbol at the end of alexx's quote shows, such statements are usually made in a humorous spirit. However, there does seem to be a true core to the feelings of inferiority conveyed therein. As Weil (1992, p. 151) argues in relation to the idealised androgynes of ancient Greek myths, which mostly represented feminised males and not masculinised women: 'within the androgynous tradition, even women are brought to see their most glorified image as that of a man'. In this tradition, the deliberate putting on of femininity is a form of sanctioned transgressive play for men, 'while it is something always risking self-contempt for women to put on "the feminine"' (Russo, 1988, p. 216). Accordingly, some Goth women appear to entertain quite strong negative feelings towards their female physique, and do indeed see the most glorified image of femininity in a man wearing female attire:

I love men in long cybery skirts, think its to do with the fact I have always lusted after having a sleek slim bod like some blokes without curves to ruin the look of an outfit. (Bat Girl, *slashgoth.org*, 13/11/02)

I vote the short skirt Taoist, you look gorgeous! At least being slim you can get away with short skirts without fear of the dreaded flab like some of us goth girls! (Kitsch Bitch, *slashgoth.org*, 12/11/02)

While Gothic norms of beauty do leave some scope for female curves to be valued, the Goth ideals of male androgyny versus female hyperfemininity can entail massive and sometimes contradictory pressures for women. Despite sensing that their version of femininity will never measure up to the kind of femininity which androgynous males can project, Goth women still have to hold on to it as they feel rebellious androgyny is not an option for them.

Conclusion

In view of the widespread assumption that 'subcultures in some form or other explore and celebrate masculinity' (Brake, 1985, p. 182), which dominated subcultural studies until the late 1980s, a subculture like Goth still seems like a minor revolution on the youth cultural front. Here, both men and women are encouraged to cherish and experiment with femininity, pulling it from the dull sphere of the domestic right into the limelight of clubs and festivals.

However, this resurrection of the feminine is bought at a cost. Through the style practice of male androgyny, Goth men can draw on the transgressive charge of gender-bending as a major source of subcultural capital, from which Goth women with their hyperfeminine style are largely excluded. Moreover, while female Goths share their marginal status in terms of the little subcultural capital accorded their (style) practices with females in overtly masculinist subcultures, their potential for transgressing hegemonic social standards seems even more restricted by the Gothic norm of hyperfemininity. Women in the heavily male-dominated Graffiti and Punk scenes have been shown to confront both general and subcultural standards of femininity through adopting traditionally masculine markers of subcultural deviance (Macdonald, 2001; Leblanc, 1999). By contrast, Goth women's potential for 'gender trouble' seems largely muted through a one-sided veneration and colonisation of traditionally feminine style codes as tropes of male transgression within the Gothic scene.

Furthermore, Gothic style norms do not so much appear to transgress or disrupt the traditional gender binary, but rather to transpose it. This transposition could be conceived as a shifting from the distinct categories of *masculinity* and *femininity* – which form the traditional binary – to the still relatively distinct categories of *male androgyny* and *female hyperfemininity* within a newly constructed binary. As Goth men colonise part of the territory of femininity through the style practice of androgyny, it seems, the stylistic domain of Goth women is in turn shifted to the extreme of hyperfemininity, as if partly to keep intact the binary and distinct structure of conventional gender. As we will see in chapter 5, (androgynous) Goth masculinity avails itself of certain strategies to assert its distinctness from femininity, thus guarding the shifted yet still intact boundary between the male and female domains of the Gothic gender binary. Yet we will also see that, viewed from a perspective other than the mere colonising of femininity, male androgyny does hold some potential to unsettle conventional gender norms, especially those of proper male appearance.

4

Female Style and Subjectivity

Leipzig, June 2003, the annual Wave-Gotik-Treffen festival. It is a very hot Saturday evening, and the streets and public spaces are brimming with black-clad creatures of the night as the venues for the festival are spread all over the city. I am on my way to the tram station to travel to the Agra, the main festival site, when a group of scantily clad girls catches my eye. All of them are wearing skimpy black PVC skirts or hot pants, with one even dressed in nothing but a skin-tight PVC bodice, torn mesh stockings and extreme high heels. Obviously I am not the only one to notice these women; their charms seem anything but lost on the group of male youths standing at the tram station, whose outfits mark them out as what Goths tend to call 'townies'. I overhear how one of them, a tall guy with a white baseball cap and baggy jeans, tries to talk the others into chatting up the girls. They ogle the one in the PVC bodice, making saucy comments about her body and dress. Prompted by their obtrusive stares and sexual banter, all of a sudden she walks up to them and starts eyeing the tall guy in a confident, almost aggressive way. I think I can even see a slight smile around her eyes. The boys instantly stop their boastful banter and fall silent, seeming rather uncomfortable with the situation. The tall one tries hard to avoid the woman's gaze and obviously does not feel like showing any more interest in the ample cleavage displayed right in front of him. As she walks back to her friends, her subdued smile turns into a broad grin – a contagious grin, it seems, as I still have it on my face when the tram finally comes.

Femininity as 'Masquerade'

So far I have discussed male and female Gothic style in terms of status and subcultural capital, evaluating gendered Goth styles from the perspective of the general norms and values of the scene. The following two chapters focus more on the subjective meanings and functions Goths assign to their styles, starting here with an analysis of hyperfemininity as a source of personal empowerment.

The issue of women's relation to style and its subversive or empowering potential is a conflicted one and remains hotly debated in feminist cultural theory. Russo (1988, p. 217) poses the question whether women are 'so identified with style itself that they are as estranged from its liberatory and transgressive effects as they are from their own bodies as signs in culture generally'. Indeed, my own assessment of hyperfeminine Goth style in terms of subcultural capital would suggest that the answer to this question is yes. However, such an assessment does not tell us everything about female Gothic style and its significance for the individuals who don it. Modern theorists of dress generally agree that the driving forces behind female style creation are multiform and cannot be reduced to the negotiation of women's role as erotic spectacle for the male gaze. Style practices also form an important tool for creative self-expression, and for actively constructing female subjectivity beyond mere gender identity. In these properties of style there resides some potential for women to reclaim dress and appearance as a source of empowerment.

For a discussion of the empowering functions of female Gothic style, the concept of *feminine masquerade* suggests itself. First introduced by Doane (1982) into film theory as 'feminine masquerade'[1] and by Irigaray (1985) into feminist literary criticism as 'mimicry', this concept stresses the subversive, disruptive potential of women who reappropriate traditionally feminine clothes with an ironic twist. As Doane (1982, p. 82) argues, femininity as a consciously adopted masquerade works to distance woman from her patriarchal image precisely through 'a hyperbolization of the accoutrements of femininity, that is through hyperfemininity'. Flaunted as a masquerade, such a parodic excess of femininity can work to disrupt the male-defined scopic regimes of voyeuristic and fetishistic looking at women so deeply ingrained in our visual culture (see Mulvey, 1992). This line of argument suggests that hyperfemininity can be a form of resistance, a strategy for deconstructing the patriarchal ideal of femininity from within rather than from an impossible position outside gender discourse.

An important characteristic of feminine masquerade or mimicry is the notion of a conscious 'ironic distance' (Silverman, 1986) – e.g. in the form of deliberate parody – from the outwardly projected image of (hyper)femininity. The female masquerader, aware of the conventions that encode her as feminine, performs femininity with a playful and critical difference, demonstrating 'that it is a role and not a nature' (Tyler, 1990, p. 193). However, some statements by my female interviewees suggest that quite the opposite is true in the case of Goth women. Instead of fabricating a conscious distance, most female Goths strongly identify themselves with the excessive femininity of their outward appearance in one way or another:

I try to keep it [i.e. her style] all feminine as well; I like being feminine. I like to look pretty as well, that's why I like the long, flowing gowns, it's elegant, and that's what I like. ... I think I've just always been a feminine person. (Batty, f, 30, Brighton)

That's why I like wearing nice clothes, just to like make myself feel more feminine. Cause I kind of look like, I think I look quite butch with certain clothes actually. I just wanna look pretty. (Fairy, f, 23, Brighton)

Both interviewees cite the wish to 'look pretty' as one of the chief motives for their feminine style, showing no intention of deconstructing patriarchal notions of female beauty. Batty furthermore insists that she has always been 'a feminine person', thus indicating that she feels no distance between herself and her feminine image; on the contrary, she seems to regard femininity as an essential part of her personality. Fairy does experience a certain distance between herself and an ideal femininity, as she thinks she can look 'quite butch' without her feminine style. However, she employs her style not to draw attention to this distance but rather to cloak it, and to make herself not only look but also 'feel more feminine'.

This discrepancy between academic notions of feminine masquerade and the subjective attitudes of Goth women towards their hyperfeminine style in a sense exemplifies the problems of thrusting a concept derived from arts or literary theory onto the empirical reality of the nitty-gritty everyday. Hence, it is further proof that due attention should be paid to the subjectivity of social agents when interpreting their style practices. Yet while the conscious intentions and motives of the people wearing a style do matter and must be considered, Holmlund (1993, p. 216) reminds us that 'masquerades change according to who is looking, how, why, at whom'. Consequently, if we want to assess their relation to hegemonic modes of representation, we have to think about how they function for specific people in specific situations. So the factor guiding an analysis should be the concrete effects masquerades have for the individuals concerned, rather than their declared intentions; this means that the notion of feminine masquerade may still hold some relevance for an understanding of female Gothic style.

Empowering Subjectivity

Many statements in my data indicate that, on the level of subjective experience, hyperfeminine Gothic style does indeed have some powerful effects on the self-images of Goth women, and also on the way they interact with other people. The following very young interviewee, for example, reports a drastic increase in her self-confidence and her ability to handle social situations due to her adoption of a – fairly moderate – Gothic style:

> I've also noticed, since I started dressing like this, I don't know, I've become more self-confident, I've really become totally more self-confident. Previously I didn't even dare to ask a stranger in the street for the time; and it's really like this, that's really astonishing somehow. And most of all, previously I was always afraid of any strangers, and now it just simply annoys me that they're staring at me. (Anthea, f, 14, Berlin)

Anthea experiences her style as empowering and protective at the same time. By increasing her confidence, it also enables her to overcome social anxieties and to deal with unwanted attention by strangers more effectively.

Similar feelings are voiced by Sarn – who prefers a conspicuous, sexy Fetish style for which she designs her own PVC outfits with tight-fitting tops and extremely short skirts – in response to my question of what her outfits mean to her:

> I think a certain amount of freedom, cause at times I used to think, I used to meet X [her boyfriend] at Euston Station or something, I used to be standing there and

Figure 5 Hypersexy fetish style: my interviewee Sarn. Photograph: Synara, www.synara.com

like, tight corset, little skirt and, you know, really Gothed up. And I think if I was like natural blonde – which I am – and wearing that, then I would get so much hassle. Yeah, but because, in a way it was an element of, you know, you could be so much more extreme but still feel safe. You know, you still get some comments or something, but, you know, you were enabled to do and be how you wanted to be and how you wanted to look. (Sarn, f, 33, Brighton)

For Sarn, her erotic yet confrontational style also holds certain protective functions in making her 'feel safe' and deflecting some of the unwanted sexual attention she might get wearing similarly revealing clothes as part of a more conventional style (e.g. blonde instead of black-dyed hair). A factor she emphasises even more is the feeling of freedom her style gives her. While conceding that her way of dressing does attract some sexualised hassle and comments, she still feels that it enables her to express herself freely without fear of social censure or direct sexual harassment.

Goth women certainly do get sexualised hassle because of their style, as we have seen in the preceding chapter. However, many of them experience their style as somehow making them untouchable for conventional men, despite inviting the voyeuristic male gaze. Its dark edge and distinct *femme fatale* overtones are seen to rattle men from outside the subculture, and thus to deter them from making direct sexual advances. The following exchange between Lady Leather and Leatherman, a Goth couple from Edinburgh, about Lady Leather's highly sexy Fetish style with a sinister twist elaborates on this logic:

LL: I like it because of the way it makes me feel. When I go out and I'm wearing rubber and shiny boots I do feel quite powerful and it does make me feel good about myself. Again, I like the attention it gives me.

L: And the fear.

LL: *laughs*

L: People, if you would wear something pink and fluffy – 'ah, look, like an easily achievable sexual target'. That's not something to achieve; whereas someone who is like really scary and really powerful, that's a lot more attractive.

LL: Yeah, if you're wearing something harsher it would deter anybody who's likely to come up and try and pull you if you're wearing something fluffy.
...

L: If you appear to be something which is unachievable, it's good for a fantasy for someone, but 'hell, I'm not gonna talk to her, she's

LL: she's a fucking scary bitch!'.

(Lady Leather, f, 21, Edinburgh; Leatherman, m, 38, Edinburgh)

Here female Gothic style – especially in its most confrontationally sexy Fetish variety – is associated with power and fearsomeness. A woman wearing this kind of sexually assertive style is seen as 'powerful' and 'scary', and

Figure 6 My interviewee Lady Leather at the Edinburgh Goth Weekend.
Photograph: D. Brill

precisely not as the easy sexual prey which conventional 'pink and fluffy' femininity signifies. While Leatherman suggests that this air of menace and defiance makes Goth women particularly attractive to men on the level of erotic fantasy, he and Lady Leather agree that at the same time it deters conventional men on the level of actual sexual advances. In this connection, it is worth mentioning that Lady Leather – who regularly wears her Fetish-Goth outfits when working as a strip dancer – further told me that while men like looking at her, she hardly ever gets pestered by regular guys trying to approach her when she goes out. Jet, a very attractive Goth woman who also prefers a sexy, Fetish-inspired style and sometimes works as a Fetish model, reports similar experiences when talking about the reactions she gets in 'mainstream' clubs:

J: I have been to some mainstream clubs, and the women, they just look and 'uh, god, what's going on there'. And the men, I don't know, it just seems like normal men have got kind of a weird hang-up, kind of like almost a fantasy about dark, kind of dom-looking women.

Me: And do these guys try to approach you?

J: I think I scare them away actually. I think they just feel a little bit intimidated that you actually dare to be different. … You know, they kind of give it, they go to their mates 'wohey, she's in a corset, wohey, she's in heels, woaah'. And you actually go up and stand next to them and smile at them, and they kind of go 'oh fuck, oh god, uh, let me out!'.

(Jet, f, 21, Brighton)

A recurrent theme in the stories female Goths tell about their style is power and control. As proposed by academic theories of feminine masquerade, Goth women – even without establishing a conscious ironic distance between themselves and their hyperfeminine image – seem to take control of their own image precisely by projecting an excessive femininity and sexiness which invites the male gaze only to confound it and keep it at a distance. In the same vein, another of my female interviewees, sporting a sexy Fetish-inspired style, explicitly links it to the notion of 'power dressing':

That's power dressing. … If I feel, like, I'm going out and I feel as if I can conquer the world, that's a feeling where you can just go and do anything. Power-dressing like that, making you look powerful as well as feeling powerful, it's very, it's good, it gives you a thrill. (Mistress Naté, f, 24, Edinburgh)

To see power represented in excessively feminine style may seem paradoxical, as power is usually held to reside in strongly masculine symbols (e.g. military uniforms, the business suit) in our culture. Yet some theorists of dress have pointed out that expressions of femininity can signify power. For instance, Wright (1995) discusses the stiletto heel – an item of clothing which epitomises a stereotypical sexy image of femininity, and hence is often regarded as reactionary by feminists – as a symbol of women's liberation rather than oppression. She argues that young women in the 1950s and 1960s used this form of footwear to distance themselves from the post-war ideal of domestic, modest and passive femininity which the parent generation embodied, instead putting across their femininity in an aggressive and explicit manner.

What is interesting about Wright's line of argument with regard to Gothic style is that she claims the meaning of the stiletto became more radical and transgressive as the style itself became more exaggerated, i.e. higher and pointier. Extreme stilettos, she argues, represented an excess of sexualised femininity in style which went beyond the bounds of what was socially acceptable for women in that era, thus becoming capable of symbolising power and a rejection of convention. This view of the stiletto is based on the notion that 'an overt representation of femaleness equals assertion' (ibid., p. 16) – a view which could just as well be applied to Goth women's excessively sexy femininity.

McDowell (1992) makes a similar point in relation to the changes which the miniskirt underwent over the decades. He argues that the shorter and hence sexier the miniskirt got, the stronger, more aggressive and menacing was the image of femininity it conveyed. This line of argument points towards the empowering potential of taking femininity and sexiness to extremes in female style. McDowell speaks explicitly of 'power dressing' and women's new confidence in this context; a blatant display of sexiness, he maintains, 'frightens as many men as it excites' (ibid., p. 177). These formulations sound very similar to the ways Goth women talk about their style. So while I have argued before that Gothic hyperfemininity does in many respects conform to conventional norms of female attractiveness and sexiness, the wilful exceeding of these norms through hypersexy modes of dress complicates the picture, making Goth women's style practices oscillate between conformity and transgressive excess.

Alternative Identities

Hyperfemininity as an empowering and protective masquerade represents a general way in which female Goths' emotional investments in their style can be understood. On a more specific level, my data further indicate that certain Goth women with marginal positions in society as well as in the subculture use their style to construct alternative feminine images and identities for themselves. Ayleen, for example, is a transgendered Goth woman who went through difficult inner struggles because of not fitting into the binary gender categories which structure our society. She sees her elegant, traditional Gothic style – with long, flowing dresses or skirts in black, ruby or purple and lots of velvet – as a chance to turn this exclusion from 'normal' categories into an affirmative statement about herself:

> Well, I did try and become, how to put it, a normal – well, probably no, that's not right, but a socially acceptable female, but I don't like the clothes *laughs*. They are so boring. ... Well, I went through a period of time with myself that

Figure 7 Alternative trans femininity: my interviewee Ayleen (left). Photograph: D. Brill

was very, I was fighting against my feelings, so I got very depressed, suicidal, I took overdoses and that sort of thing. That was a very dark period of my life, and I got out at the other side by allowing myself to express myself via my, just my guitar playing or band playing and stuff, or the way I presented myself to the society in general. You know, it's a statement about myself: 'I don't fit in your category, this is what I look like, this is who I am'. (Ayleen, f, 38, Brighton)

Ayleen also told me that the flashy version of femininity many transgendered women go for was simply not for her; Gothic style enables her to construct an image for herself which conveys femininity without trying to emulate conventional female fashions. Sappho, a lesbian Goth who also prefers a traditional style with long black skirts and velvet tops, feels similarly alienated from the masculinised style norms of the lesbian scene. For her, Gothic style has been a way of holding on to her femininity while fully acknowledging her lesbianism:

> Well, especially as a lesbian I find, well, I'm one who's kept up keeping her hair long for years and years all the same. Well, I still remember in the beginning, well, I'm the only one, more or less the only one who's never cut her hair short of all the ones I know, yes, and of course I'm keeping this up partly because of my Black sentiments, well yes. I'm lesbian because I like the feminine and don't like something like kind of an imitation of maleness. (Sappho, f, 33, Leipzig)

Big women are a particularly interesting case of females from marginal groups who construct alternative images and interpretations of femininity for themselves through Gothic style, mainly because they are regularly discriminated against not only in general society but also in the subculture. Gunn (2007) argues that the 'death chic' dominating Goth beauty ideals values extreme slimness and hence works to marginalise bigger people, especially women. Despite its rhetoric of free self-expression and tolerance, strong undercurrents of discrimination against overweight women definitely exist in the Gothic subculture. A posting on *de.soc.subkultur.gothic*, for example, insults big girls as 'the barrel girls with their I'm-gonna-choke-you cleavages and their flabby arms in much too tight medieval dresses' (Sina Wartmann, 27/01/03).

Although other postings in the respective thread disagreed with this statement, the fact remains that, while I have met some very confident, assertive bigger females on the scene who take obvious pride in their female curves, overweight women often experience unease or even shame when going out to Goth clubs. A thread on *Gothiccommunity.de* started by an obese girl gives voice to the feelings of such women. Accounts of feeling ashamed to turn up at Goth clubs because they do not meet the ideal standards of beauty, of being treated in subtly derogatory ways by some other Goths, and of progressively losing one's self-confidence indicate that many big women feel partly excluded from the subculture. A statement posted in response to a woman who deplored that the cult of slimness pervading our culture also surfaces in the Gothic scene is particularly telling:

> Also is an understatement.... By now I'm getting the feeling that more and more "Blacks" especially at events like the WGT [Wave-Gotik-Treffen] and such like are JUST ONLY interested in one's figure... might be my paranoia, but I think a trend is discernible... you're no longer a human being if you don't fit into XXS in PVC and leather... I think this is perverse... and it just only aggravates the situation for me. (Ygramul, *Gothiccommunity.de*, 28/04/03)

However, a thread like this also functions as a safe space in Gothic Internet forums where overweight women can express their feelings, experience solidarity and, most importantly, construct alternative values and standards for Goth femininity. For instance, *slashgoth.org* contains a thread aptly entitled 'Plus Size Goth', where a big girl enquires about how to become a plus-size Goth model and gets lots of constructive tips and encouraging reactions from other Goths. The thread also contains quite a bit of direct criticism of what at least some members of the subculture regard as a stereotypical 'anorexic' Goth body ideal. Moreover, such criticism regularly advances alternative interpretations of what constitutes a truly 'Gothic' ideal in style. As the following statements indicate, Gothic as an ideal can be reclaimed against the grain of subcultural beauty standards – by women who do not meet these standards – through recourse to the deeper ideology underlying subcultural style practices, namely nonconformism, free self-expression and acceptance of people who differ from the norm.

Some people do not at all seem to understand that being fat is also a bit of what Gothic means. Being different from the norm, tolerance only for tolerance. You want people to be open and reach out to you and not to depreciate you because of the way you look. (hen-mir, *Gothiccommunity.de*, 28/04/03)

I want those bras with booster cups but apparently as a 36DD I am not allowed to have them! The whole size debate boils down to one thing – conformity. As most goths do not want to conform, is it then anathema to be made to conform to the fashion industry's notions of what different sizes should be wearing. (Anonymous, *slashgoth.org*, 28/09/02)

These women take the liberty to interpret 'Gothic' their own way, instead of feeling alienated from it because the beauty norms of the subculture have imbued it with some values and meanings which exclude them. Importantly, the anonymous poster of the second statement points out that the attempt to regulate or prescribe dress styles according to body size is 'anathema' to the Gothic spirit of nonconformism. She obviously does not want other people – be they Goths or not – to decide for her what she should or should not wear.

Of course it requires much confidence to take this defiant stance towards people inside and outside the subculture. Clothes which emphasise unusual physical features draw even more attention to these features, an effect many overweight people want to avoid. However, Gothic style can also work to boost the often fragile self-confidence of big women through exactly the opposite mechanism. As the following statement by an overweight female about the way outsiders react to her appearance illustrates, it can be used to deflect unwanted attention from the body to the conspicuous clothes and accessories adorning it:

But it has one big advantage that now everyone is bitching about my Black appearance, because previously (when I was still dressing fairly normally) I had to put up with remarks about my overweight all the time: fat pig, fatarse, big hulk, a bum like a brewery horse, this kind of stuff, these were words that really hurt me and during that time also destroyed a lot of my self-confidence! Nowadays they stare at my piercings and my gear and nobody says anything about my figure any more! (DarkSister, *Gothiccommunity.de*, 21/01/03)

Claiming Androgyny

We have seen how some big women reinterpret 'Gothic' by claiming its ideological connotations of free self-expression and nonconformity for themselves against the grain of the dominant body ideal held in the subculture. Hyperfeminine appearance – and the rejection of female androgyny that goes with it – is a norm far more deeply ingrained than slimness in Gothic ideals of beauty. Although one of the godmothers of Goth, Siouxsie Sioux of Post-punk band Siouxsie and the Banshees, used to display a strong penchant for androgyny and gender play, androgynous women are conspicuous only for their absence on the current scene.

However, during my research I encountered one woman who takes obvious pleasure in thwarting the unwritten subcultural rules of female appearance by switching between highly feminine and fairly plain, androgynous modes of dress. The case of this woman warrants a more in-depth analysis, as it points to the liberating potential which both androgyny and hyperfemininity as a masquerade can have for Goth women if donned strategically – a potential that certainly exists but is not often realised in practice.

Petit Scarabee is a beautiful woman with long, flowing hair who usually likes to wear richly decorated velvet dresses and elaborate make-up when going out to Goth clubs. Yet sometimes she opts for the exact opposite in her style, wearing things like black combat trousers, an army shirt and a cap with her hair bound back. She gave me the following account of her unusual style practices and the way they fit in with her personal interpretation of Goth:

> Some days I want to be really feminine, some days I prefer to be quite simple. If I want to dance more or if I want to be comfortable and, I don't know, sometimes, some days I feel more like my masculine side comes out. And then I want to wear simple things and big boots and, well, big clumpy boots and T-shirt and army stuff. ... The Goth scene also allows me to bring these two sides of me, balance these two sides of me, masculine and feminine. I've never really thought about it much, but that thing that some days I like to be feminine, some days I feel like being masculine, I'd never really be able to bring it that much in normal clothes. It's more intense in Goth clothes, I think, cause, I don't know, because it's such an important thing to dress up. (Petit Scarabee, f, 26, Edinburgh)

Figure 8 Petit Scarabee in her 'masculine' guise (left). Photograph: D. Brill

Petit Scarabee feels that Gothic style enables her to express both her 'masculine' and her 'feminine' sides in a very intense way precisely because dressing up is an important element of Goth. In an environment where people of both genders normally dress to the nines, the otherwise rather trivial act of deliberately dressing down is a deviation from an expected standard. It can hence be experienced and perceived as transgressive, especially if done by a woman who perfectly embodies the subcultural ideal of hyperfemininity in her usual style.

Theorists of feminine masquerade as a subversive sartorial strategy for women have stressed the importance of unmasking femininity as a 'put-on' which 'can easily be taken off' (Tyler, 1991, p. 52), as 'a mask which can be worn or removed' (Doane, 1982, p. 82). To deliberately assume and flaunt femininity as a mask can be empowering for a woman precisely because it implies she does not always have to wear it: 'To put on femininity with a vengeance suggests the power of taking it off.' (Russo, 1988, p. 224) As we have seen, however, Goth women usually do not regard their hyperfemininity as something simply put on; on the contrary, they tend to strongly identify themselves with their feminine image. So while Gothic hyperfemininity with a *femme fatale* twist offers scope for a conscious flaunting of femininity as a subversive and distancing masquerade which can be taken off at will, this specific potential is not often realised in practice.

Yet Petit Scarabee stands as an example of someone who takes control of her own image by putting the patriarchal mask of femininity on and off as she pleases, thus confounding ingrained norms of feminine appearance in the subculture and in society at large. Another interesting aspect of her playing with androgyny comes through in a statement made in response to her boyfriend talking about his style in terms of rebellion against certain attitudes he dislikes:

> I think the way you say you react against things you don't like, it might be a bit of the same with me when I stand out my masculine side because I really hate girls who are really 'ninini' *in a high-pitched voice*, talking about make-up and boots all the time, who are really overly girly. ... Usually these girls follow their boyfriends and they have no passion and they just do their, they usually go club-bing and getting dressed up and 'ninini'. And when I dress more masculine I just feel like, I almost feel strong compared to these silly 'ninini'-girls – and I like that. (Petit Scarabee, f, 26, Edinburgh)

Through distancing herself from women inside and outside the subculture who in her view embody a derivative and vacant image of femininity,[2] Petit Scarabee claims female androgyny as a source of rebellion and strength for herself. In doing so, she implicitly lays claim to the masculinist tradition of rebellious androgyny, which is normally reserved to males in the Gothic scene. On the subjective level, androgyny thus has an important empowering function for her; however, it should be noted that there are no subcultural rewards or recognition for such acts of female gender-bending. As I have shown before, Goth women's style is judged mainly by aesthetic criteria, and the cultural rele-vance of female gender play is not acknowledged. Consequently, an androgy-nous style does nothing to boost a woman's subcultural capital – a thesis further confirmed by Petit Scarabee telling me that her boyfriend tends to urge her to dress up more often, and that she herself prefers a very dressy style for their own monthly club in order to look 'more impressive'.

As Coates (1997, p. 63) argues: 'Signifiers of rebelliousness and sex signify differently ... in terms of gender performativity. When a woman appropriates performative aspects of the "wrong" gender, discursive correctives are imme-diately introduced.' Such discursive correctives in the form of being deemed less impressive and attractive by others are obviously at work in the subculture, but without discouraging Petit Scarabee from her playful flaunting of both hyperfemininity and androgyny as masquerades. So it comes as no surprise that she has also formulated her own interpretation of gender-bending in Goth, written for her homepage long before our interview:

> Look at Goths: It seems that the distinction between men and women becomes more subtle/ambiguous than the "normal" one. Make-up and skirts are no

longer associated with women. The men wearing make-up and corsets don't look like women; the distinction is deeper than that. It is more interesting. Where lies the distinction? Can you tell? This style as well suits me better. I find myself quite masculine; I usually get along better with men than with women; but I usually look very feminine wearing long velvet clothes, although I do like wearing old clothes, army trousers and ripped tights, which I find more masculine. ... To me, the femininity/masculinity distinction should always be more subtle; this should become normality. (Petit Scarabee, f, 26, Edinburgh) [from: http://www.finsternis.org.uk/Vio/index2.htm (retrieved 18/05/02)]

This quote presents a view of male androgyny in Goth as potentially liberating not only for men but also for women, because it can work to loosen up common gender stereotypes and to sever gendered sartorial signifiers from their rigid association with either femininity or masculinity. In Petit Scarabee's eyes, the fact that traditionally female elements of style like skirts, corsets or make-up are freed from their exclusive links with femininity in Goth frees her from the exclusively feminine connotations of such style elements as well. She may usually look 'very feminine' according to conventional standards, but the standards she sees represented in Goth make it possible to go beyond such banal distinctions and introduce more ambiguous and 'deeper' definitions of gender categories.

This interpretation of Gothic gender norms stands in stark contrast to my discussion of gendered Goth style practices in terms of subcultural capital, where I argued that male androgyny often serves to tie women in the subculture even more closely to common standards of femininity rather than to liberate them from such standards. Yet this does not mean that these two interpretations directly contradict or exclude each other. Petit Scarabee's statement is not intended to describe the way Goths in general conceive of their style – though I am sure many Goths would agree with it as an ideal the scene should aspire to – but what 'Gothic' means to her personally. In fact she herself points out that it might be overly idealistic, and partly reflects her initial enthusiasm upon discovering Goth. However, this idealistic view should not be discounted, as it points to the radically liberating *potential* for gender subversion inherent in Goth and its style practices. This potential may hardly ever be realised by women in the subculture, but it is still there as a chance to be seized.

Conclusion

As the other two main threads of this chapter – namely alternative identities constructed by minority women and female androgyny as empowering – concern highly individual phenomena, I restrict the concluding discussion to hyperfeminine masquerade as a collective strategy of empowerment used by Goth women. Feminist cultural theory has hotly debated the possibilities and dangers of the tactical, ironic use of stereotypical feminine imagery as a strategy of emancipation. One basic problem with such a strategy is that trying to differentiate 'hyper'-femininity from a supposed 'standard' femininity, be it in theory or in practice, is fraught with some tricky definitional as well as ethical questions which cannot be easily solved (see Tyler, 1990, 1991).

Moreover, with notions of masquerade as an excess of conventional femininity there is always the question of whether the masquerading woman 'subverts the patriarchal feminine by unmasking it' or simply 'reinscribes the patriarchal feminine by allowing her body to be recuperated for voyeurism' (Kaplan, 1993, p. 156). Women in male-defined subject positions like the porn actress, the strip dancer or the prostitute – and more recently even chart-topping singers like Britney Spears – have always been making highly sexualised, hyperfeminine spectacles of themselves, apparently without disrupting the voyeuristic male gaze.

Of course female Gothic style is not quite the same as the sexy hyperfemininity projected by such figures, although Goth women draw on some of their taboo connotations. Both the motives and intentions behind Goth hyperfemininity and the actual look adopted differ significantly. Doane (1982) explicitly aligns masquerade as an excess of femininity with the cultural trope of the *femme fatale*, a trope strongly resounding in female Gothic style and the discourses surrounding it. According to Doane, the *femme fatale* is seen by men as evil incarnate, and hence threatens to disrupt the masculinist regime of erotic looking.

Other theorists do not always share this overly positive appraisal of this cultural trope. Susan Butler (1987), for example, regards the *femme fatale* as a familiar ideal convention for representing threatening aspects of femininity within the safe bounds of a patriarchal imagery. She argues that by invoking this fairly conventional trope, the threat of feminine independence can safely be 'converted into the traditional male projection of the dangerous lady' (ibid., p. 124). Walser (1993, p. 119) also sees the *femme fatale* as a fairly traditional female subject position, as 'women are encouraged by a variety of cultural means to think of appearance as their natural route to empowerment'. On the subjective level, however, Goth women's hyperfeminine style with a distinctly dark twist forms a powerful source of confidence, strength and protection for these women. Their style may look attractive to ordinary men, but at the same time it intimidates those men and keeps them at a distance. So Goth women's feminine masquerade partly works to confound and deflect the male gaze of scene outsiders. Its relation to the gaze of male insiders, that is Goth men, is more complex and marked by a higher degree of voyeuristic recapture – a topic I discuss in chapters 6 and 8.

5

Masculinity in Style

Brighton, spring 2003, a club in the town centre called Lowlife. This is Brighton's main monthly Goth night, and, as always here, I encounter some of my former interviewees. This time it is Sarn who comes up to say hello to me, the female half of a couple I interviewed a few weeks earlier. As I remember from the interview that the two were nearly inseparable, I am quite surprised that I cannot spot her boyfriend anywhere. 'Come and meet Synara,' says Sarn with a wicked laugh, and I follow her to a tall, slender woman in very unusual Fetish gear sitting at the bar, who has already caught my eye earlier. I am happy that Sarn is finally going to introduce me to her, as I have long been thinking about asking her for an interview but never quite picked up the courage to talk to her. At the bar, Synara greets me with a warm smile and a gentle handshake. She is wearing a tight black PVC bodice and something like a long, obviously custom-made wraparound PVC skirt, straight jet-black hair in girly bunches and moderate yet meticulously done make-up; only the pint of lager standing in front of her seems slightly out of tune with her elegantly girlish appearance. 'Hey, nice to see you again', she says to me as she puts her arm around Sarn's shoulders, and instantly the scales fall from my eyes. In fact the mysterious Fetish woman I have always been too shy to approach is Sarn's boyfriend – the guy who turned up at our interview in an old leather coat, plain, loose-fitting, fairly scruffy black clothes, with a tangled ponytail and stubble instead of make-up on his face!

Gender Benders

Male androgynous style has already been discussed as a major source of status and subcultural capital on the Gothic scene. Of course this view of male androgyny is limited and one-sided as it only focuses on the micropolitical level of subcultural norms or values, without taking full account of the disruptive potential which male androgyny may hold in relation to the macrostructures of power at work in society at large. We have to remember that our culture still censures androgyny in male style in most areas of everyday life, be it in the workplace or in the leisure sphere. The tradition of glamorous and transgressive androgyny on which male musicians – and by extension male Goths – have long drawn can only function as a rebellious accessory in modern pop culture precisely because it is still largely outlawed in ordinary male style and behaviour.

Members of conspicuous subcultures may not always be able or willing to express in words the meanings they invest in their styles. Yet the fact remains

Figure 9 Male femininity: my interviewee Synara. Photograph: SaRn Satino

that they choose to wear flamboyant and transgressive styles of dress in spite of – or maybe even because of – existing social norms which tacitly prohibit such displays in many public spaces, especially for males. A glamorous, androgynous style may win Goth men high status and recognition within the subculture. However, the same style can be interpreted as an abdication of superior masculine status from the perspective of general social norms.

Woodhouse (1989) argues that as Western culture is phobic about male effeminacy, a man sporting feminine style elements defines himself as deviant and inferior. The construction of masculinity is based on an inflexible gender identity, which demands the rejection of traditionally feminine traits of behaviour and appearance precisely because masculinity is valued more highly than femininity. The rigid demarcation of clothing along gender lines helps to establish and secure a superior masculine status by providing a visible outward sign of male supremacy. It follows that 'the man who wears feminine clothing announces his deviancy, his demise as a male and his fall from the grace of superiority' (ibid., p. 14), thereby loosening up the rigid boundary between genders and undermining the male claim to supremacy. The following humorous anecdote by an effeminately styled male Goth about walking home from clubs shows that androgynous Goth men can produce quite a bit of 'gender trouble' in the eyes of general society:

> I'm tall, with long blonde hair, and tend to look very effeminate in full make-up. So, walking home, drunken eejits [idiots] think they've just spotted a long-legged blonde bombshell. Regularly, one of said eejits would walk up if I was waiting to cross the road and make some lacivious comment, to which I'd respond, in deepest voice, "Sorry, mate, I'm a guy", to which they'd turn bright red and have to walk back to friends who were generally in fits of laughter. (Girl the Bourgeois Individualist, *uk.people.gothic*, 30/11/02)

Gutterman (2001) points to the great potential residing in heterosexual men who identify with femininity to subvert and disrupt existing gender norms. While women and gay men are restricted to fighting the categories of gender and sexuality from marginal cultural positions, straight men with an interest in disrupting these categories 'can work to dismantle the system from positions of power by challenging the very standards of identity that afford them normative status in the culture' (ibid., p. 64). This subversive potential of men who consciously refuse patriarchal positions of power is also recognised by Silverman (1992, p. 389), whose book *Male Subjectivity at the Margins* valorises male subjectivities which venture into the marginal domain of femininity. She regards these alternative or deviant masculinities, which 'not only acknowledge but embrace castration, alterity, and specularity' (ibid., p. 3), not as a simple masculinist colonising of feminine territory but as a crucial site for renegotiating gender constructs and relations.

The embracing of spectacle and flamboyance by men is a central characteristic of the Goth subculture. Masculinity as aesthetic display and object of the erotic gaze is not only inscribed in Gothic style codes, but also forms an integral part of the subjectivities of many Goth men. The following statement expresses sentiments voiced by quite a few of my male interviewees:

> Well, a man surely has to mind his appearance, I mean otherwise he's not at all attractive to the other sex, well. I mean there really has to be enough sex appeal so that you can just say 'hey, he's really good-looking'. And men also shouldn't

be so uptight that they can't say of themselves that they find another man good-looking, I think that's really crap, too. Well, I mean you don't have to be gay or bi for this. You can always tell, and when then some bloke comes along and somehow says to another guy 'hey, I can't tell if the shirt suits you', for example, then I could really blow my top. Well, for me this is just simply this, this kind of like 'oh my God, I mustn't say anything wrong now, otherwise everyone will think I'm gay'. (Ozzy, m, 18, Bonn)

Since the Romantic era, decorating the body has been both an obligation and a privilege reserved to females. For many women, self-adornment has provided an outlet for creativity and a way to symbolically handle female identity (Ganetz, 1995). In the Gothic subculture, this traditional female privilege is also extended to men. Vanity is seen as a virtue rather than a vice in Goth, and men are allowed and often even expected to experiment a lot more with hairstyles, clothes and make-up than the restrictive norms of straight male style in other social circles would ever permit. One of my interviewees, for example, concludes from his own experiences at the Whitby Gothic Weekend that male Goths are at least as keen on traditionally feminine pastimes like shopping, dancing and dressing up as the women:

The main event itself is two days of drinking, dancing, live bands and shopping, and the guys are at least as bad for it as the women are. I mean, some – not all of them – will spend just as long if not longer doing their make-up, will agonise over what to wear, will unashamedly get up onto the dancefloor. (Brain Hurts, m, 24, Edinburgh)

The androgynous male style codes of the subculture partly free Goth men from the shackles of traditional masculinity, enabling them to indulge in pleasures normally branded taboo or at least improper for men in our culture. Of course style codes for young males in Western cultures have generally become less restrictive over the last few decades. The changes in men's fashion in the 1980s in particular have introduced style commodities into popular male culture which render possible new expressions of masculinity (Mort, 1988; Winship, 1987a). Contemporary urban culture is rife with erotic representations of the male body and images of moderate male androgyny (McDonald, 1997; Whiteley, 1997a).

These changes in male fashion and in the construction of masculinity in youth culture as a whole are certainly implicated in the gender politics of male Gothic style, insofar as they both enable and are enabled by such subcultural expressions of gender and sexual fluidity. However, the androgynous style and the related attitudes of Goth men sometimes go well beyond the bounds of what is deemed acceptable even in our current, fairly liberal cultural climate. Many male Goths are openly critical of the homophobic squeamishness which typically fuels negative attitudes towards male vanity and eroticism in straight men. While the male body as erotic spectacle is far from being displayed by all men in the subculture, it is generally tolerated and even valued. Goth men in sexy gear usually attract positive rather than negative attention on the scene.

A related aspect of male androgyny in Goth is the issue of what Mort (1988, p. 223) dubs 'style-led sexual politics'. The question is whether innovations in gendered style codes can actually change the gendered subjectivities of men. While this issue remains hotly debated, one cannot ignore 'the profound identification of men's and women's appearances with their expected gender roles' (Foote, 1989, p. 146). Our ideas about how men and women should look form an integral part of the powerful and pervasive system of culturally shared values regulating what is 'appropriate' male and female behaviour. Apparently, male androgyny in Goth can and sometimes does go beyond mere appearance. For quite a few Goth men, embracing feminine elements of style goes hand in hand with embracing certain aspects of feminine subjectivity. In line with Silverman's (1992) marginal male subjectivities, these men consciously identify themselves with femininity in espousing traits like sensitivity, empathy and even weakness – traits which are traditionally coded as female and normally deemed unfit for men in our culture:

I like the marginal, the weak, art and nature. My sensitivity is longing for the empathy of a sensitive woman. (personal ads, *Orkus*, 10/02, p. 136)

For a while I was wondering if I might be gay, so many things seemed to point in that direction, as I have a pronounced feminine streak. … I'm not gay, heaven knows I'm not *smile* and by now I even just see it with some sense of pride that I've managed to integrate my feminine side a fair bit into my personality. Simultaneously with the development of my feminine side my masculine side has developed as well then. And that's definitely a good thing. (bloodfever, *Gothiccommunity.de*, 09/11/02)

In both these quotes, men implicitly or explicitly identify themselves with the feminine. The second statement again presents a man who seems to have no problem with the 'gay' associations ascribed to effeminate men in our culture; however, obviously he still feels the need to stress quite emphatically that he is not gay. Moreover, while embracing the feminine, he lays claim to masculinity at the same time by stressing that his masculine side has developed alongside his feminine one.

Hidden Class Struggles

Goth men in general often appear to have a rather conflicted relationship to masculinity as a cultural construction. The term 'real men' is regularly used in a clearly ironic way in the newsgroup *de.soc.subkultur.gothic*, for example.

Moreover, many of my male interviewees explicitly distance themselves from masculinity by stressing that they have no wish to come across as particularly masculine or that they dislike traits like toughness and manliness, an attitude almost unanimously shared by female Goths. A closer analysis of such statements, however, reveals it is a particular *type* of masculinity – rather than masculinity as such – from which Goths of both genders distance themselves.

> I don't think I've ever met a Goth woman who hasn't had a footy-shirt wearing townie chat them up at some point of their lives. It's something that never ceases to amuse me; I mean, why on earth would we want to choose some trainer-wearing lout who thinks a guy wearing make up is a "poof" over a man we can share our cosmetic bags with? (Jane Bennett; *Meltdown* 13, Spring 2003, p. 38)

> Could you honestly see the average Ben Sherman-wearing townie decked out in a frilly shirt and leather trousers? … Just imagine it: "Sorry mate, I can't have a fight with you today 'cos I'll chip me nailvarnish and the missus will 'ave a go at me when I get home…" or better "Oh shit, my lacey cuffs have just fallen in my pint of beer and I've smudged my lipstick across my face… no I look like Marilyn bleedin' Manson… poof!" (Natasha, *slashgoth.org*, 03/10/02)

The masculinity such statements berate is characterised by certain recurrent features. The dumb, beer-guzzling 'townie' or 'lout' in football shirt and trainers who hates effeminacy and is always ready to pick a fight epitomises the opposite of everything the aesthetic and ideology of the Gothic subculture stand for. Such descriptions of thuggish 'townie' lads can be seen as middle-class caricatures of working-class masculinity. The contempt Goths level at this type of masculinity is expressed most strongly in statements which link it to earlier stages in human evolution and present a caricature of a Neanderthal or ape-man:

> [About the typical hecklers who shot abuse at Goths:] Their means of communication seems to consist of a mass of guttural grunts and bellicose bellowings probably a regression to a form of proto-language. The lurching, swaggering gait and the frequent displays of belligerent arm and fist waving compound the picture of a comic-book ape-man creature. Maybe those ubiquitous baseball caps conceal the prominent brow ridges characteristic of an earlier stage in human evolution? (Capain M, *uk.people.gothic*, 01/12/02)

> I just find that this, this typically masculine demeanour that machos have, that's just like an ape. That's nothing more than a monkey that can speak. For me, well, I mean we're all evolving, yes, and I don't think that this uptight, super-masculine demeanour, with hairy chest and whatever, sitting with legs apart, right, I just find that, first of all it doesn't look particularly good. … I can't imagine that a woman – a normal one at least – prefers a guy who has a super-hairy chest, a gold chain,

and then while he's watching the football and drinking his beer belches all the time, for example, I can't imagine that. (Ozzy, m, 18, Bonn)

Of course such statements could be interpreted as a plain attempt by a middle-class identified social group to defend its superior status against elements of the underprivileged working class. However, Goths' hostility towards the type of masculinity ridiculed here is not entirely without reason. I personally witnessed unmotivated aggression by football hooligans against Goths at the informal Goth gatherings taking place near Cologne Cathedral in the early 1990s, until the police finally banned Goths from using this space as it seemed too difficult to protect them from the large numbers of football fans flooding the city when the local team had a match. Moreover, verbal or physical aggression towards Goths by the type of men described above indeed seems mainly directed at the effeminacy and perceived gayness of the scene.

In his seminal text *Distinction*, Bourdieu (1984) has demonstrated that class conflicts are often transposed onto the level of gender; in certain circumstances, 'anxieties about class status and belonging are sublimated into and played out through the categories of masculinity and femininity' (McNay, 2000, p. 43). This is exactly what seems to be happening when working-class identified social groups or individuals like football hooligans attack Goths verbally or physically, and likewise when middle-class identified Goths strike back by ridiculing and deprecating certain modes of working-class masculinity.

Affirming Masculinity

Historically, the association of femininity with spectacular display and masculinity with sartorial sobriety so deeply ingrained in our visual culture is a fairly recent development. Until the late eighteenth century – previous to what Flügel (1950) dubbed the 'Great Masculine Renunciation' – upper-class males used extravagant dress to display power and privilege. In scopic terms, masculinity was hence not defined as exerting the male gaze at the female 'other', but as commanding the gaze of the lower-class 'other' (Silverman, 1986). Ornate dress was mainly a class rather than a gender prerogative during former centuries. Moreover, the elegance and flamboyance of male dress often surpassed that of female dress, thus defining spectacle as a male rather than a female attribute. It follows that 'power can invade spectacle, and disinvest from the gaze – that spectacle, in other words, can function phallically' (ibid., p. 153). In historical periods which espoused narcissism and effeminacy in male style, the ruling aristocracy and powerful occupational groups like judges, doctors and solicitors typically wore the most ornate dress. Ash (1995, p. 36) sums up this historical relation between sartorial display and male power in the simplifying but apt equation that 'the more supposedly "effeminate" the male appearance, the more power could be wielded'.

This discussion is highly pertinent to the ornate dress of androgynous Goth men. We have already seen that Gothic male androgyny can function in a fairly conservative way by affirming traditional masculine values like courage and confidence. In academic analyses of gender politics in Rock music culture, there is a tradition of stressing the negative and even misogynist effects of male androgyny (e.g. Reynolds and Press, 1995; Simpson, 1994). Male Glam Rockers and Heavy Metal stars are seen as appropriating the glamour and mystery of the feminine to the male body in order to affirm their heterosexual male power over women and other men. This view of male androgyny may be overly pessimistic; yet the fact remains that many Goth men display a striking need to affirm their (heterosexual) masculinity through certain discursive moves precisely when talking about their androgynous style. For instance, Phill White – singer of British Goth band the Narcissus Pool and voted 'Sexiest Male' in *Meltdown*'s readers' poll of 2001 – writes in an article for a *Meltdown* 'Male Fashion Special':

> I didn't always wear make up but I noticed I got laid far more when I did, which pretty much decided it for me! ... Obviously I've had numerous jibes and comments on the street but then I've never worried what narrow minded idiots think. I've also been fortunate that I'm big enough to look after myself. I once ran a would-be mugger head first into a telephone box without so much as smudging my blusher! (Phill White, the Narcissus Pool; *Meltdown* 13, Spring 2003, p. 38)

Insofar as Phill here rhetorically produces himself as an object of female desire, the first part of his statement could be taken to advance a progressive new image of masculinity. However, the way he expresses this is arguably a rather masculine one. Even in a sexually liberal environment like the Goth scene, a woman would be less likely to give 'getting laid more' as her prime motive for wearing make-up. Women in our post-feminist cultural climate usually resort to a rhetoric of self-fulfilment and self-expression when talking about their make-up, insisting they are primarily doing it for themselves and not to attract men. Admitting that one wears make-up mainly to attract sexual partners – even if half in jest – without being regarded as 'cheap' and silly remains a largely male prerogative, and probably has as much to do with traditional boys' talk of sexual prowess as with renegotiating masculinity as erotic spectacle.

The second part of Phill's statement juxtaposes a direct affirmation of a very masculine trait – namely the cultural expectation that a man must be able to defend himself and his way of life with physical force if necessary – with a rhetorical nod to the very feminine obsession with keeping one's make-up intact. Independence and self-mastery are generally recognised as desirable traits in a man, as masculinity encourages competition for status and emphasises defiant achievement (Easthope, 1986). While Goths generally reject fights and aggression, obviously it can still be an important status thing for a man to present himself as ready and able to fight back when attacked. This is further confirmed by the following statement by a male Goth, who made it clear before that he normally shuns fights:

> There are groups of townie thugs who are really scared of me. Even when it's about 10, 12 people, I don't give a shit, I can walk right through them and they make way for me, cause they're just scared stiff that I might again clobber any one of them in such a bad way that he can hardly stand on his feet anymore. I might look frail, but I'm, when I blow my top people should really keep their distance, then I'm sometimes even scared of myself. (Ozzy, m, 18, Bonn)

Ozzy manages here to distance himself from the 'townie thug' masculinity Goths regard as antithetical to their aesthetic and ideology at the same time as he discursively affirms his own masculinity. By claiming that, despite his frail physique, even the outwardly masculine and aggressive 'townies' who used to shout abuse at him for his effeminate style have come to fear him, he produces himself as somehow more masculine than those caricatures of vulgar masculinity. This discursive move of affirming one's masculine status precisely through distancing oneself from the type of vulgar, aggressive 'townie' masculinity described above can also be traced in the following quote:

> I remember walking through one town with two very beautiful women, one on either arm, who were taking me to bed. This guy comes up and says 'fucking poofter', and I'm thinking: Ok, I may be wearing thigh-length stiletto heel boots, skin-tight shiny black trousers and looking drop dead gorgeous; you're calling me a fucking poofter, which is insulting to me and insulting to gay people; I'm taking these two beautiful women, rather these two beautiful women are taking me home to bed, and you're going to come out of your martial arts macho class and no-one's gonna look at you twice. And so ok, I may be a fucking poofter but, evolutionary [sic] speaking, I'm sexually very successful and so uh, ok, take it for that. (Leatherman, m, 38, Edinburgh)

Even more explicitly than Phill White, Leatherman links his androgynous style to (hetero)sexual prowess in this anecdote. Moreover, he maintains that he is far more successful on the heterosexual terrain of attracting women than the aggressive macho men who insult male Goths as 'poofs'. Having sex with two attractive women at the same time is certainly one of the favourite wet dreams of omnipotent male fantasy. By claiming he has easy access to what 'townie' men also want but cannot have, Leatherman implicitly assigns himself a higher masculine status. The language of evolutionary success he uses discursively produces him as something like an alpha male in terms of sexual prowess, relegating the men who meet the traditional criteria for this position – i.e. aggression and physical strength – to inferiority.

To summarise, while traditional masculinity as such is not valued in the Gothic subculture and openly disparaged in its 'townie lad' variety, traditional masculine values like courage, confidence and even sexual prowess are cherished and regularly affirmed despite, or rather *through*, the androgynous style of Goth men. Here the case of Leatherman is particularly telling, as the interview with him and his girlfriend first brought this phenomenon to my attention. I had initially asked him for an interview when I spotted him at the Edinburgh Goth Weekend decked out in martial leatherwear, as I thought it would be interesting to include such a fairly atypical male Goth with a hyper-masculine style in my sample. During the interview, however, it transpired that the frilly, rather skinny-fit velvet top his girlfriend Lady Leather was wearing originally belonged to him, and that he used to sport a very androgynous style when he was younger and thinner. At my surprise at discovering this side to him, because he is now quite sturdily built and comes across as strongly masculine, he explained:

> I think masculinity, it's not about 'look at how big my muscles are, look at how broad my shoulders are', it's about confidence. It doesn't matter whether you're being confident wearing the kind of leather I'm wearing, which is more like armour than leather, or whether you're standing up dressed in like skin-tight PVC jeans and thigh-length stilettos and a frilly shirt, with black eyeliner on and your hair all slicked back – it's still a confidence thing. And you're saying 'I don't care what you're thinking of me, I like who I am, I like how I look, and I'm very comfortable with it', and that's an aggressive thing cause people don't like people who are comfortable with how they look, people find that very threatening. (Leatherman, m, 38, Edinburgh)

Leatherman explicitly links androgynous male style with a display of masculine confidence and even aggression. Indeed he suggests that, in terms of courage and defiance, his former effeminate style was very close to the outwardly masculine, martial leather style he prefers now. Despite their contrary appearances, Leatherman's two different styles share a common substance for him in that both demonstrate male confidence. It should be noted, though, that Leatherman draws on a very similar discourse when talking about his girlfriend Lady Leather's style, describing it as 'scary' and 'powerful' (see chapter 4). This indicates that the courage and confidence linked with transgressing conventional norms of dress can function as a general subcultural value in Goth regardless of gender, although it is more often and more explicitly associated with male Gothic style.

However, we have already seen in chapter 3 that Goth men's claim to subcultural transgression through the style practice of male androgyny is paramount. Androgynous style definitely functions as a marker of masculine status in the Gothic scene. Male Goths who sport it see themselves and are seen by other Goths as courageous, confident and defiant in the face of social norms which

Figure 10 Masculinity in full armour: my interviewee Leatherman. Photograph:
D. Brill

censure male androgyny. But the fact remains that androgyny only works as a masculine status criterion within Gothic circles, while other straight men still tend to see male Goths as emasculated, sissy and poofish. Yet there exists a further, indirect way for Goth men to affirm their masculinity, namely by asserting their (hetero)sexual prowess through the attraction which Goth women possess for conventional men. Males from outside the subculture often find hyperfeminine Goth women very alluring. The desirability of their female friends and girlfriends to other men can help male Goths to restore their masculine status even in environments where male androgyny and sissiness are outlawed, as the following remark by a Goth in the military – speaking about the reactions of his comrades to his moderate Gothic style – indicates:

> Most guys didn't give a shit about it, those that were wary would soon change their tune when i showed em picks of some of the girls I went clubbing with and my girlfriend – then they were begging to come along to Slimes [Slimelight, a well-known London Goth club]. (Gadge, *slashgoth.org*, 07/10/02)

When asked about the reactions they get at work, other male Goths stated that while their colleagues usually cannot understand their choice of dress and general lifestyle, they are almost always keen on photos of female Goths and juicy anecdotes about amorous adventures on the Goth scene.

> I also have kind of like a reputation for being the crazy one. Well, I often notice with some colleagues that they're like looking up to me with like partly admiration and partly with, with like, well, affirmation; well, kind of 'yes, you're living your life after all, and ha ha, and your things with women, and blah'. (DeEm, m, 31, Bonn)

As with Leatherman and his two beautiful playmates, success in attracting desirable women here works to boost masculine status not only within the subculture but – at least subjectively – also towards outsiders.

Negotiating Boundaries

In the preceding section, we have seen how the emasculating meanings commonly assigned to male androgyny are being contested by Goth men in order to affirm their masculine status. What is more, the proper boundaries of androgynous male style – and the definition of androgyny itself – are subject to constant negotiation within the Goth subculture. Gothic style norms for male androgyny are not set in stone, but can and will be interpreted in different ways by different individuals. Some male Goths take obvious pleasure in sometimes being mistaken for girls by outsiders when dressed up, and discussions in Gothic Internet forums regularly contain humorous anecdotes about such incidents. We have already encountered one such man, Synara, in the narrative introducing this chapter. Here are two more examples of Goth men who fully embrace what I would call unlimited androgyny or male femininity in their style:

> If I wear a skirt or dress or whatever I have no qualms to walking down the street like that. Sometimes I'll go shopping with my daughter and people will assume I'm her mother. Kinda funny. (The Malfated, *slashgoth.org*, 11/11/02)

hmm, i came to the conclusion that there isn't enough male gothic clothing about, but then i just ended up crossdressing and i prefer that to the way i would have dressed otherwise anyway. ... masculine-ish skirts are possible. i wouldn't wear one but i think they're cool. i'm stuck with nice girlie gear now and happy with it. (Andrasazel, *slashgoth.org*, 24/01/02)

However, even in this subculture which cherishes androgyny as a male status symbol, such a wholehearted embracing of effeminacy is the exception rather than the rule. The majority of Goth men who sport feminine style elements like skirts or make-up prefer to differentiate – or even strictly distance – their style practices from cross-dressing, drag or transvestism, and stress that they have no wish to be seen as feminine. Of course the complex mixture of masculine and feminine styles and traits male Goths typically practise is far from inherently reactionary; in fact Garber (1992) accords modes of dress which are deliberately mixed or contradictory in terms of gender a particular subversive potential. Yet we will see that in Gothic male dress such a mixing of gendered attributes in many ways works to affirm masculinity and binary gender.

Now I wouldn't want to look androgynous somehow when I'm wearing a skirt. I think my skirt is a pretty and handy piece of clothing, but that doesn't mean I make myself up to look feminine when I'm wearing it. (Frank Lachmann, *de.soc.subkultur.gothic*, 19/05/03)

Well, I started with a kilt-style skirt as I just thought it's particular design would suit me better than a bona-fide skirt, rather than any desire to keep masculinity intact. The long combat skirt I got was another step, but I don't think you'll be seeing me in a PVC mini anytime soon. As far as I'm concerned, I'm a man who sometimes wears a skirt (and it's certainly not every time I go out), I'm not a cross-dresser by any means. (EOL, *slashgoth.org*, 12/11/02)

The quote by EOL, which is part of a heated discussion in an Internet forum thread about male Goths wearing female clothes, is particularly interesting in this respect. As Tyler (1991, p. 36) points out, 'anxiety about being "normal" with respect to gender can be consistent with patriarchal gynephobia when it takes the form of the repudiation of femininity'. Anxieties about gender, she argues, lie behind the frequent insisting on a masculine 'true' gender identity by many drag queens, who also tend to stress they do not really want to be mistaken for women. In EOL's statement – which came in response to a female poster suspecting that Goth men's preference for kilts and so-called combat skirts rather than more feminine designs was due to latent homophobia – the same kind of anxieties can be traced. EOL rhetorically fends off the suggestion that his liking for masculine skirt designs reflects masculinist and anti-gay sentiments, but all the same he insists on strongly distancing his sartorial practices from those of cross-dressers. A similar discursive mechanism is at work in the following quote by Freiblut, a man who looks very androgynous according to other postings:

I also occasionally wear a skirt, I think they're totally brill, well, the ones that reach to the floor, in addition to the fact that they're comfortable... other than that I mainly wear kilts... and one just can't claim that the old Scotsmen were gay, just the contrary, there our muscle-shirt-wearing and beer-drinking mega-men (I mean what like supposedly is called "masculine" here, as it where) might as well just instantly pack up and leave *smiley icon*! (Freiblut, *Gothiccommunity.de*, 16/11/02)

Like EOL, Freiblut manages to reject crude 'townie' masculinity while at the same time distancing himself from the gay, emasculated associations which a skirt on a man has in general society.

Moreover, the Goth men quoted here practically rule out certain all too feminine garments or styles as proper male gear. A PVC mini on a man simply seems a step too far in the direction of cross-dressing proper. By contrast, kilts or combat skirts – i.e. long, straight-cut skirts with a flap at the front, often with chains and buckles – with their air of medieval or futuristic warriors are explicitly marketed as 'men's skirts' by Gothic shops, and hence deemed proper even by males who normally reject androgynous style. The strongly masculine connotations of a term like 'combat skirt' facilitate the marketing to men of a type of garment traditionally coded as female. As Freiblut's statement indicates, the men wearing such skirts seem very aware of these connotations. In another posting, EOL describes a fake leather kilt-style skirt he customised using a razor and fishnet fabric as working 'in a fetish-warrior kinda way' (EOL, *slashgoth.org*, 11/11/02).

The following interviewee – whom I spotted at the Wave-Gotik-Treffen wearing a custom-made combat skirt with lots of chains and buckles – goes even further in trying to masculinise a type of garment traditionally associated with femininity:

Me: And what exactly do you like about the skirt?
S: The chains are brill, and the buckles, I think yes. And it's really comfortable to wear, and above all it's also cut in a way that, because most skirts that are like available, most skirts for men, they're still a little too feminine in my opinion. There something harsh is proper, kind of that they come across like a little harsher on a man, you know.

(Samael, m, 21, Leipzig)

In Samael's eyes, even the men's skirts available in Goth shops are still somewhat too feminine for a man to wear; he prefers a skirt which comes across as 'harsh' and precisely not effeminate.

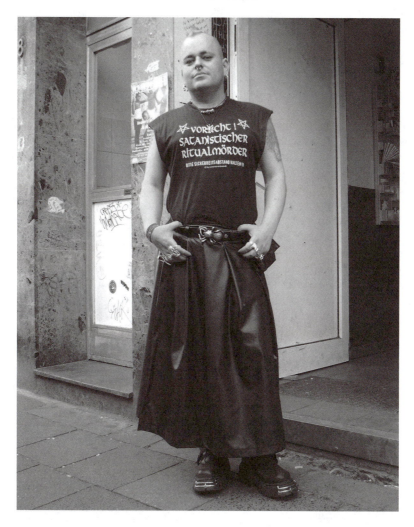

Figure 11 Striking a cool pose in a men's skirt: my interviewee Muckel.
Photograph: D. Brill

This insistence that wearing skirts or make-up does not necessarily have anything to do with femininity is fairly widespread among Goth men who don traditionally female elements of style. There is a strong tendency to rid these elements of their feminine connotations both in actual design and in the meanings attached to them. Many male Goths insist that if they put on make-up for going out, it is a particular style of make-up not supposed to look feminine. The standard make-up for Goth men is a generous dash of eyeliner below the eyes and blackened eyebrows. Some men do more elaborate make-up, but only rarely does it resemble typically feminine styles. Accordingly, one of my female interviewees likened the way most male Goths do their styling to 'stage make-up'.

Paoletti and Kidwell (1989) argue that truly androgynous dress has never existed for adult men and women throughout modern history, as there is continuing pressure to retain some distinguishing features between male and female styles. Distinctions can be maintained 'both by keeping a few symbols tightly bound to masculinity or femininity and by transforming borrowed symbols' (ibid., p. 159). In the Gothic subculture, this pressure to keep male and female styles distinct is also still at work, despite its ideology of gender-lessness. Goth men are often eager to retain a discernibly masculine appearance, hence trying to guard the sometimes thin and permeable boundaries between masculinity and femininity in Gothic style codes (e.g. by only wearing 'masculine' types of skirts). Many Goth women also invest heavily in keeping these boundaries intact. While there are some who like men to look extremely effeminate – just as there are some male Goths who like styling themselves that way – most female Goths insist on certain distinguishing features as well, even if they generally prefer androgynous men:

> Long hair and a bit of eyeliner is one thing, men trying to look like women is another. I like them to be kind of feminine, but still with their big boots – big chunky boots, yeah, and T-shirt and tight jeans and long hair. ... I don't like men in heels, I think they look silly – especially when they fall over. Or especially when they try and fight and they've got handbag and heels, it's just like watching two drag queens, it's just – no! (Jet, f, 21, Brighton)

> Miniskirts also don't look particularly good on men. On men it should like always look kind of like somewhat cyberpunk-shaman-like if they start wearing female clothes, you know. ... Because then it looks quite impressive, then it just looks really kind of 'aha!', you know, and not simply like a queen. (Rai, f, 19, Bonn)

Obviously, most Goth women still like their androgynously styled men to be proper men and not drag queens. The mental pictures invoked by Jet – men falling over when trying to walk in high heels, and attempting to fight with handbag and heels – are particularly telling. Despite their humorous tone, these pictures draw on deep-seated cultural notions of what men and women are like underneath the styles they wear. Men are supposed to be ready to fight (although Goth men hardly ever fight with each other) and to walk in a rather ungainly way in female gear like high heels. This implies such gear is somehow at odds with male nature, that is with what is deemed proper and natural male behaviour.

Such a humorous invocation of gender stereotypes is also employed by Goth men to negotiate the tension between the overt display of vanity in Gothic style and their claim to a masculine identity. While many Goth men embrace male vanity as a virtue rather than rejecting it as a feminine vice, some are very reluctant to admit they are vain. Invoking male gender stereotypes – especially the cliché that men are neither able nor willing to care much about their appearance – can work as an indirect rhetorical tactic to defuse the emasculating notion of excessive vanity.

> Well, I would wear a skirt in the summer if I was able to put on some make-up without then looking like having committed a failed suicide attack in the cosmetics department ... and wasn't too lazy to buy clothes anyway. (Sebastian Dill, *de.soc.subkultur.gothic*, 19/05/03)

As in this humorous pleading of incompetence and laziness in the traditionally female sphere of style and beauty, male Goths sometimes downplay the attention they pay to their appearance and the energy and time they invest in it. For instance, while Goth women often state they like wearing skirts or dresses because they make them look more beautiful and feminine, men tend to stress they wear skirts mainly because they are 'comfortable'.

Vanity or Virtue

The attempt to define their sometimes elaborate style practices as something other – and in particular something more masculine – than vanity seems an important strategy male Goths employ to keep their masculine identity intact. While many Goth men proudly admit to being vain, others emphatically deny that male Gothic style is about vanity. My interviewee Jiad, for example, used to serve in an elite military unit and has even customised pieces of his former uniform (e.g. his army dress hat) for his Goth gear. While not looking particularly androgynous, he puts much effort into his appearance; yet his own view of male Gothic style practices is very far from notions of feminine vanity:

> I wouldn't really call it vanity. Well, I mean, you know, I don't know, I've been in an environment where people had to dress for each other, and at least in this military environment they used to call it self-respect or pride, personal pride in appearance. (Jiad, m, 45, Edinburgh)

Jiad does not see the effort he puts into his style as a sign of indulgent vanity, but interprets it against the backdrop of his experiences in the military. For him, taking care of one's appearance is a mark of self-discipline and pride.

Both male and female Goths sometimes engage in a playful and rather ironic toying with military chic, often set off by feminine style elements like make-up. A more serious stylistic flirtation with militarism and sometimes even totalitarianism, however, is entertained by male Goths – especially those of the

Industrial and Neo-folk factions – much more frequently than by female Goths. A telling example is the conversation between two Neo-folk fans dressed in army-style black shirts and trousers which I overheard by chance at the Wave-Gotik-Treffen. One of them, who was also wearing some historic army badge, told the other with an air of manly bravado about the frequent negative reactions his outfit attracts because of its alleged fascist connotations – crucially not only from outsiders but even among Goths and other 'Alternative' types.

Obviously, a militant or military style not only works as a plain affirmation of a tougher, non-androgynous mode of masculinity but also functions for some Goth men as a signifier of an ultimate rebellion or transgression. With such a style, a man can show his rebellion against common cultural norms and also express his defiance of perceived norms and trends within the subculture. This form of defiance clearly surfaces in the following statement by a male Industrial fan about his preferred style:

> Now I like military stuff, I like to wear a smart shirt and tie, uniform, or some-times I just wear normal suits and tie, and I really like the smart, more like formal dress. ... As Goth became more Rock and it was just long hair, with beards as well which I don't like, and then it even really goes towards Heavy Metal and just kind of hairy, scruffy Metal people. So maybe I'm partially reacting against that. With Industrial music there's a definite sort of discipline and order there, which also goes towards the politics and that of the Neo-folk scene. And I think, I don't know, I think when you're wearing a uniform and you look very stern and austere possibly you command a certain degree of respect. (Deception Boy, m, 24, Edinburgh)

Deception Boy, who used to sport a more flamboyant Cyber style before switching to the no-nonsense look he prefers now, sees his adoption of military and other formal dress partly as a defiant reaction against the influx of 'hairy, scruffy' styles from the Alternative Rock and Metal scene into the Gothic subculture. Moreover, he actively embraces its militaristic connotations of discipline, order and respect – connotations which are anathema to most other Goths and Alternatives.

In terms of style politics, adopting a 'stern and austere' uniform-style appearance to express one's defiance seems strongly at odds with the playfully defiant flaunting of male androgyny espoused by large portions of the Gothic scene, as it promotes a very traditional mode of masculinity. However, both kinds of practices can be found under the by now large and fractured umbrella of Goth, whose various factions sometimes differ markedly in their stylistic and ideological outlooks.

Figure 12 Masculinity in uniform: my interviewee Deception Boy. Photograph:
D. Brill

Cultural Differences – Enter the Teutonic He-man

We have already encountered the Industrial/Neo-folk faction as a subgroup
under the Gothic umbrella whose gender politics are strikingly different from
those promoted by general Goth ideology, in hailing a militaristic image of

masculinity. There are many other subgroups and trends – most notably certain genres of Metal and Techno – which have fed into Goth and influenced its styles and ideologies, also in terms of gender politics. For instance, many German Goths in particular enter the subculture via the route of Metal, bringing some of the heavily 'macho' style elements and values of that scene with them.

Quite a few factions and trends in Goth differ between countries and regions, sometimes with a marked impact on the subcultural politics of gender. One of the most striking observations in this context concerns male androgyny in Gothic style. While androgyny as an ideal of male beauty is generally espoused by Goths – and seen as highly desirable by female Goths in particular – the two countries I researched diverge markedly in terms of Goth men actually adopting androgynous styles. The UK scene boasts a much higher proportion of androgynous males as well as a higher rate of men who take androgynous style to extremes. This difference is not absolute but conspicuous enough to be instantly noted and regularly commented on by Goths who travel between both countries. For instance, a German music journalist reporting from the Whitby Gothic Weekend for an older issue of *Sonic Seducer* remarks that, in comparison with German events, 'the large number of people who suggested through their outfit not to be heterosexually inclined was conspicuous' (Thomas Abresche; *Sonic Seducer*, 06/01, p. 41).

So it comes as no surprise that Goth women in Germany regularly complain that the effort Goth men put into their appearance has dwindled over the last decade. Many female Goths deplore that there are fewer and fewer long-haired, creatively styled men on the German scene, and that most men now turn up at Goth clubs just wearing ordinary black trousers and a band T-shirt. The majority of the women, by contrast, tend to take their feminine styling to extremes. The following observations by a male interviewee summarise these complaints:

> With the boys I've noticed that the willingness to like do themselves up properly and so on, it's declining I think. Many just think: well, take a black T-shirt out of the cupboard and a pair of black trousers, and that'll do. And, well, the effort one used to put into it like, I don't know, only a couple of years ago, like with eyeliner and then back-combing one's hair and so on, that's got rarer. It's also because of the advent of that Electro scene, there it's just like more the kind of uniform simplicity that's called for, you know, and so that's getting more and more. And the girls, by contrast, they now attach more and more importance to like expensive, well, big, voluminous, expensive skirts and a nice corset to go with it. ... I think there once was a time when boys and girls used to spend about the same amount of time in the bathroom, but that's decreased again. (DeEm, m, 31, Bonn)

DeEm suspects that the rise of the Electro/EBM faction in German Goth in the 1990s is partly responsible for the decline in glamour and androgyny in male style. While Electro music with its harsh, pounding beat features prominently in Goth clubs throughout the world, Germany is its stronghold. Moreover, the male-dominated German Electro scene has generated its own style codes. While British – and to a lesser extent other European and US – Electro fans tend to sport elements of flamboyant Cyber gear, German EBM style's militant, hypermasculine imagery with cropped hair and muscle shirts is completely opposed to Gothic androgyny with its stress on long hair and delicate fabrics.[1] This masculine, militaristic EBM style also promotes a different male body image; the skinny, frail ideal body venerated in Gothic androgyny is replaced by the traditional masculine ideal of a muscular, sturdy build:

> On boys I also like the somewhat more militant style; but for that the person also has to be a bit more muscular accordingly – well, it doesn't look good when like some skinny, small bloke turns up like in army trousers and with a bare chest or a muscle shirt and an EBM crew cut. (Muckel, m, 30, Cologne)

Matching the harsh, repetitive beat of its music, the Electro/EBM scene has also developed its own dance styles, consisting of either a repetitive, stomping march of three steps forwards and backwards or an almost Punk-style moshing at concerts. Such dance styles stand in stark contrast to the traditional Gothic style of slow, sweeping movements, and they directly affect the women on the dance floor or in the audience. As in Rock music culture, aggressive movements by bigger and physically stronger males can function to exclude women from the front of the stage or from a packed dance floor (Leonard, 1997).

At the Wave-Gotik-Treffen, I met two girls whom I asked for an interview on discovering that one of them had sprained her wrist at a DAF (a prototypical Teutonic EBM band) gig. She told me that an audience mainly consisting of 'bullnecked, bald-headed, partly muscly, partly just plain fat, bare-chested men' (Hail, f, 19, Leipzig) slamdanced without consideration for the weaker or smaller people around them and hence brought her to the floor. Interestingly, Hail's description of the DAF audience resounds with the negative characterisations of vulgar masculine bearing from which Goths usually distance themselves and their subculture. Via the Electro/EBM faction, obviously this type of rough, aggressive 'townie' masculinity normally despised by Goths finds inroads into the scene and its spaces.

In contrast to these developments, the Cyber style popular mostly among British Goths offers ample scope for androgyny. However, the type of androgyny espoused here differs markedly from that of traditional Gothic style. With its penchant for UV-reflective, sleek materials and brightly coloured hair extensions, it works to neutralise gender difference rather than to highlight femininity and sexuality:

Figure 13 Teutonic Electro/EBM style: my interviewee Eddy. Photograph: D. Brill

I don't know, in Cyber it sort of seems this thing to do with this ultra-skinny, waif-like look, and at some point the sexuality side of it almost disappears, so you're not quite sure what they are. (Geek, m, 34, Brighton)

Cyber Goths of both genders aim for a playfully artificial, futuristic look in which eroticism is secondary despite the use of skinny-fit, skimpy clothes. Instead of being highlighted, gender and sexuality sometimes 'almost disappear' in Cyber style.

Conclusion

The main thread running through this chapter is the tension between androgyny and conventional masculinity in male Gothic style and the rhetoric surrounding it.

As to the issue of 'alternative' masculinities expressed through Gothic style, the tenor of my findings is two-sided. Male androgyny can be an expression of a progressive, softer and more emotional ideal of masculinity in the case of some Goth men. Yet most of them rather employ it to assert a fairly traditional masculine identity, either by imposing restrictions on androgyny in male style or by redefining its meaning from associations of effeminacy to notions of masculine power and defiance. Both mechanisms work to demarcate male Gothic style practices from female ones, thus keeping intact the unstable and constantly negotiated boundary of the shifted Goth gender binary of male androgyny versus female hyperfemininity.

The fact that Goth men use androgynous style to affirm traditional masculine values like confidence, defiance and sometimes even sexual prowess leads to a seemingly paradoxical effect. From this perspective, the supposedly feminine appearance of male Goths functions partly as a display of masculinity. To use the words of feminist artist and critic Mary Kelly (1996, p. 217) – who observed the same paradox in artistic avant-garde movements – Goth men could be said to 'assume the masquerade of transgressive femininity as a form of virile display'.

With respect to the cultural differences discussed, however, it has to be said that, despite this critical appraisal of male androgyny, I see its partial decline in Gothic style as a negative development in terms of subcultural gender politics. While I have pointed out the problematic aspects of androgynous male style in Goth as excluding women, I have also stressed its liberating and progressive potential. Certainly, Goth men can and often do use androgynous style to gain subcultural capital and to affirm traditional masculine values. Yet there are still certain progressive aspects to such an unconventional way of affirming masculinity, as it profoundly rattles traditional conceptions of proper male appearance. As we will see in the next chapter, regardless of androgyny Goth men can draw on other, far more conventional sources to affirm their masculine status in the context of heterosexual gender relations.

6
Gender Relations

New Year's Eve 2002, Bochum, the Matrix club. Many Goths from the Cologne/Bonn area have travelled to the densely populated Ruhr Region to celebrate this night in one of the biggest Goth clubs in Germany; so have I and a female friend of mine. We arrive shortly after the doors have opened, and all three dance floors are still empty. To kill time, we take a seat close to the entrance to watch the people entering the club. Boredom obviously makes us bitchy, and we do not fail to notice just how many beautifully styled fairy queens and Fetish princesses walk in with boyfriends we jokingly classify as 'substandard'. We spot a girl with elaborate make-up and a big hairdo, wearing a black satin corset richly decorated with velvet ornaments, high platform heels and a short skirt with a transparent lace insertion at the back which displays her half-naked buttocks. Her boyfriend is a geeky guy with short brownish hair in a band T-shirt, plain black trousers and worn-out army boots. Another girl, with the body of a model and a beautiful face framed by extremely long ruby hair, is holding hands with a stocky EBM type who looks about twenty years older than her. True, there are two or three dark princes who come close to the male Gothic beauty ideal of long hair, fine make-up and androgynous dress. Yet invariably these rare creatures are in the company of even more ornately styled girlfriends, who resemble the Goth princess ideal to perfection. 'Great prospects for just a common single woman like me,' my friend grumbles sarcastically. We laugh and move on to the main dance floor, which is pretty crowded by now.

A Heterosexual Space

While issues of style feature prominently in subcultural studies, the question of male–female relations has been sidelined by much research into subcultures and gender. Without doubt, flamboyant styles form an important facet of conspicuous subcultures in terms of gendered self-expression and deserve in-depth analysis. However, such an analysis should be coupled with an examination of actual heterosexual relations as 'the primary site where gender difference is re-produced' (Hollway, 2001, p. 272).

Macdonald (2001) and Leblanc (2002) have described the male-dominated Graffiti and Punk subcultures as 'resolutely heterosexualist' spaces, where men construct stereotypical tough and dominant images of masculinity for themselves and relegate female members to equally stereotypical inferior roles as either camp followers or sex objects. Conversely, we have seen that Goth as a more gender-balanced subculture promotes an ideology or fantasy of genderlessness, cherishing femininity and male androgyny. Yet despite this ideology of gender being immaterial, in many respects the Gothic scene clearly presents itself as a heterosexually gendered space. While traditional masculine poses like macho bearing and physical violence are normally outlawed on the scene, on a more subtle level it still functions as a turf where men 'fight' for territory and women. The following responses to the question whether it was easy to meet people on the scene describe this state of affairs first from a male and then from a female perspective:

L: The London scene, it's like 'no, fuck off', it's very cliquish.
LL: I don't find that.
L: And that's a very gender difference. If you're male in the Gothic scene in London you are completely excluded if you don't know people in the Gothic scene. ... If you're a female in the Gothic scene in London what happens is people will talk to you. ...
Me: But why do they accept women and not males?
L: I don't know, it's a culture, a male-dominated culture; that's not the same and that's like a straight question. If you're a strange female in the area, then it's gonna be half the population in that area trying to get to know you. If you're a strange male in that area, then it's two halves of the population trying to distance you. There's the male half trying to say 'I don't want you to know people here because you're gonna become competition'; there's the female half saying 'I don't know who the hell you are, therefore I can't trust you', and so you become very isolated.
        (Leatherman, m, 38, Edinburgh; Lady Leather, f, 21, Edinburgh)

Men are no problem. You go to a Goth club and you're a new Goth, and they just go 'wohey, noone's been there before, right – who's gonna pounce first'. Women are just, you know, they get really defensive, all their defences just kind of spring up, and they're just like 'oh, no-no-no, we don't, no-no', and they just try and dig up as much dirt as possible. ... When I moved back down [to Brighton] I used to go to clubs by myself, and the men just used to giggle and come over and, you know, or fight each other or, you know, just as they do with any girl that goes down there. It's kind of like a territorial thing: 'wohey, she's on our patch, right; who's eligible; who's single, right; you can't have her because you' – it's ridiculous. But the girls, they're just, they can be so nasty. Well, you get interest from a guy and a girl would like him, and loads of girls will be friends with her, and even if you weren't interested in the guy at all, all these girls just hate you. And everyone knows her, and then all of a sudden you become this demon bitch from hell. (Jet, f, 21, Brighton)

Both Leatherman and Jet describe the Gothic scene as a culture marked by territorial claims and competition of a decidedly heterosexual shape, with Leatherman even explicitly calling it a 'male-dominated' culture. The differences and similarities between the male and female perspectives from which this territorial culture is viewed are particularly interesting here. Leatherman states that it is hard for male strangers to gain the trust and acceptance of both Goth men and women, though for different – and stereotypically gendered – reasons: the men want to guard their territory against fresh competition, and the women are wary of trusting men they do not know. Both interviewees agree that it is easy for women to get the men in the subculture talking to them, and hence to be accepted and included in the scene fairly quickly. As Jet points out, however, the heightened interest displayed by male Goths towards new females can also back-fire, in the sense that already established women may see female newcomers who are popular with the guys as competition and treat them like enemies.

Both statements characterise Goth as a culture with deeply traditional heterosexual gender roles and relations, where men fight each other for terri-tory and eligible females, and where women try to guard their claims to the exclusive attentions of eligible males against female newcomers. No wonder that a lesbian couple I interviewed – with a more distanced view of male–female relations – described the gendered behaviour codes and especially the courtship norms within the scene as 'totally heterosexual' in terms of who ogles whom and who makes advances at whom. These gendered norms can also be traced in the ways some club promoters and journalists describe and advertise certain features of Gothic club events. The first of the following quotes is about a London Goth club called Perversion; the second describes the atmosphere of the Goth events at a venue called Kulturruine from the point of view of one of the organisers:

> Craziest of all, though, was February's competition. One DJ deck was placed at each end of the dancefloor and, for two hours, Slimelight DJ Judas had to cross the entire length of the room to change each and every track. On live cameras, any girl who could make him VOLUNTARILY miss the next track was to be awarded £500 IN CASH!, which went to the DJ should he resist for the whole set. (The Stranger; *Kaleidoscope* 14, Summer 2003, p. 46)

> But the very special charm is afforded by the erotic atmosphere, provided for by so many beautiful princesses that there's hardly a dry eye in the place, and the willingness of the (male) guests to communicate which is coupled with that. (Mozart, Umbra et Imago; *Sonic Seducer*, subscription bonus calendar 'Columbus 2002', p. 18)

These descriptions portray the events as resolutely heterosexual and promote very traditional gender roles regarding eroticism and seduction. At the club called Perversion, despite the air of sexual transgression this name conveys, even the apparent playfulness of the competition described here cannot cloak the conservative nature of the roles assigned to men and women in this game. The male DJ is to heroically resist lots of attractive female punters trying to seduce him into missing the next track. The prize to be awarded for successful resistance in the case of the male or successful seduction in the case of the females in fact rewards the culturally deeply ingrained gendered values of male stoicism versus female seductiveness. The implied gender roles in the portrayal of the Kulturruine Goth events come across as no less rigid and traditional, with the women being responsible for providing erotic charms by virtue of their beauty, and the men letting themselves be charmed into finally doing the talking and approaching the women.

While such descriptions are fairly isolated cases and by no means representative of the Gothic club scene as a whole, the one-sided exploitation of female eroticism they convey seems a more pervasive trend. In Germany in particular – and also in the US (Weinstock, 2007) – it has become common practice to advertise Goth events with scantily clad Fetish-Goth girls on flyers, posters and magazine ads (see also chapter 8).

Sluts against Sexism

However, despite their conservative import the above quotes also hint at one progressive feature of the Gothic scene in terms of gender relations, namely the wide acceptance and even promotion of open, direct displays of a self-deter-mined female sexuality. Many sociological studies (e.g. Macdonald, 2001; Stombler, 1994) have shown that in most contemporary cultural and subcul-tural spaces male-defined gender role norms still curtail female sexual expres-sion and behaviour. In the Gothic scene, by contrast, a self-determined expressing and acting out of female sexuality is regarded as a natural entitle-ment by most women, and crucially also by most men. Here, the widespread double standards of male and female sexual behaviour do not seem to apply. Goth women do not have to worry about gaining a reputation for a promis-cuous sex life, at least not a bad one. On the contrary, a 'slutty' reputation can in fact work to enhance rather than lessen the status of a female Goth:

> I've like noticed that sluts, or that the word 'slut' is a rather positive label in the Gothic scene. ... Also the behaviour pattern that's behind it; well actually, you can't get this term pinned to you in a negative sense because of your behaviour, and I think that's a positive thing really. Perhaps you even gain in status. (Satyria, f, 25, Berlin)

In the course of my research, I met a lot of confident and obviously self-determined women who express and live out their sexuality in a very direct, one could even say aggressive, way. Many of them indeed seem to have a fairly high status within the subculture. For instance, Lady Leather earns her living as a lap dancer in a strip club, and she convincingly described the feelings of control and superiority over the men ogling her which she enjoys when dancing there in her Fetish-Goth gear. Mistress Naté regards 'being a sadist' in the

erotic sense as an important part of her Goth side and takes pride in co-organ-
ising private S&M parties. In the Gothic subculture, it is generally accepted for
both men and women to indulge in the free play of sexual pleasures if they
choose to do so, and for many Goths transgressing conventional norms of
eroticism and sexuality constitutes a hallmark of the scene.

Another facet of this free expression of female sexuality on the Gothic scene
is the highly sexualised style that many Goth women adopt. Certainly not with
the same political consciousness as the feminist Riot Grrrl movement (see
Leonard, 1997) but with clear similarities in the practices employed, female
Gothic dress can work to challenge notions of female display. For instance,
some Goth women sport black dresses with words like 'slut' or 'bitch' printed
all over them, thus 'publicly confronting the viewer with the very terms
designed to prohibit female display and curtail sexual activity' (ibid., p. 235).
While in our culture at large certain styles of female dress are held to signal
sexuality in a way which invites sexual harassment (Wilson, 1985), this pernicious link between sexy female dress and sexualised hassle is partly broken in
Goth clubs. Here, women can dress up in very alluring gear without fear of
unwanted sexual advances on the part of Goth men:

> Like females will dress in a way that they would never do in a straight club –
> male sort of alcohol, you know the sort of clubs that people go to – and they can
> dress up, and they can feel fantastic in what they wear, and people will really
> appreciate what they wear, and that's it, that's all it is, and it's great. ... Some
> women do dress up to look really fucking sexy, and they love it and they love the
> attention, but know that in a Goth club they'll not be hassled, they'll be admired
> but not hassled. (Veeg, m, 40, Edinburgh)

> I think the difference is that in a Goth club you don't get hassled and people
> don't make silly comments – If you wear fishnet to a normal club, people would
> ask if you're a whore. (Petit Scarabee, f, 26, Edinburgh)

The same phenomenon has been observed by Hodkinson (2002) and
Schmidt and Neumann-Braun (2004). Hodkinson concludes that on the Gothic
scene modes of erotic attire are usually not interpreted as a sexual come-on but
'valued more in terms of their subcultural aesthetic qualities' (ibid., p. 51). This
reading – which echoes Pini's (2001) portrayal of Rave as a safe space for sexily
dressed women – may be overly idealistic considering my interviewees' statements about the Goth scene as a turf for competitive heterosexual courtship.
Yet it does have a point in that the way Goth women talk about the difference
between traditional clubs and Gothic clubs is very similar to what Pini
observed among female Ravers.

Pini regards the regular distancing on the part of Raving women from what
they see as a 'cattle market' mainstream as an expression of a specifically
female critique of the traditional gender codes and the predatory, sexualised

Figure 14 'Slutty' with attitude: a female interviewee at the Wave-Gotik-Treffen. Photograph: D. Brill

atmosphere in ordinary clubs. Similarly, Goth women's recollections of visits to 'mainstream' clubs abound with references to drunken, obtrusive 'townie lads' who 'thought it was their given right to grope any unattended female' (tatyana, *slashgoth.org*, 19/09/02). As we have seen, Goths are generally very critical of such vulgar modes of traditional masculinity, and certainly Goth women's fear of being harassed by such men is one reason for this aversion.

However, while Gothic spaces are commonly portrayed as havens of safety for females, they are not entirely free of obtrusive male behaviour. Subcultural spaces are not sealed off from the outside world, and as the door policies of Goth clubs differ widely, it is quite common for non-Goth males with dubious intentions to gain entrance into these spaces. Occasionally, male outsiders hassle girls in Fetish dress in a Goth club, probably inspired by the pornographic stereotype of 'easiness' they associate with such gear. Goth men do not normally behave like that, partly because the Gothic community functions almost like a small village in terms of social control and could punish such misbehaviour with exclusion. Arguably, this social control makes the scene much safer for women than many ordinary clubs. However, the embracing of sexual transgression, which is a hallmark of the subculture, has one serious downside in that it may be exploited by 'predatory' individuals to take advantage of 'young, impressionable minds':

> There's a lot of very young, impressionable minds on the scene. ... And, I mean, because it's all like pushing boundaries forwards, its transgressive nature, all that sort of thing, and yeah, in some senses, say if someone is predatory in this scene they can find a lot of prey amongst these fresh, impressionable young minds. And I mean basically if they camouflage themselves in the avant-garde costume of the scene they can have access to people in different generations and age groups, who may be impressionable and easily manipulated. And yeah, I think that's a bit of a downside of the scene, but from another point of view it is inclusive, and that, it's not limited to any particular generation. (Jiad, m, 45, Edinburgh)[1]

Subcultural 'Sugardaddies'

On a positive end note, Jiad characterises the Gothic scene as 'inclusive' in terms of being open to different age groups and not segregating people according to generations. This idea of inclusiveness across social categories like age strongly accords with what Bradby (1993) calls the 'Utopian discourse' of openness and inclusiveness pervading Rave culture. Bradby (ibid., p. 165) points out that this discourse centres 'around the mixing on the dance floor of social categories across which marriage is discouraged', and names age as one of the most important of these categories. However, the quite common and socially accepted age structure of heterosexual relationships among certain well-respected people in current and former societies – e.g. ageing male rulers, politicians and stars with massively younger wives or lovers – proves that relationships across age boundaries are accepted in our culture as long as the woman is younger than the man.

This one-sided 'openness' of the age boundary, where it is deemed socially acceptable for older men to go out with younger women but not vice versa, is basically the same in the Gothic subculture. There is nothing 'Utopian' really about the kind of age inclusiveness which Goth represents in terms of heterosexual courtship practices. Although many Goths claim that for them age simply does not matter, this declared 'ideology of agelessness' is not at all borne out by the reality on the ground. While there are quite a few Goth couples where the man is significantly – sometimes a whole generation – older than the woman, I have yet to meet a couple where this fairly traditional age structure is fully reversed.

The explanations given by Goth men in particular when asked about possible reasons for this state of affairs usually reflect the typical discourses about this topic circulating in general society. The simplistic biologism of popular evolutionary psychology with its postulate that females prefer seasoned males who have proven themselves in life, and the rather elastically interpreted truism that men mature later in life than women, feature prominently in such explanations. However, the explanatory value of such societal discourses is limited if we want to get at the actual motives of male and female Goths for tending to choose partners according to a very traditional and conservative age structure. The following statements which flowed from general conversations about amorous adventures on the scene prove far more illuminating.

> DE: Well, you know, I also have the reputation that for the last 15 years I've always had like girlfriends who are about 16, 17 – just that way back then I was 17 as well.
>
> Me: How does that come about then?
>
> DE: Don't know, it just happens somehow. They always feel that I've got a lot of experience already, like 'hey, he's got long hair, right, he must have been growing it for ten years already' and so on.
>
> (DeEm, m, 31, Bonn)

> Of course there are also some little minxes then who really dig it – I'm actually going to call them little minxes for now, you know – who really dig it that I've reached a certain age accordingly and have been on the scene for a long time; who then also, don't know, who then find the length of affiliation within the scene attractive. That happens as well, that's got nothing to do with looks at all. Or you look extremely freaky, better than the ones in their age group, I'd just say, I mean the boys, cause they possibly aren't able or willing to live it out so much cause they're still living with their mums or have just finished school somehow or whatever. (Muckel, m, 30, Cologne)

Both interviewees agree that, up to a point, for men a higher age – and especially a long involvement in the Gothic subculture – can function as a source of subcultural capital on the heterosexual courtship market, as it holds a certain attraction for some younger females relatively new to the scene. Moreover, meeting subcultural standards of style (e.g. long hair or an 'extremely freaky' look) can be a further important source of status and desirability for older men, even if physical beauty as such declines. Every city where I observed the scene seems to boast at least one ageing 'Übergoth' with extreme styling who is notorious for attracting a string of young, beautiful girlfriends despite notable shortcomings in terms of physical beauty. For instance, one specimen in Berlin sports well-groomed long hair despite being half-bald and projects an image of a vampire count; one in Brighton even wears a long-haired wig to hide his baldness; one in Edinburgh often displays a very androgynous style (e.g. tight corsets).

In my experience, ageing female Übergoths with such pulling powers are conspicuous only by their absence on the scene. The mechanism of attracting partners, and in particular younger partners, mainly by virtue of one's long-standing, outwardly visible involvement in the scene seems mostly a male privilege. It does not usually work for Goth women, who are hence excluded from the rewards which long-time involvement in the scene can earn for Goth men on the courtship market:

> Well, of course it bothers me as a woman who's growing older that this mechanism doesn't work for me *laughs*. Cause you just have to admit that the younger men are just more attractive. Well, but unfortunately it doesn't work in this case. And, well, in the scene you just tend to get it a lot that these old-established scene gurus, who are also past it already as far as age is concerned, then tend to have like underage girlfriends. And I think that the girlfriends tend to, I mean, they turn a blind eye to the age difference cause they're expecting that someone who's been on the scene for so long, you know, can also introduce them appropriately then; and that she herself attains a certain status by just going out with someone who's just very well established on the scene, you know. ... Well, and I think that's just something you just also see a lot in normal society. Well, there you know that there's a certain percentage of women who just also tend to – men who present a certain symbolic status tend to be taken in order to establish oneself; that is by the quickest possible means, not necessarily the most pleasant, I must say *laughs*. (Umbersun, f, 29, Bonn)

Umbersun draws a direct link between the traditional custom of women 'marrying up' – i.e. choosing a man of high social standing – to enhance their own status and the subcultural phenomenon of young female scene newcomers trying to gain recognition by taking an older, well-established male partner. This traditionally female means of increasing one's status through association with people (mostly males) who already possess a high status in the relevant cultural grouping is referred to by Bourdieu (1984) as *social capital*.

Of course relationships in the Gothic subculture will rarely be based on such conscious calculations; yet this model can help to explain a seeming incongruity in the relation between age, gender, status and courtship on the scene. We have seen that many Goth men draw on the discourse of popular evolutionary psychology to explain or justify the mechanism whereby older males can attract younger females. Let us now take a basic postulate of pop evolutionary psychology – namely the idea that women choose seasoned males who have gained enough wealth and status to provide for their women or families

– as a metaphor of how social factors have shaped courtship norms, rather than in its deterministic original sense. Even then, this postulate does not seem to make much sense in the context of the Gothic subculture. While some older Goth men have got the common trappings of success and status in the form of a well-paid job, many who manage to pull younger, attractive women actually lack the traditional status criteria of our capitalist society, as they are unemployed or in low-paid temporary jobs.

In the Gothic subculture, however, men can obviously draw on other sources of status and capital which more than make up for this lack, especially a long-standing, intense involvement in the scene as DJ, promoter or simply active member. Properly employed males often lack the time to engage fully in the scene and also face certain restrictions in the more permanent aspects of subcultural style (e.g. long hair, tattoos, piercings). Males without such constraints can invest much time and effort into Goth and hence gain subcultural capital through extreme looks and active involvement. Ironically, despite the Gothic subculture's esteem for formal education and success, those men whom conventional society would class as 'losers' may thus be in a prime position to achieve a high standing within the scene and its courtship market.

Gendering Subcultural Capital

While Goths can be quite reluctant to talk about their scene in terms of subcultural capital, they generally agree that the main status criteria which count regardless of gender are productive involvement in and sheer length of affiliation to the subculture. People who contribute to the scene by running clubs or shops or by organising festivals are widely admired. A notable finding in this connection is that at least in smaller, not overly commercial national or regional Goth scenes like the UK one, female involvement in production and organisation is high in comparison with many other music-based subcultures (see Cohen, 1991; Thornton, 1995). On the Edinburgh scene, for instance, 'Ascension' club co-organiser and 'Underground Nation' shop owner Julia and 'Edinburgh Goth Weekend' organiser Morag are among the most prominent individuals.

However, it struck me that at Gothic festivals, and especially in the clubs, there tend to be far fewer older (i.e. over thirty) women than men. Single Goth women of that age who frequent clubs and events are particularly rare, whereas there is a large number of older men who are very active on the scene. While older women are accepted in the subculture, I suspect the rewards and pleasures of active subcultural membership partly decline with age for females, which is not the case for males. Meeting a partner may not be the prime motivation for going to Goth events, yet heterosexual courtship still plays a major role on the Gothic scene. As we have already seen, in this area single older women may feel marginalised in Goth, just like in most other sections of society.

Traditionally gendered norms of status attainment still hold quite powerful sway over how males and females are viewed and positioned in society. While 'men are more frequently judged by their social status, intellect or material success, women are commonly defined in terms of their appearance and relationship to men' (Betterton, 1987, p. 7), a truism confirmed even by the most cursory glance at common media representations of men and women. Such gendered norms of judging status also apply in the Gothic subculture to some extent, as indicated by the following statements about the qualities which can win a man or a woman popularity and admiration on the scene.

E: Well, you just get the best example in all the clubs, you know; what always, what's just always in demand among the women is any one of those DJs, or anyone who plays in any of those bands, yes. That's just something special for all the kiddies, I'd just put it like that. *laughs* ...

Me: And what about the women?

E: Well, I mean a woman just simply has to look good and that's enough, you know. *laughs* And everything else just comes automatically, so to say. Yes, but it's true. *both laugh*

(Ed, m, 35, Cologne)

My boyfriend de-jays and helps run clubs, he's run clubs in the past as well, and he's very admired and looked up to, well, because of his age and experience and also, you know, cause of the way he's got his make-up down to a fine art and his clothes are lovely and, you know, he knows all, he knows his music and stuff. ... For women, a lot of the time I think it's aesthetics, it's the way you look and stuff. Although men, it can be the same for men to an extent. (Persephone, f, 21, Edinburgh)

Mirroring the status quo in general society, success, knowledge and experience in the subcultural sphere form major sources of cultural capital for Goth men, while women are judged mainly by physical attractiveness. Beauty and styling still seem particularly important in the definition of femininity rather than masculinity on the Gothic scene. Here, just like elsewhere, a woman's status and character are often judged by her looks. However, in some ways the gendered norms of winning status are more relaxed in Goth than in many other sections of society.

Firstly, gender parity in terms of the importance accorded to styling and physical attractiveness is greater, as the scene promotes flamboyance for both genders. The social pressure to meet certain ideals of beauty which women routinely face in our culture is at least partly extended to men. Personal ads in Gothic magazines and Internet forums often feature women explicitly looking for men who fulfil the standard male Goth beauty ideals of long hair and slimness, and quite a few men who 'apologise' in advance for lacking these assets. On the courtship market of the Gothic scene, looks are obviously an important source of capital for men as well as for women. Yet the crucial difference is that Goth men can more than compensate for shortcomings in that department by drawing on other sources of subcultural capital like organisational activities and experience, which are just as well convertible into heterosexual desirability for them.

A second area where the gendering of status attainment seems less rigid than in other sections of society is precisely this sphere of organisational or productive involvement. For instance, some of the biggest British Goth enterprises are run by females; there is 'Whitby Jo', for example, who organises the main British Goth festival, and Natasha Scharf, who runs the leading British Goth magazine, *Meltdown*. Contributing to the scene through club or festival promotion, DJing or publishing is an important source of subcultural capital for Goth women and men alike. However, this form of capital can be converted into a currency which counts on the heterosexual courtship market only by men. Women who organise events or produce subcultural media are paid the same amount of respect as their male colleagues by fellow Goths, but I found no hints in my data that such activities do anything to boost their desirability.

The more commercial German scene is a special case, as it has spawned quite a few successful subcultural entrepreneurs, nearly all of them male. In contrast to the infrastructure of the British scene, where there is not much money to be earned through Goth, the main German Gothic festivals, magazines and clubs are firmly in male hands. Of course the fact that here financial success can be achieved *within* the subculture affects the value of this traditional male status criterion for Goth men. Professional involvement in the scene enables some of them to don the trappings of both conventional financial success and full subcultural prestige; thus, professional success can work to boost subcultural capital.

A Beauty Contest?

For female Goths in any country, physical beauty and elaborate styling remain by far the most important means of status attainment. While having loosened up the codes of male appearance, the Gothic subculture has not overcome the traditional 'emphasis on physical attractiveness as the measure of a woman's value' (Paoletti and Kidwell, 1989, p. 158). In our society, physical beauty functions as a chiefly female form of capital in Bourdieu's sense, a source of status called *corporeal capital* (Skeggs, 1997). While femininity is generally not a strong asset to trade and capitalise on, investments in it can yield relatively high profit in some areas – most notably on the heterosexual courtship market, where the trading value of physical attractiveness is particularly high for women. Hence, the sphere of beauty and style normally forms the main arena of competition for recognition and status among women.

While many Goths are reluctant to talk about their subculture in terms of competition, a few Goth women admit to being jealous of attractive females who get more attention. Notably, it is mainly female Goths who are described or describe themselves as competitive:

Some females will try to look as good as they humanly can to maybe, maybe be the best-looking female there, to get all the admirative stares from the men and women. (Mistress Naté, f, 24, Edinburgh)

Goth men, by contrast, often portray themselves as somehow 'beyond competition'. There is a link to the notion of 'hipness' in Thornton's (1995) sense as a source of subcultural capital here, as to be really hip involves projecting an air of being above mundane things like competition. Women in the Gothic subculture apparently have to compete for status in a more directly observable arena than men. Female subcultural capital resides mainly in highly visible factors like corporeal capital (i.e. physical beauty, styling) and social capital (i.e. who, that is mainly which *men*, they associate themselves with), while males can more easily shift their status struggles to seemingly less superficial spheres (e.g. expertise in subcultural fields of knowledge, like music).

Writing about women's magazines, Winship (1987a) argues that their focus on beauty and style promotes the idea that to achieve 'individuality' for a woman primarily means using beauty products and fashion in the right way to express her personality. Consequently, 'any achievement of "individuality" has a somewhat hollow ring, barely registering on a "higher" masculine scale of values' (ibid., p. 64). Males gain a status of individuality by virtue of their character and actions, so the logic goes, whereas females' main route to distinction is styling and appearance. This logic is not entirely, but at least partly, reflected in the Gothic scene, where looks and especially style are important status criteria for both genders, but still more important for women.

While we have seen that hyperfeminine Gothic style can be empowering for women, it can also work to make those who are not willing or able to conform to this ideal feel inferior and excluded on the scene. The following female interviewee, for example, sensed that many of the women at a big Goth club event she attended were trying to emulate the ideals of dark yet hypersexy feminine beauty promoted in certain Gothic media (especially *Orkus* and *Sonic Seducer*) to perfection, a realisation which made her feel uneasy and out of place:

S: Well, I was there, was feeling uneasy at this event as I like realised this, because I had the feeling that I don't style myself like that, I do try to make myself look good but not in that way, I don't dress that sexily. And just because of that so I fail to meet the ideal and hence don't have such great chances, and, well, am already a step below in the hierarchy of attractiveness. Well, I knew that I don't want to look that way, that I'm different and so on, but I was still feeling inferior and had the feeling not to be so attractive for the people there. ...

Me: And this hierarchy of attractiveness, how is it structured?

S: At the top of the hierarchy are the women who are made up very femi-
      ninely, of course, who, well, are dressed as sexily as possible, yes. And the
      less you meet the classic ideal of beauty, which actually also applies in the
      mainstream – that doesn't differ much then, only in the colour of the
      clothes one wears – so if you deviate from the ideal of beauty then you
      aren't so attractive in the Gothic scene as well, exactly like in the other
      society.

                                                          (Satyria, f, 25, Berlin)

Skeggs (1997, p. 104) points out that subcultural standards of beauty and
style can 'invoke hierarchies of corporeal and cultural capital' within a scene
at the same time as they challenge stereotypical representations in broader
culture. Appearance is simultaneously a site of pleasure and strength and a site
of anxiety and regulation for women. In Goth, this conflicted relation of
women to their style and appearance is very evident. While the sexy, hyperfeminine dress codes of the subculture pose a challenge to stereotypical nice
and passive images of femininity and can hence empower their wearers, they
can also cause anxiety and feelings of inadequacy for women who do not
measure up.

The 'hierarchy of attractiveness' described by Satyria points to the importance of standard ideals of beauty for Goth women. The styling of female
Goths may often seem weird or freaky to outsiders; yet for such a – usually
rather moderate (e.g. long hair with shaved sides, thick black eye make-up) –
freaky styling to be deemed attractive within the subculture, classic ideals of
feminine beauty in the form of symmetrical, fine facial features have to be met.
Just like in general society, deviations from this ideal have to be masked rather
than set off through the use of make-up by female Goths if they want to
enhance their attractiveness for the opposite sex.

For Goth men, looking freaky can sometimes work to enhance status and
desirability – a phenomenon I dub the 'Marilyn Manson effect', as this artist
also manages to appear attractive by enhancing the naturally freaky aspects of
his look (e.g. by wearing bizarre make-up and differently coloured contact
lenses). On women, by contrast, apart from a mildly weird yet still beautiful
styling, a freaky look is regarded as undesirable. Contrary to widespread
popular opinion, female Gothic style creation mainly revolves around meeting
certain standards of feminine attractiveness and sexiness, rather than aiming to
look conspicuously freakish or menacing. When asked about how they see
female Gothic style, male Goths tend to join in the 'female empowerment' rhetoric that Goth women appear strong and command respect. However, certain
off-the-record remarks I picked up suggest that Goth men's interest in the
hyperfeminine masquerades of female Goths resides mainly in their erotic
appeal, rather than in their alleged subversiveness or empowerment for
women.

Beauty and Courtship

As already implied by this observation, Goth discourses on gender relations and the importance of physical beauty can be conflicting and sometimes contradictory. For instance, one woman I asked about a Gothic singles party in Berlin she had attended described the atmosphere there as a 'meat market'. In her view, most of the women were dressed so as to present their bodies and were there mainly to get attention for their looks and not their personality. In sharp contrast to this critical view, a male interviewee portrays the Gothic scene as a haven of more cerebral and less superficial or body-oriented relations between the sexes:

> What I also kind of think is that like the, these ideals of beauty are different there. Well, I'd just say the percentage of intellectuals is like pretty high there, and also among the girls. Then you talk to someone, and much is going on like on an intellectual level. ... Well, I'm certainly not exactly the slimmest and most handsome man here, I do have my 190 pounds I'm carrying around with me at a size of 5'7". But when I look at like women with whom I like – well, I had a long-term relationship with one of the most beautiful women in the whole town of Bonn. And, well, there it was just no problem that I wasn't like the epitome of a good-looker. Well, when I like look at, like couples like from the Gothic scene, there are totally ugly girls, for example, just to put it like that, with a totally pretty bloke. Or vice versa, that one of those blokes who, where I think 'for heaven's sake, what does he do with his looks', is walking hand in hand there with like an absolutely beautiful, like a fairy-girl. (DeEm, m, 31, Bonn)

According to DeEm, the choice of partners on the Gothic scene is motivated by intellect and personality rather than by purely aesthetic factors for both men and women. However, maybe it is not accidental that such a positive assessment – which also invokes the familiar ideology of genderlessness in claiming that the chance to attract partners way out of one's league in terms of looks is open to males and females alike – is advanced by a man. From a female perspective things can look quite different, as the following Internet forum posting by an overweight Goth woman shows:

> The only thing that's making me really, really sad is that soooooo many people are always preaching tolerance but on the other hand can't seem to accept my appearance. Men above all. Most depressing are snide words by men with whom I fell in love. I wasn't attractive enough, something along these lines. (Niobe, *Gothiccommunity.de*, 18/02/03)

Polhemus (1988, p. 65) maintains that girls in conspicuous subcultures 'wouldn't think of going out with a boy who wasn't as completely, creatively and outlandishly adorned as themselves'. However, this claim is not backed up with empirical data, hence reflecting subcultural ideologies of gender equality rather than the reality of gender relations within them. While there certainly are Goth women who make great demands on the looks and styling of potential partners, couples where a very attractive and elaborately styled female goes out with a rather plain male are quite a common sight. Contrary to DeEm's appraisal, however, couples where this traditional status quo is reversed are all but non-existent on the scene.

Just like in general society, where received wisdom has it that women should go by character in choosing a partner whereas men are tacitly granted the privilege of judging by character *and* appearance, making unflinchingly great demands on the looks of erotic partners is mainly a male prerogative in the Gothic subculture. While in theory Goth women almost unanimously prefer well-groomed, slim, tall men with long hair, fine features and an androgynous touch, in practice they seem far more ready than the men to lower or even completely forgo their demands in the looks department. Androgyny frequently remains a seemingly unattainable ideal of male beauty for Goth women, who are often prepared to opt for a partner not even remotely resembling the ideal they so passionately rave about.

Above all a beautiful (male) person should have long hair, and a wonderfully long face with hollow cheeks, white skin and endlessly long fingers (+ fingernails) but these are just only nice to look at, I don't know, for a boyfriend I don't want to have a delicate guy... then I'd always be afraid that I break something *g* my boyfriend certainly suits me quite well there (ValisLacrimarum, *Gothiccommunity.de*, 14/03/03)

I'd better realise that I'm growing older and that this doesn't do my body so much good. And nevertheless I've got more and more clear-cut conceptions of beauty. Yes, hands and eyes are important to me, too – and long, dark hair. But... these are just the partners of my dreams, dreams being the operative word. In life things happen differently after all, you know; there I can rave about a man like Johnny Depp at one moment, with long black hair and fine features. And in the very next moment there's one standing in front of me with short blond hair and crude features and I'm in raptures. After all, usually the nice thing about dreams is that they don't come true and so always remain nice dreams, untouched by the profanity of the everyday, you never have to take them down from their pedestal cause they're snoring or distributing their socks all over the place. (Audrey, *Gothiccommunity.de*, 15/03/03)

While ValisLacrimarum simply states she does not really want a delicate man as a boyfriend, Audrey gives a more complex explanation of the difference between ideal and reality in her choice of partners. She similarly insists that there is a demarcation line between 'dreams' and 'life' she would not want to cross so as to leave her fantasies untarnished by the profane reality of an actual relationship. Yet she casually mentions another factor which could be operative here, namely her realisation that her own beauty declines as she grows older; this realisation might make her feel no longer entitled to make great demands on the looks of potential partners. Appearance as a chiefly female form of symbolic capital depreciates with age, as the ideals of femininity demand youthful beauty. These traditional criteria of female sexual attractiveness – youth and beauty – seem the main form of capital on which Goth women can trade on the courtship market.

Heterosexual desirability is a powerful factor in the sense of self of many women, who see it as a validation of themselves as it confirms individual and sexual identity (Ganetz, 1995). Desirability represents a way in which feminine cultural capital is confirmed as worth having, thus legitimising the value of performing femininity. Yet it also 'offers to masculinity the power to impose standards, make evaluations and confirm validity' (Skeggs, 1997, p. 112). In our culture, the 'habitual notion that what men think of women is the ultimate criterion of femininity' (Butler, 1987, p. 121) still holds powerful sway over the self-images of women, and many tacitly regard being desired by men as a primary source of cultural validation. As we have seen, Goth women partly collude with these cultural standards. However, the following statements – about why there is more choice of Gothic clothing for women than for men – prove that some female Goths see right through this mechanism and its hidden workings within their subculture, and attempt to break its sway by laying it open.

> I suspect that the reason for this problem is the same as the reason that there is more clothing for females in pretty much every subculture, group, whatever. It's because aesthetics are considered to be primarily the domain of the female. ... there's the fact that it is generally assumed that males are more aesthetically motivated in choosing lovers, and that females are utterly obsessed with being chosen as such. (okan'e, *slashgoth.org*, 23/01/02)

> Another reason there are more fashions for women is probably because women are expected to worry their pretty little heads about fitting in so as to get themselves a man. Or am I just being cynical? (Eviscera, *slashgoth.org*, 24/01/02)

Gender Roles

Even more than the gendering of subcultural capital, gender role standards in Goth go the whole spectrum from deeply traditional archetypes to playful role reversals, with many shades of grey in between. One area where the tensions inherent in the gendered images and behaviour codes of the subculture can sometimes be directly observed is the Gothic dance floor. Dance, which is an important mode of self-expression for male and female Goths alike, is usually associated with the feminine in Western culture (Hanna, 1988; Klein, 1992). However, dance styles can differ widely in the gendered connotations they carry, ranging from softly flowing 'feminine' movements to harshly stomping 'masculine' ones. In certain environments, men tend to adopt forms of dance whose 'almost purely physical (as opposed to aesthetic) component' makes them seem almost like a workout (Amico, 2001, p. 362). On Gothic dance floors as well, the styles men and women display are often quite strongly demarcated along gender lines.

K: A typically masculine behaviour is someone who's wearing Docs [Doc Martens boots], perhaps with leather trousers, too, a muscle shirt, and then stomping on the dancefloor, across the dancefloor to an EBM track – Rammstein, for example. Many people dance in a very typical fashion to Rammstein tracks, who just, you know, well, want to demonstrate strength by posing with legs apart; strength, unbendingness, power, perhaps violence, something of this kind. I would also call that a typically masculine behaviour. Although women dance like that as well, of course that also happens, but it's clearly just a minority. So it's almost always just men who dance like that, who also take pleasure in acting that role, you know. ...

Me: And what's like the usual female dance style?

K: Staying at one single spot more or less, hardly moving, very intensely waving their hands about in the air, for example, well, and swaying with the upper body in some cases. Rather, well, trying to appear fairylike, elfin, arcane, mysterious, something of this kind.

(Kasch, m, 35, Bonn)

Kasch interprets the typical male and female dance styles he observed as expressing the dancers' desires to project images of hypermasculine power and strength or hyperfeminine grace and mystique. These images conjure up fantastic archetypes saturated with gendered meanings – e.g. vampires, warriors, fairies – which form a major medium of identification and self-presentation in the Gothic subculture. Some of the dark, mythical archetypes invoked by Goths have progressive and empowering implications in terms of gender. The figure of the 'black goddess' Lilith, for example, is celebrated in a Goth magazine article as epitomising 'the independent, rebellious, raging and deadly woman' who 'hits the phallic pride of patriarchy' (*Orkus*, 06/03, p. 108).

Others, like the vampire, have conflicting or even reactionary connotations. On the one hand, the vampire symbolises a subversion of traditional binary gender; the creature fuses and confuses the gendered categories of penetrating and receptive, as the mouth with its penetrating teeth is the primary erotic orifice of male and female vampires (Craft, 1989). On the other hand, the vampire stands for the dominance of the masculine over the feminine, because most vampire tales feature a male protagonist as the 'Great Original' who creates 'female surrogates who enact his will and desire' (ibid., p. 218). Chris Pohl, a star on the German Goth music scene, obviously draws on the latter interpretation in stylising himself as an erotically dominant 'vampire' in his relationships with women:

> I often *bite* a woman to put her on a par with me, to carry her away into my realm and to share all sorrow and joys with her. The price for this is often also that she has to give up the life she's led so far and to change her ideas completely. (*Orkus*, 09/02, p. 19, original emphasis)

This statement – while certainly owing as much to the mise-en-scène of Pohl as a cool yet romantic Goth artist as to his personal views – reflects a very traditional conception of gender roles in heterosexual relationships: the male as active, dominant and powerful versus the female as receptive, submissive and malleable. The implied suggestion that a woman needs to be elevated from her lowly position by the action of a man to be finally 'on a par' with him and able to share his visions betrays a deeply reactionary view of gender relations, at least on the level of fantasy.

Similarly, the gendered archetypes invoked in Gothic personals (which are a popular feature of *Orkus* and *Sonic Seducer*) often imply regressive ideal images of masculinity and femininity. There are hordes of 'lonesome warriors' and 'lonesome black knights' looking for their 'princesses' or 'elves' of the night; there are male 'vampires' and 'wolves' roaming the personals pages for fresh female prey, and there is also many a 'little Goth girl' or 'fallen angel' yearning for her 'Lord of Darkness'. These archetypes have long become standard fare in Gothic personals, to such an extent that many Goths now use them with an ironic twist to distance themselves from what they see as hackneyed clichés. Goth men and women who do not fit in with these stereotypically gendered ideal images often take them as negative points of reference in their own ads:

> [female:] No, I'm not looking for my Prince of Darkness and neither am I a little fallen angel. (*Sonic Seducer*, 03/03, p. 74)

> [male:] Don't worry, I'm neither fraught with any kind of macho image nor looking for a dark "Barbie dolly"! (*Orkus*, 04/03, p. 138)

Renegotiating the Roles

The critical and ironic use of gendered Gothic stereotypes by people who refuse such limited heterosexual roles already indicates that quite a few Goths of both genders attempt to renegotiate received gender roles. Naturally, many of those who defy the gendered clichés of Goth – e.g. the very rare women who reject hyperfemininity outright – are located at the margins of the scene. However, instances of a striking openness towards experimenting with gender roles and relations can also be found at the very heart of the subculture, most notably in the sphere of style but also in the sphere of gender identity and trans-sex identification. As the following examples from these two spheres illustrate, such progressive renegotiations of gender roles can go quite far but often still remain trapped within the traditional binary conception of gender:

> I don't think it took me any less time to get ready than it took my (ex) g/f... Having said that, I think women consider it their duty to take at least 30 minutes longer than their male partner to get ready, no matter *how* long the guy actually takes. (Taoist, *slashgoth.org*, 11/11/02)

> I actually went out with a transgender, which was refreshing cause I had enough of men, and it was so nice to go out with someone knowing behind closed doors it was a bloke, but out on the street we could communicate like women. And it was a refreshing change he didn't think like a bloke, he had none of that testosterone crap *laughs*. I mean cause she was doing hormone replacement tablets she was more sensitive, very caring, very loving, very tearful for the reason she took her tablets. Maybe it was just nice to go out with someone who wasn't gonna treat me like the opposite sex as such; someone who actually appreciated me for who I was and not trying to get and reap me into bed, you know. And I find that a lot with blokes, their testosterone is a funny thing, I would never like to have it *laughs*. ... But, I mean, we split up in the end because we were finding we were actually falling for each other and that wasn't what I wanted. I mean, who'd carry the bouquet for goodness' sake *laughs*. (Batty, f, 30, Brighton)

Taoist is a very androgynous man who attaches great importance to styling and takes obvious pride in his vanity. Yet still he suggests that, in his experience, women feel compelled to surpass their male partners in the time and effort they put into their styling. This alleged female behaviour pattern seems to be a ritualised mode of achieving femininity rather than to grow out of pre-existing gender differences in making-up habits; as Taoist humorously insists, many women consider it their 'duty' to take notably longer than their male partner regardless of the actual time he takes.

Batty's story about her relationship with a preoperative male-to-female transgender is more complex and warrants closer analysis. As we will see in the following chapter, Goths in general are very accepting of transsexualism and queer sexualities. I have already mentioned the transgression of conventional boundaries of sexuality as an ideal highly valued in the subculture. Here, this ideal works as a benign force advancing tolerance and understanding – and even veneration – for people who do not fit in with the traditional binary concept of sex and gender. As Batty told me, her relationship with a trans-gender was widely accepted and sometimes even admired on the scene, and she herself obviously also sees it as a perfectly natural thing and a positive experience.

However, despite this openness towards sexualities which cross or blur the traditional sex-gender binary, Batty's talk about her transgender ex-partner and their relationship is still steeped in explanations and metaphors hailing from this very binary. While the switching between the pronouns he/she in her account indicates that she experienced the relationship as blurring sex and gender boundaries, the way she tries to make sense of this experience falls back on strict binary categories and traditional biologistic discourses. The difference between a 'sensitive, caring, loving, tearful' woman in a man's body and 'blokes' with primitive sexual urges is explained in terms of hormonal factors, namely as an effect of the hormone therapy the transgender was undergoing versus the high testosterone levels of normal men. The humorous invocation of a traditional heterosexual wedding scenario – where it would not be clear who performs the female role of carrying the bouquet – to explain the break-up of an otherwise satisfying relationship further reveals the operation of deeply conventional discourses.

Not surprisingly, even for the most open-minded Goths – just like for anyone in our society – it seems difficult to think beyond the deep-rooted traditional binary concept of gender. However, the Gothic scene also offers instances of a playful yet fairly thorough reversal of gender roles, most notably in the sphere of styling and vanity:

I personally like dating lads whose make up kit is better than mine...and it normally is hehe I don't even mind being ready 1 hour before him :) (Princess Thais, *slashgoth.org*, 18/11/02)

R: Going shopping with Ozzy, that's like, like straight from a cliché, a bad clichéd book for women.

O: *laughs*

Me: Come on, tell me.

B: Well, 'does this suit me?' and 'how does that look then?' and 'should I buy this?; oh, I don't know, I probably look fat in it' *all laugh*.

O: Yes, it's really like that, you shouldn't let me do my shopping on my own.

B: For hours on end! You know, I walk into a shop, say 'well, I like this, how much is it?', and then if the price is okay I try it on and then I buy it, you know. So there's not much to discuss. But Ozzy *rolls her eyes*.

(Rai, f, 19, Bonn; Ozzy, m, 18, Bonn)

These rather light-hearted episodes of gender role reversal may seem trivial in comparison with the ingrained binary structures commonly governing heterosexual relations both within and outside the subculture. Yet the symbolic power of such playful renegotiations should not be underrated. Radical changes in gender roles and relations will not readily happen even in a subculture which promotes the transgression of traditional boundaries of gender and sexuality. However, obviously some seeds of change have already fallen on the dark, fertile soil of Goth, and the subtle renegotiations of gender roles taking place there could well point the way to more open-minded, more playful and above all more equal relations between the sexes.

Conclusion

This chapter has portrayed the Gothic scene as a mainly heterosexual space and shown that its gendered courtship norms, status criteria and role standards oscillate between progressive and reactionary tendencies.

As to the analysed links between courtship and status, it can be said that Goth men are partly freed from the shackles of common cultural status criteria for men in the form of occupational and financial success, and can draw on other forms of (sub)cultural capital if they fail to meet those.[2] Crucially, these alternative modes of winning status – androgynous or otherwise extreme styling, long-standing and active involvement in Goth – also have a high trading value on the heterosexual courtship market of the scene. By contrast, Goth women's means of status attainment, or at least the capital they can trade upon on the courtship market, remain closely tied to the traditional criteria of female sexual attractiveness, namely youth, physical beauty and feminine styling.

In contrast to certain insider accounts of the Gothic subculture, which portray it as a space where 'absolute equality ... between men and women' (Wallraff, 2001, p. 41) is the rule, this state of affairs is symptomatic of one fundamental inequality between the sexes in Goth. Men can partly escape the pressures of hegemonic masculinity through experimenting with androgynous style and drawing on alternative sources of status within the scene. Women, however, remain largely restricted to the standards of traditional femininity, both in their hyperfeminine appearance and in their means of status attainment linked to it.

Moreover, the fact that Goth women's status on the heterosexual courtship market hinges mainly on their beauty and sexiness, while Goth men can afford to neglect their appearance and mobilise other sources of capital instead, replicates a deeply conventional scopic regime of desirability where women 'pose' for the male gaze. We have already seen that the *femme fatale* mode of hypersexy femininity projected by many Goth women can work to partly deflect the male gaze of scene outsiders, who may find it mildly threatening. Yet it seems fully recuperable by the gaze of male insiders, who simply find its dark edge erotically attractive. This scopic regime – or, more precisely, its operation in Gothic media – will be further discussed in chapter 8.

7

Queer Sexualities

Brighton, spring 2002, one of the city's most legendary gay pubs called the Harlequin. The pub is hosting its popular Saturday night Eighties party, which always draws a very mixed crowd. Along with young to middle-aged gay men in trendy clothes, lesbians ranging from sporty to rustic, and ageing drag queens in fanciful dress, the local Goth community has chosen this particular party as one of their weekend haunts. Currently there is only one monthly Goth night in town, and certain niches within the flourishing gay scene – which embraces flamboyance and androgyny just like Goths do – naturally suggest themselves as alternatives. At a table next to the tiny, crowded dance floor I spot Lowlife, one of the DJs and organisers of Brighton's Goth club. I am very surprised to learn that the Skin-Punk guy sitting next to him is his long-term boyfriend, as it had never occurred to me that he might be gay or bisexual. Later on, a friend introduces me to a tall, slender woman dancing elegantly in a flowing black velvet dress, whom I have long wanted to ask for an interview: Ayleen, a male-to-female transgender with an eventful subcultural biography reaching from early Punk to her current Hippy-esque take on Goth. Tonight, my first night at the Harlequin, it seems to me that there is a huge overlap between queers and Goths in Brighton. However, this impression wanes over the next few weeks as I get to know more and more of the local Goths. In fact, Lowlife and Ayleen remain the only real connecting links between the two scenes whom I happen to meet during my years in Britain's 'gay capital'.

Berlin, summer 2004, the Zyankali Bar, a bizarre Kreuzberg drinking den resembling a cross between a stalactite cave and a B-movie set with lots of ghastly, tacky horror film props all over the place. I have come here tonight to meet the monthly les-bi-gay Goth gathering taking place at this bar. When I finally spot a table with black-clad people, I am welcomed by Erinnys, a woman with black dreadlocks, who turns out to have launched this gathering more than two years ago. Asked about what inspired her to start such a minority group within a minority scene, she replies: 'Well, I felt extremely isolated both on the Gothic scene and on the gay scene as I never really met like-minded souls, but I had a feeling that there simply *must* be more of us in Berlin than just little me. So I started classified ads in the Goth press and the local gay press, and in some Internet forums. At first we were only three or four people, but obviously there's some demand for this kind of thing'; she smiles, pointing to a new arrival who can hardly find a spare seat at our crowded table. Later that evening she introduces me to some of the other regulars. There is Tee, a transgender woman with fine facial features and brown dreadlocks; Sal, a middle-aged bisexual female with long, pink-dyed hair; the couple Sappho and Shiva, who both sport long black hair, flowing velvet skirts and lace tops; Moore, a gay man in his twenties with a ponytail displaying his undercut; and Nada, a lesbian with short peroxide blonde hair, a band T-shirt and black combats. The group of people at the gathering is extremely diverse, but with time I learn they have one thing in common. In the various conversations I have with the individuals meeting here, I pick up that there is a subtle sense of exclusion from the 'straight' Goth world. While they as queers generally feel accepted on the Gothic scene, there is also a feeling of their sexual identities somehow being trivialised through playful co-optation there – a notion I decide to trace further in my analysis.

Goths and Queers

In the discursive structure of our culture, the concepts of gender and sexuality are closely linked and intertwined. Judith Butler's (1990) notion of the *heterosexual matrix* with its dictate of heterosexual romance as the main sustainer of binary gender difference illustrates how 'the discourses of gender and sexuality are entangled and mutually sustaining/informing' (Gutterman, 2001, p. 62). Consequently, a discussion of sexualities in the Gothic subculture is a vital part of a thorough analysis of gender and Goth. Having examined the structure of male–female relations on the scene in the previous chapter, this chapter sheds light on the practices and attitudes of Goths towards queer sexualities. While the narratives introducing it give a flavour of my forays into the subcultural niches where Goth and queer culture overlap, the following analysis focuses more on what could be called the sexual mainstream of the – mainly straight – Gothic scene.

Sexualities are a highly popular topic among Goths that regularly pops up in casual conversations, Gothic Internet forums and in my interviews. Virtually every Goth forum I came across during my research contains at least one thread about queer sexualities (mostly bisexuality, but also homosexuality); likewise, many of my interviewees spontaneously brought up the issue of sexualities on the Gothic scene. As we have already seen, sexual openness and transgression are important general Gothic values or ideals. Goths usually entertain a high degree of tolerance and acceptance towards unconventional sexual (e.g. gay, lesbian) or gender (e.g. transgender) orientations. Moreover, even though the majority of the scene – which is still overwhelmingly heterosexual[1] – does not really subscribe to such orientations,

Goths often display a strong identification with gays, transsexuals and other sexual minorities. For instance, gestures of solidarity with sexual minority groups often come through when Goths attempt to distance their subculture from alleged right-wing tendencies. While traces of a militaristic, sometimes fascist aesthetic are embraced by certain factions of the Gothic scene, most Goths rail against such tendencies and voice decidedly anti-Nazi sentiments. These sentiments are often flavoured with direct or indirect declarations of identification and solidarity with sexual minorities:

First off, I can't imagine why a nazi would be involved in the Goth scene as it is full of Girly men and many people are gay, lesbian, transgendered, bisexuals, etc. Dont they hate us?? The thought of being a nazi lad wearing a skirt is ridiculous. (Princess Thais, *slashgoth.org*, 18/11/02)

I thought skinheads stopped wearing Doc Martens [a make of boots popular among Goths] years ago. Ever since girls, gays and goths appropriated them, no self-respecting bovver boy would be seen dead in DMs. (Captain M, *uk.people.gothic*, 09/11/02)

The alignment of Goths with the feminine (i.e. 'girly men' or girls) and the sexually marginal (i.e. homosexuals, transgenders, etc.) is put forward here as the main reason for Goth being practically incompatible with neo-fascist elements.[2] Equally prominent is the fact that these statements explicitly bracket the Gothic scene with those of sexual minorities like gays, lesbians and transgenders, thereby displaying a strong identification or at least solidarity with such marginal groups. Crucially, such a verbal espousal of sexual minorities is not mere lip service but is also borne out by the actual relations between the different scenes or groups concerned. In smaller cities in particular, where subcultural scenes are limited in their scope and hence likely to build communities of interest with like-minded groups, Goths and gays or transvestites often share the same spaces, and they peacefully coexist or even mix at certain events.

As Hodkinson (2002, p. 55) has pointed out, open displays of homoeroticism are generally accepted and sometimes even venerated in Gothic circles, an attitude he partly explains as a response 'to regularly being in a cultural environment in which the division between males and females was significantly blurred by subcultural style'. Indeed, I observed a few gay men in non-Goth dress happily mingling with Goths at some Gothic clubs in smaller German cities, probably because the Gothic scene is one of the few non-gay spaces where they do not have to hide their homosexuality. Conversely, an example of a gay venue that is welcoming to Goths is the Harlequin in Brighton, which I described in the introductory narrative.

The paradoxical image of 'a nazi lad wearing a skirt', which is invoked by Princess Thais to attest that neo-Nazis are strongly at odds with Goths and gays alike, indicates that the solidarity between Goths and sexual minorities has a lot to do with the extravagant and gender-bending dress styles frequently adopted by both scenes. Many Goths seem to see the risk of getting abuse from conventional people for sporting alternative, flamboyant styles of dress, which they share with sexual minorities like gays and transsexuals, as a strong link between the two groupings. As the following two interviewees who combine Goth and queer identities – one male Goth in a same-sex relationship, one transgender Goth woman – suggest, the fact that Goths regularly experience abuse for their style of dress and other cultural preferences can work to engender more tolerance, openness and understanding in their own scene:

> I think if someone's gonna walk down the road in PVC and big boots and make-up, they're already opening themselves up to criticism and abuse from other people. And if you have to put up with that in the outside world then you, maybe perhaps you become a bit more tolerant within your own scene. (Lowlife, m, 26, Brighton)

> People [in the Gothic scene] tend to be a bit more accepting of individuality. We have to be, I mean because the people are expressing themselves in their way, so if you don't like the way somebody else is expressing themselves, then what right have you to express yourself? You know, so we have to be more accepting, we have to be more open. (Ayleen, f, 38, Brighton)

Moreover, the affinity between Goths and certain sexual minorities in terms of flamboyant dress and the social censure that comes with it is not just a one-sided impression on the part of Goths. While people from sexual minority groups are certainly not as numerous on the Gothic scene as Princess Thais' above statement would have it, the gay, lesbian or transgender Goths among my interviewees unanimously stressed that the tolerant and open-minded climate of the subculture enables them to live out their identities openly and without fear of reprisal in Goth spaces. In rural and conservative areas, in particular, the solidarity between both scenes seems very strong. As Samael – a straight interviewee originally hailing from a small Bavarian village – told me, the few gay people in his village always greet him with a friendly smile when they see him in his Gothic gear. In his view, they appreciate the fact that someone else also dares to look different from the norm; although their colourful, flashy dress style differs markedly from his own, 'they just laugh cause they know exactly what it's like to be gawked at' (Samael, m, 21, Leipzig).

A Genderless Utopia?

Beyond its general openness towards and solidarity with different sexual minorities (gays, lesbians, bisexuals and transsexuals), the Gothic subculture fosters a striking affinity with bisexuality. Goths often portray their scene as a haven of free-floating bisexual desire, as something like a 'genderless' space where partners are chosen for their looks and character regardless of gender. I have already pointed out that academic theories of bisexuality (e.g. Eadie, 1999; Garber, 1999) tend to celebrate this sexual identity as radically liberated from the shackles of binary gender. Many of my interviewees' statements about the supposed bisexuality of the Gothic subculture echo such claims for its radical potential to break down traditional gender categories. The well-liked trope of androgyny is often invoked explicitly or implicitly in these statements, partly to illustrate and partly to explain the widespread adoption of bisexual identities and practices in Goth:

J: Sexuality on the Goth scene is very very bizarre. Most Goth guys have tried another guy and most Goth girls have tried other girls. It's, they all look so similar and lovely. ... I don't know, it's just on such a regular basis, you know, different genders of people are attracted to the same gender just because of the way they carry themselves and the way they look and the way they behave, and it's just to do with the whole Goth scene and what attracted them in the first place. And if someone, you know, regardless of what gender they are is what they're looking for, things happen. It's true.

Me: So you think gender is not that important then on the Goth scene?

J: I don't think it is, no. All my friends, I think practically everyone I've hung around with for years and years and years has tried the same-sex scenario. And if you speak to them and they say they haven't, I know they're lying *laughs*.

(Jet, f, 21, Brighton)

It's very androgynous, so when you get that you're automatically cutting the boundaries down, isn't it; as soon as you got a bunch of people in a room and sometimes you look at a bloke and you think 'is it or isn't it?'. And then because of that you have already questioned the boundaries of sexuality, and it becomes less of a problem. I think people in the Goth scene look at each other as people before they look at each other as a bloke or a girl. Well, hopefully – at least I like to think it's like this. (Lowlife, m, 26, Brighton)

Both Jet and Lowlife stress that on the Gothic scene a person's appearance – in which common markers of gender are often blurred through androgynous styling – and character are far more important for partner choice than gender. In fact, gender is described as generally mattering very little in the subculture. The differences in appearance between men and women are smaller than in other sections of society, so the logic goes, which makes the 'boundaries of sexuality' set by the heterosexual matrix that normally structures our culture more permeable.

In the discussions about bisexuality which are common fare in Gothic Internet forums, Goths seem to agree that their scene boasts an exceptional proportion of bisexual people, and that it provides an atmosphere which is highly conductive to experimenting with gender and sexuality. Again and again, the 'androgynous element' of the subculture is put forward as the main reason for Goths' openness to bisexuality. Another discourse frequently invoked in this context is the notion of a self-defined outsider status, and the relative immunity from common social censure that comes with it. Such an

Figure 15 Girly fun in the ladies': my interviewee Jet (right). Photograph: D. Brill

outsider status is seen as enabling Goths to indulge freely in the bisexual impulses which most other people also feel but do not dare to act out. The following attempts at explaining why so many Goths are supposedly bisexual can serve to illustrate both these discourses.

I would imagine it's the androgynous element – anyone attracted to that is probably more open-minded about sexuality. (Lady Lazarus, *slashgoth.org*, 28/02/02)

I think it's probably due to having an open mind… for most goths anyway. I seem to find that most people are just a little bi … but there are a lot of social pressures on people that make them want to conform. Being seen as a freak already has it's advantages in some regards. (~StormAngel~, *slashgoth.org*, 28/02/02)

As one important facet of the general open-minded attitude towards sexuality and the prizing of sexual transgression which characterises the Gothic subculture, bisexuality seems to form a central social value in Goth ideology. In the case of Lowlife, whom I have quoted above, the claimed openness of sexual boundaries on the Gothic scene also finds a direct expression in his actual love life; he has had a male partner for years, but also used to have girlfriends. However, such a matching between a declared ideology of genderlessness in terms of sexuality, on the one hand, and the way sexual relationships are lived, on the other hand, turns out to be the exception rather than the rule among Goths.

As we have to note again at this point, the discourses of gender and sexuality circulating in the Gothic scene can be competing and sometimes even contradictory. Jet, the woman quoted directly before Lowlife at the start of this section, provides a particularly striking case in point. The part of our interview used here portrays the Gothic subculture as a space rife with bisexual opportunities and experiences, a space where common heterosexual courtship norms with their binary gender structure no longer hold sway over the free expression of desire. Yet this image of Goth as a progressive microcosm where the traditional gender binary is transcended and largely gender-free sexual choices are enabled stands in sharp contrast to another statement by Jet. In fact, I used a different part of the same interview at the start of chapter 6 precisely to illustrate the rigidly gendered courtship norms pervading the subculture. That statement is all but antithetical to the one quoted here, characterising Goth as a deeply heterosexual space where gender actually does matter a lot in terms of social and sexual relations.

The direct contradiction between the notion of the Gothic scene as a decidedly heterosexual space advanced in chapter 6 and as a realm of non-binary sexual orientations introduced in this chapter of course demands closer scrutiny. Despite many Goths describing their subculture as a haven of freefloating 'genderless' desire, the overwhelming majority of Goth relationships are heterosexual. Same-sex couples are an accepted part of the subculture, and hence can live out their sexuality freely and without fear of social censure; yet still they are only a small minority. While girls holding hands and 'snogging' on the dance floor are a fairly common sight in Goth spaces, actual same-sex relationships among Goths of either gender are rather rare. An exchange between two anonymous posters – in response to the claim that a good thing about Gothic bisexuality was the ease with which one could find a date regardless of gender – perfectly captures the true state of courtship patterns in Goth clubs:

Date? Possibly. Random snog on the dancefloor? Most definitely. Actual relationship with someone of the same sex? Not very likely in my experience. Not at all bitter and twisted… (Anonymous, *slashgoth.org*, 01/03/02)

I know: at least one very good friend of mine has that problem at the moment. It just winds me up about how many Goths say they don't see gender as an issue but still have all their actual relationships with the opposite sex. (Anonymous, *slashgoth.org*, 02/03/02)

The first poster complains that while it is fairly easy to find a superficial flirt with a same-sex person on the Gothic scene, it can be very difficult and frustrating if one is looking for a proper same-sex relationship. The second poster even more directly calls into question the popular Goth ideology of genderlessness, by pointing out that many Goths who claim to find gender irrelevant for partner choice still have heterosexual relationships only. The obvious incongruity is that while many female Goths in particular claim a bisexual identity, there is not much going on in the way of actual same-sex relationships on the scene to warrant these widespread claims.

Apart from the naturally fractured and blurred character of real-life discourses, we have already seen in the discussion of Gothic androgyny as genderlessness that there can be marked differences between a proposed ideal and the reality on the ground. Here again, the descriptions of the Gothic subculture as a virtually genderless space advanced by Jet and others represent an ideal or ideology rather than the actual reality of common Goth gender relations. Contrary to Jet's humorous suggestion that some Goths she knows might deny having had erotic encounters with the same sex despite having tried the 'same-sex scenario', in my experience Goths – at least female ones – are more likely to do exactly the opposite. It will become clear in the course of this chapter that claiming a bisexual identity or at least some bisexual experience is anything but detrimental to Goth women's status and can in fact work as a source of female subcultural capital.

Bisexuality as a cherished ideal of the Gothic subculture can promote the vision of a genderless Utopia, where erotic choices are severed from the normative heterosexual pressures of binary gender. This Utopian vision shines through Lowlife's rather cautious view of the scene as a space where people 'look at each other as people before they look at each other as a bloke or a girl', for example. Whenever discussions of bisexuality take a more personal form, much bolder formulations abound; quite a few female Goths in particular seem keen to stress that, for them, gender is of absolutely no account for partner choice. As the following statement illustrates, the alleged naturalness of bisexuality in all human beings is often invoked in such verbal celebrations of 'genderless' love.

For me … the only thing that counts is the PERSON one loves, NOT the gender. Love just happens where it happens, and it'll happen if you let it. I firmly believe that ALL human beings are bisexual from birth. (LadyGiverny, *Gothiccommunity.de*, 17/09/02)

This enthusiasm for bisexuality as a force of love which transcends and displaces artificial gender boundaries is not only typical of Goth discourses but also shared by many academics writing about bisexuality (see chapter 2). A study by Ault (1999) into the discourses surrounding bisexual identity, however, can help to put things back into perspective and alert us to the difference between theoretical ideal and empirical reality which surfaces again here. Ault found that while many of her bisexual respondents 'do believe in the transformative potential of bisexuality as instability, anti-binarism, and indeed fluidity, the ways in which they describe their own bisexual selves constantly undercut that potential by reinscribing bisexuality within binary frameworks of gender and sexuality' (ibid., p. 167).

Bisexual discourse – be it academic or subcultural – typically aims to code the bi category as destabilising and denaturalising the dominant discourses of sex and gender. Yet theorising bisexual identity as subverting binary gender proves simpler than realising this subversive potential in practice. In fact it makes more sense to speak of bisexual*ities* rather than bisexuality when trying to stake out the multiple and hybrid identities the term stands for (Pramaggiore, 1996). There are many different forms of bisexual desire and practice and, despite the regular invocation of the ideal of 'genderless' love by theorists of bisexuality and bi-identified Goths alike, not all of these forms match that ideal.

That bisexuality in Goth does not necessarily equal genderlessness, here meaning the notion that gender is irrelevant for erotic choices, is evinced by the markedly skewed gender balance of bisexual identities and desires on the scene. Crucially, there are far more female Goths who claim a bisexual identity than male Goths; two girls 'snogging' are a standard sight in Goth clubs, yet one rarely sees Goth men do the same. Moreover, Goth couples who express a desire for bisexual experiences (e.g. in the personal ads sections of *Orkus* and *Sonic Seducer*) nearly always fit the standard threesome pattern of a decidedly 'straight' male and a 'bisexual' female looking for another bisexual female to play with. While ads of this type are not unusual in Gothic personals, I did not come across any ad in my research where this fairly conservative arrangement – which keeps the active and penetrating role of heterosexual masculinity perfectly intact – was reversed into a 'straight' woman and a 'bisexual' man looking for another bisexual man.

Despite all the talk of transcending or subverting restrictive heterosexual gender norms, bisexual desires and practices which really call into question traditional binary definitions of femininity and masculinity – and particularly those which threaten heterosexual masculine identity – are fairly rare on the Gothic scene. The bisexual discourse of choosing partners regardless of gender, which is an important part of Goth ideology, may reflect a sincere ideal or wish on the part of the people who voice it. However, Ault (1999, p. 180) reminds us that this discourse rests on 'a sexual cosmology oddly oblivious to feminist criticisms of the categorical differences in power and privilege between women and men in this society'. The genderless Utopia of fluid sexualities promoted by Goth ideology frequently seems to succumb to a social reality still structured by the privileging of heterosexual, mostly male-defined desire.

The Bisexual Norm

Bisexual orientations usually have a marginal status in straight and gay culture alike. The culturally ambiguous bisexual category is difficult to inhabit because it gets social censure from both heterosexuals and gay people (Ponse, 1998). Bisexuals tend to appear as stigmatised 'others' in dominant sexual discourses, negated and silenced by heterosexual majority culture and gay subculture. Hence, bi women's awareness of negative stereotypes of bisexuals normally discourages them from marking themselves as bisexual in both lesbian and straight social spaces, lest they may experience reprisal, loss of status and feelings of exclusion.

Paradoxically, in the Gothic subculture – despite its heterosexual structure in terms of actual courtship and relationship norms – exactly the opposite situation presents itself. Here, we can observe an apparent reversal of the dominant value discourses on sexuality. At least on the level of professed identification, bisexuality forms a dominant norm rather than a marginal position of otherness among Goths, especially among female ones. This bisexual norm is humorously yet aptly captured in one woman's gut reaction on finding out that most of her Goth friends appear to be bisexual:

> My only worry was that for some freaky reason, I wasn't bi!!! (Eviscera, *slashgoth.org*, 28/02/02)

Many Goths seem convinced that their scene is mainly bisexual, sometimes even to the extreme of claiming they have hardly ever met a Goth who is not bisexual. As the second of the following quotes – both taken from Internet forum threads started by a gay or lesbian Goth looking for like-minded people – shows, some Goths are well aware of the normative character of the bisexuality ascribed to their scene, and invoke it in an ironic way.

> Let me get this straight, you can't find a gay/bi goth girl on the goth scene? I can't remember the last time I was with a straight girl, girls who like girls are everywhere. Hence the joke "Why are so many goths bi? Because they can't tell the difference either" (Preacher, *uk.people.gothic*, 28/10/02)

> Gay and lesbian goths? That's terrible. I thought all us goths were supposed to be bisexual :-P (Anonymous, *slashgoth.org*, 27/02/02)

One striking point about these and similar quotes is the fact that the bisexual norm proposed here not only ignores the obvious dominance of heterosexuality in actual Goth gender relations but also works to exclude or marginalise homosexual orientations. As replies to requests by gay people for tips on how to meet like-minded Goths, the statements basically work to deflect attention from the issue of homosexuality on the scene, instead making the cherished trope of Gothic bisexuality the main topic of discussion.

Another common reaction to such requests by gay Goths is the notion that, unlike in mainstream culture, 'the scene is so accommodating to gay ppl that there is no need for any "special" clubs or groups' (*s*, *slashgoth.org*, 27/02/02). This is certainly true as far as the subculture's openness and acceptance towards same-sex relationships and practices is concerned. However, when it comes to courtship the situation is quite different. In fact none of the same-sex loving Goths I encountered during my research had met their partners on the Gothic scene as such. Gay and lesbian Goths looking for a relationship usually have to resort to the conventional gay scene or its media. The situation of same-sex loving Goths is slightly better on the relatively big and diversified German scene, where they have managed to carve out certain niches for themselves *within* the Gothic subculture (e.g. Web forums, regular meetings, sporadic clubnights in some bigger cities like Berlin). However, the fact remains that, despite the supposed bisexuality of the scene, ordinary Goth clubs do not seem to be a good place for finding a same-sex partner. An anecdote by a lesbian Goth – about an attempt at same-sex flirtation gone wrong – indicates one major reason for this:

> The really confusing thing last night was when I was talking to a girl I have chatted up in the past. Her (very drunk) friend came over to me and asked if I was bisexual so I said "no" and she ran away before I could point out that it's men I don't go for. And it's not the only time that has happened. (Gina, *slashgoth.org*, 06/03/02)

Gina complains about having experienced a certain scenario more than once on the Gothic scene – namely that, on saying she was not bisexual, other people automatically assumed that she must be interested in men and not women. In a sense, the other girl turning away when Gina answered in the negative is a reaction which implicitly denies her a homosexual identification. By tacitly assuming that somebody who is not bisexual must be heterosexual, both the normative bisexuality of the Gothic subculture and the general cultural norm of heterosexuality are confirmed and reified, while homosexuality is negated and excluded. Although same-sex practices and relationships are generally accepted and sometimes even venerated in Goth circles, some Goths seem to find it difficult to conceive of an exclusively homosexual identity.

Moreover, people who claim such an exclusive liking for the same sex tend to be portrayed by bi-identified Goths as artificially 'restricting' themselves, and hence not able to experience the 'true', genderless nature of unfettered desire and love. This mildly condescending attitude surfaces in the following response to a posting by a gay man who stated that, after going through an initial bi-phase, he could not imagine having a relationship with a woman any more because he has never felt as deeply for a woman as for a man:

> I think these thoughts really have nothing to do with true love anymore. ... Love is love... and there I really don't care about gender... it's a pity that you've already changed in this respect... in my view... restricted yourself... *negative smiley icon* (LadyGiverny, *Gothiccommunity.de*, 08/01/03)

Self-evidently, this kind of criticism could also be applied to people who define themselves as exclusively heterosexual. However, perhaps it is not accidental that the first gay person to post in the respective thread gets this scathing response, while the many self-defined heterosexuals before got much milder reactions (e.g. the question of whether they could really never find a same-sex person attractive). Just like Gina's case, this instance suggests that Butler's 'heterosexual matrix' is not necessarily overridden by the bisexual norm pervading the Gothic scene. Probably without any conscious intention to privilege heterosexual over gay orientations, such reactions indicate that the norm of heterosexuality so deeply rooted in our culture still partly skews the vision of a genderless bisexual Utopia which many Goths hold.

The following quote by another bi-identified Goth woman – about the notion that homosexuals in particular often refuse to accept bisexuality – displays a similar condescending attitude towards people with allegedly 'restricted' sexual orientations. Moreover, here the categories of heterosexual and homosexual are moved to a common margin. This discursive move even more explicitly works to establish bisexuality as legitimate and superior 'against a newly constructed and now stigmatised collective other, the monosexual' (Ault, 1999, p. 181).

> Are these people [i.e. the homosexuals] jealous because they, who on the surface act so unconventionally, are really exactly as restricted as the heterosexuals? Because we bis arrogate the liberty to ourselves to take a slice of every cake? (Audrey, *Gothiccommunity.de*, 03/01/03)

While it should be acknowledged that such statements by bi-identified individuals partly work as a defence against the – similarly exclusive – negative rhetoric they get from some elements of the gay scene, this quote also performs a much more problematic kind of discursive work. Ault (ibid., p. 180) argues that a certain form of affirmative bisexual discourse sets up an alternative binary system of 'bisexual' versus 'monosexual' in place of the heterosexual gender binary, thus installing bisexuality as a dominant category: 'This discourse moves bisexuals from the margin to the center, where bisexuality and bi identity become normative and gay and heterosexual people are constructed as relatively depraved.' Whether through essentialising and universalising bisexuality as the only legitimate form of 'true love' (see LadyGiverny), or through a more typically subcultural championing of bisexuality as the only sexual orientation which is truly 'unconventional', liberated and transgressive (see Audrey), this type of affirmative and elitist bisexual discourse is much in evidence in the rhetoric Goths use when talking about sexualities.

Bisexuality and Status

Regarding the norm of bisexual identification on the Gothic scene, one central question still remains: why is it that the trope of bisexuality assumes such a highly desirable status in a mainly straight subculture? The crux of the issue is that, arguably, there is a tendency among female Goths in particular to claim a bisexual identity even if they do not actually feel sexual desire for other women. For instance, one Goth woman – who proclaimed her bisexuality earlier in the respective thread – comments on a posting by an exclusively heterosexual woman who wrote that she liked to look at beautiful people regardless of gender but that there was 'no sexual desire' involved:

> Exactly. I mean, although I have a liking for the female sex as everybody knows, I'm well able to look without dribbling. *smiley icon* For instance, there's a whole string of actresses I can hardly take my eyes off (e.g. Julia Roberts or Sarah Michelle Gellar, Christina Ricci, Alyson Hannigan and Alicia Witt). But I haven't ever felt the desire to personally get into sexual contact with any one of these women – there I rather watch a love scene with them and an attractive man. :grin: And if that's one like Johnny Depp or James Masters, **then** I maybe start dribbling... *gg* (Audrey, *Gothiccommunity.de*, 06/12/02)

Considering the bisexual identification of its author, this statement advances a rather bloodless notion of bisexuality, namely one which is rid of any actual sexual desire for another woman and supposed to exist on a purely aesthetic level. For sexual desire to be sparked, the presence of a man seems necessary – an idea which further confirms the privileging of heterosexuality in many bi-identified Goths' conceptions of desire and eroticism.

Of course my aim here is not to tell 'real' from 'fake' bisexuals; as post-structuralist gender theory (see chapter 2) has deconstructed the notion of an 'authentic' sexual identity, construed as a core of a person existing prior to that person's sexual identification and performance, this would be a futile undertaking anyway. I want rather to get at the reason why many female Goths in particular are keen to claim a bisexual identity, when actual desire for both sexes does not always seem to be the prime motive. Certainly, part of the reason lies in the close link Goths routinely draw between Gothic androgyny and the widespread bisexuality ascribed to their subculture. At least some female Goths seem to conflate being bisexual (i.e. liking both men and women) with their penchant for androgynous males (i.e. liking femininity in men). Some statements in my data indicate that quite a few Goth women take their general preference for androgynous men – or the fact that, in their view, their current male partner has an androgynous look and personality – as confirming their claimed bisexual identity.

The elitist, affirmative discourse of bisexuality outlined in the last section gives us a further hint as to why projecting a bisexual identity, that is an identity which has a rather low status in most other straight and gay sections of society, can prove so desirable among Goths. As we have seen, this discourse sets up bisexuality as the only truly nonconformist, free and transgressive sexual orientation, qualities which are highly valued in the subcultural sphere with its general ideal of transcending or transgressing common social norms. Consequently, an image of bisexuality can function as a source of status and subcultural capital on the Gothic scene, a source which seems particularly attractive for female Goths. Some of my interviewees, who have observed the frequent sight of two girls – often even girls who attend the club with their boyfriends – staging a 'bisexual' performance together on a Goth dance floor, more or less directly point to this potential function of a bisexual image.

A lot of women think it's a good way to pull men by looking bisexual, seeming a lot more kinky and adventurous than just being, you know, straight. The guys do like the idea of girls together, so, you know, they'll be more turned on if they see you getting off with another girl, and a lot of girls use that to their advantage, so it kinda goes both ways. So a lot of girls will, you know, flirt with you to the point of snogging you and stuff and that sort, but as soon as you, if you wanna take things further then you find that they're not actually genuinely bisexual or gay, they're just, you know, doing it basically to attract men and shock their friends *laughs*. (Persephone, f, 21, Edinburgh)

I mean, I don't want to disrespect anybody, but you do wonder sometimes how deep it actually goes, or if it's just being said because it's, it looks cool or whatever and it's the latest thing to do, I don't know. But it does seem to be quite a shallow thing: two really attractive girls will be snogging each other just cause it's, because it causes, I don't know, it makes people look at them more, doesn't it. I don't know if it's shock value or it's trendy, I don't know what. (Lowlife, m, 26, Brighton)

While one of the main attractions of bisexuality for female Goths is certainly the sense of pleasure, play and erotic adventure it can afford, its additional subcultural perks should not be underrated. As Persephone suggests, appearing bisexual can make a Goth woman look more 'kinky and adventurous' than a conventional straight sexuality. It can thus work to boost both her capital on the heterosexual courtship market, as men like watching two girls together, and her general subcultural capital by virtue of what Lowlife calls the 'shock value' of homoeroticism. Lowlife's statement further hints that, at least for the former of these two functions of bisexual displays to take effect, one other condition has to be fulfilled: the girls involved must be attractive according to the standard Goth beauty ideal of hyperfemininity.

The second function, a general increase in subcultural capital through a seeming transgression of conventional sexual norms, is more complex and warrants closer analysis. Being able to 'shock your friends', as Persephone puts it – or, even better, to shock your parents – has always been a potent measure of subcultural transgression, and transgression or rebellion forms one of the most important sources of subcultural capital. As an anecdote by a female Goth about a discussion with her parents shows, an open display of homo-eroticism has the power to convey just such a transgression or rebellion against social conventions, even if it is merely implied and not actually performed:

> We were again talking about the boys I do like but my parents don't. But then I had the nerve to be really cheeky and started talking tough: "Perhaps I should find a woman for myself! How would you like that, if I suddenly turned lesbian?" (MorghaineLeFay, *Gothiccommunity.de*, 25/01/03)

Obviously aware of its transgressive and threatening potential, MorghaineLeFay invoked the trope of homoeroticism as a provocative gesture towards her parents. Having something up your sleeve to shock your parents – and other agents of conventional society – has always been a main value of youthful subcultures, and although the Gothic scene spans a wide age range, the prizing of transgression is one of its central ideals. That an image of bisex-uality can function as a status criterion in this context seems almost self-evident in view of the radically liberating and transgressive potential ascribed to this sexual orientation in certain popular and academic discourses. Theorists of bisexuality often use expressions like 'freedom' (Pramaggiore, 1996), 'resis-tance' (Garber, 1999), 'disruptive potential' or 'dissident desires' (Eadie, 1999) in their raving celebrations of a supposedly fluid, unrestricted and unlimited sexuality.

It is not surprising, then, that bi-identified Goths draw on the same discourses of a sexuality which 'transgresses rules, breaks down categories, questions boundaries' (Garber, 1999, p. 141) when talking about their bisexu-ality. A particularly telling example of such discourses is the following state-ment about the genesis of bisexuality, advanced by a bi-identified Goth woman who had posted a lengthy scientific explanation of homosexuality and trans-sexualism before. After having explained the latter two sexual identities in purely biochemical terms by the amount of testosterone released during pregnancy – a bio-psychological theory she presents as immutable fact: 'There we are entirely slaves to our chemistry' (10/10/02) – she offers a personal theory of bisexuality:

> What I have to say about this is my own opinion, here I can't offer scientific find-ings .... I personally think that bisexuality is the only volitional possibility for decision. Who knows, perhaps the hormones have a say here as well. But I believe that someone who calls himself bisexual is really heterosexual or homo-sexual, but doesn't let instilled patterns and moral standards that someone once set up restrict himself in his pleasures. (Audrey, *Gothiccommunity.de*, 11/10/02)

In view of her elaborate scientific account of transsexualism and homosexu-ality as being caused by extreme and less extreme levels of testosterone during pregnancy, respectively, it would seem more logical if Audrey tried to explain bisexuality in similar terms (i.e. as caused by even less extreme testosterone levels). Yet she makes clear from the start that she has no interest in presenting bisexuality as just another twist in the 'enslaving' biochemical machinery to which she attributes other sexual identities. She rather contrasts bisexuality with the biological determinism she sees at work in monosexual orientations, declaring it the only sexuality in which the humanist ideal of a free will – and the freedom to make a conscious decision about one's own pleasures and desires – is possible. In Audrey's description of bisexuality, the progressive bisexual discourses of freedom, unrestricted desire and transgression of received moral standards are all much in evidence. These are discourses which reflect typical subcultural values, and hence can work to set up bisexuality as a potent source of subcultural capital.

Interestingly, Audrey also draws on certain reactionary discourses about bisexuality in making her point. Namely, she cites the notion that bisexuals do not really exist in the natural order of things but are '"really" gay or "really" straight' (Eadie, 1999, p. 128), and the closely related notion that bisexuality is an identity into which one cannot be born but which one chooses (Ault, 1999). These discourses, often used by the Religious Right to code bisexuals as the 'ultimate perversion', are given a new twist in the affirmative bisexual ideologies advanced by bi-identified academics and Goths alike. In an environ-ment like the Gothic subculture, which holds sexual freedom and transgression as one of its central ideals, the notion of a sexuality which is freely chosen and coded by conservatives as an ultimate perversion of course assumes a very posi-tive value. There seems to be a tendency among Goth women to claim this cherished transgression and 'difference' for themselves as a way of winning recognition and status within the scene:

> I know bisexual women (however, regarding them I suspect that it's just a fashion thing, the attempt to forcibly break with all traditional values... I mean, they're still only going out with men) ... I think that's exactly the root problem, you see,

that enough people probably just pretend to be different in order to be recognised as an autonomous character! (Niobe, *Gothiccommunity.de*, 09/11/02)

Accusations of 'just pretending' and not being genuine are among the most common bi-phobic discourses in gay and straight circles alike (Ponse, 1998) and hence have to be treated with caution. Apart from the fruitless question of whether Goth women's bisexuality is authentic or not, however, Niobe's allegation that some people may use the air of transgression and difference it affords to claim recognition as an 'autonomous character' does have a point. In a reflexive essay on bisexuality, Hemmings (1999, p. 193) demands 'an honest examination on the part of bisexuals themselves of their own personal and rhetorical investments in reifying binary structures, and in presenting themselves as radical subjects or living embodiments of "difference", merely by virtue of being bisexual'. Hemmings is critical of this prizing of 'difference' for its own sake, as the idealising of outsider status – or, as she puts it, 'the competition for exclusionary honours' (ibid., p. 197) – which bisexual discourses often promote can work to reproduce binary structures rather than displace them.

The concept of transgression has long been part of the construction of bisexuality in progressive academic and popular discourses. Yet in times when stars like Britney Spears and Madonna mime a French kiss on stage at the Grammy Awards in a calculated attempt to spark media attention, the power of this kind of 'difference as transgression' to challenge dominant discourses of sexuality and gender certainly has to be questioned.

'My Girlfriend's Girlfriend'

While female homoeroticism is generally seen as highly desirable among Goths and can form an important source of subcultural capital, the status of male homoeroticism is far more conflicted. We have already seen that although expressions of same-sex desire among men usually do not incur social censure in Goth spaces, such expressions are rather rare. Moreover, if we revisit the discursive strategies which male Goths use to negotiate the proper boundaries of androgyny for themselves (see chapter 5), a certain form of latent homophobia can be traced in some Goth men's strong insistence on distancing their own identities and practices from those of gays or transvestites.

All this points to the idea that, despite the subculture's general openness towards queer sexualities, there exist some undercurrents of male-focused homophobia in Goth. It is very rare that Goths openly acknowledge or display homophobic attitudes; yet some Goth men still seem to entertain a deep-seated squeamishness about male homoeroticism. While such squeamishness is certainly not shared by all men in the subculture, quite a few male Goths display traces of it in their efforts to rhetorically defend and affirm the decidedly heterosexual nature of their masculinity. A rather extreme example of such an affirmation of heterosexual masculinity through a rejection of male homosexuality is provided by Peter Steele – singer of Gothic Metal band Type O Negative and once one of Goth's most desired males – in a Goth magazine interview statement about what inspired him to write a song called 'I Like Goils [Girls]':

> When I'd done the photos for "Playgirl" seven years ago, many fans came to me with the magazine for me to sign it. Among others, some homosexuals as well. When they gave me the magazine I noticed that the pages were sticking together... you understand... And they slipped me their phone numbers. That as such isn't a bad thing, you know. What bothered me was that they acted quite pushy and aggressively at that. I gave them to understand: "Hey, I'm really flattered cause it's a nice compliment – no matter if it comes from a man or a woman. But I return such compliments ONLY to women." (*Orkus*, 06/03, p. 29)

Of course Steele's idea of writing a special song just to declare he feels no homoerotic desire but only likes 'goils' – a song which contains offensive, openly homophobic lyrics – is quite an extreme measure to fend off any suggestion of male homosexuality and to affirm heterosexual masculinity.[3] As will become clear in the next section, his attitude is far from representative of Goth men's general views on male homosexuality, and also for that matter contrasts with the more positive ways in which some other bands popular among Goths (e.g. Placebo) have taken up this topic in lyrics or videos. Steele's interview statement about the song is slightly more subtle and hence more revealing. Here he resorts to the more politically correct rhetoric of feeling 'flattered' by gay male attention and not considering it a 'bad thing', but not without quite graphically expressing his disgust for gay men's sexuality in the claim that the pages of the erotic magazine were 'sticking together'.

Obviously, it is the thought of being treated as an object of male desire which bothers Steele most – a thought which seems unbearable and threatening to most heterosexual men and typically gives rise to homophobia. As a man, being used as a visual turn-on for masturbation and being wooed in a 'pushy', aggressive manner by other men threatens to displace the traditional active/passive dichotomy of male/female erotic roles (see Kaplan, 1983). Consequently, it can undermine masculine gender identity, whose imperative is to be sexually active and precisely not receptive. Weeks (1985, p. 190) points out that masculinity 'is precariously achieved by the rejection of femininity and homosexuality', which pose a constant threat to hegemonic male identity and hence have to be fended off. A more or less explicit homophobic rhetoric, along with a display of (hetero)sexual power over women, is a standard strategy men use to defuse the emasculating threat of male homoeroticism.

In view of the second part of this strategy, namely the display of sexual possession of and power over women, it comes as no surprise that Steele's Type

O Negative – along with quite a few other Goth bands – are far less squeamish about exploiting the erotic charge of female homoeroticism. One of Type O Negative's biggest hits, tellingly entitled 'My Girlfriend's Girlfriend', celebrates a love triangle between an (obviously straight) male hero and his two bisexual playmates; the cover of their album *Bloody Kisses* shows the faces of two women close together in sexual ecstasy; the band has even used a graphic depiction of a lesbian '69' position as T-shirt artwork. So while Steele anxiously guards his own masculinity against being sexually objectified by gay men, he and his band happily engage in using fetishised images of lesbian sex for heterosexual male titillation. I seriously doubt that Steele would have any qualms about Type O Negative CD covers and merchandise which feature such images getting 'sticky' from being used by heterosexual men in the same way as gay men allegedly used his *Playgirl* photographs.

I have pointed out before that the sexual possession of more than one woman is a potent wet dream of heterosexual male fantasy. This fantasy is catered to by quite a few big names in Goth music. In the same vein as Type O Negative's 'My Girlfriend's Girlfriend', the all-male German Goth band Umbra et Imago have a song called 'Viva Lesbian'. This title may sound like a political espousal of lesbianism, but with lines like 'it's so beautiful to watch you', the song seems more concerned with fetishising lesbian sexuality for heterosexual male consumption. Umbra et Imago's erotic stage shows work to the same logic, with two semi-naked women providing visual titillation with a strong homoerotic flavour, while singer Mozart – who remains largely dressed – controls the action like an overseer who only takes the most prestigious acts upon himself.[4] Blutengel, another big name on the German scene, use similar displays of female homoeroticism on stage and in some of their artwork. Even the music theatre project Kains Kinder by self-styled 'dark poet' Martin Sprissler peppers its performances with female-on-female actions.

While the artists concerned typically see a transgressive element in such displays of homoeroticism, the fact remains that the use of pseudo-lesbian poses tailored to male consumption has long been a staple of male-centred heterosexual pornography with its reactionary gender politics. In fact the way bands like Umbra et Imago and Blutengel use female homoeroticism in their stage shows does nothing to question the traditional status quo of male heterosexuality and sexual dominance, but rather serves to affirm it by pandering to the male gaze and its omnipotent fantasies. The female-on-female imagery they employ seems hardly more than 'a male representation of lesbianism to sell the product' (Whiteley, 1997c, p. 271). Needless to say, male homoeroticism, which could work to rattle the male erotic gaze and unsettle the norm of male heterosexuality, is usually eschewed in this imagery.

Figure 16 'Lesbian' display in a Gothic stage show. Photograph: Daniela Vorndran, www.vorndranphotography.com

Proud to Play Gay

Male homosexuality poses a serious threat to hegemonic male identity, which is partly based on the performance of an active, non-receptive sexual role. Hence, an open embracing of homoeroticism by men could work to call into question traditional modes of masculinity, and to displace the naturalised status of male sexual and cultural dominance. While we have seen that the Gothic subculture – just like society in general – harbours currents of homophobia towards male same-sex eroticism, its tendency to criticise or ridicule the 'gay panic' haunting traditional straight masculinity is often even stronger. When discussing how some male Goths link their androgynous style with a critique of conventional masculinity (see chapter 5), I have already pointed out that quite a few Goth men seem to have no problem with acknowledging male homoeroticism. The general openness of the Gothic scene towards queer sexualities, along with the fact that many male Goths consciously run the risk of being labelled as 'poofs' for their androgynous style, obviously do lead to a partial relaxing of sexual norms for men in subcultural spaces. Veeg, a sexually open-minded male interviewee, describes the atmosphere in Goth clubs as follows:

> Goth clubs allow you to be something, to express parts of yourself where you – you couldn't go into a straight club and be a Goth, you'd be beaten up. Cause, you know, you couldn't go and sort of momentarily appreciate another male and give him a hug and a kiss, and then both knowing it's not going anywhere, it's just momentary appreciation, it's saying 'wow, you look fantastic'; you can't appreciate in that way, you can't be androgynous. ... The last [Goth] club I went to I was sitting next to a particularly heterosexual guy, X, who defines himself as being 100% straight, and quite happily cuddling up and kissing Y cause he wanted to be cuddled and kissed. But there was no sexual desire as such, it was just a nice thing to do, momentary appreciation of a friend, and he was totally cool with that. You wouldn't get that in any other club. (Veeg, m, 40, Edinburgh)

As Veeg points out, on average Goth men are less squeamish about and more open to playful instances of same-sex flirtation than many other straight men. While extreme displays of male homoeroticism (like 'snogging') are a rare but generally accepted sight on the scene, lighter forms of male-to-male contact with a homoerotic touch – like an appreciating gaze, a close embrace or a kiss on the cheek – are quite widespread and frequent in Gothic spaces. Among Goths, even the normally taboo confession to finding other men attractive and erotically appealing seems an acceptable thing for a man to do:

> I'm not gay, but I sometimes catch myself saying to myself when I see men I find attractive: "wow, he just really looks sweet as sugar and like someone to fall in love with". Just a question to all the other 'men'.... do you also sometimes get something like this? (BlackThoughts, *Gothiccommunity.de*, 29/03/03)

The openness with which BlackThoughts, a man who does not define himself as gay, talks about his latent erotic desire for other men is notable and quite unusual for a non-gay environment, even in the anonymous sphere of the Internet. Obviously, he does not care much about keeping his masculine identity intact by denying the homoerotic feelings he sometimes experiences, an impression further confirmed by his setting the word 'men' in quotation marks. However, it has to be said that while less extreme admissions of occasional homoerotic feelings are not rare among male Goths, BlackThoughts' frank confession seems a step too far for most Goth men to follow. Tellingly, the only approving replies to his posting did not come from men, but from women who stated that they sometimes feel the same way about other women despite being heterosexual.

Moreover, it is striking that, despite their open-minded and positive stance towards male homoeroticism, the last two quotes have one feature in common which is partly at odds with their otherwise gay-friendly tone. Both in Veeg's description of the general atmosphere among males in Goth clubs and in his anecdote about a 'particularly heterosexual' man hugging and kissing a friend, it is stressed that the males involved are not gay, and that it is normally clear from the start that male same-sex flirtation in Gothic spaces does not 'go anywhere'. Even BlackThoughts' more intimate confession of desire for other men is introduced with the emphatic statement that he is 'not gay'. While naturally there exist some gay or bisexual men in the Gothic subculture, the seeming alignment of quite a few male Goths with traces of homoeroticism does not reflect an actual identification with bisexuality, let alone gayness, in most cases. As the following male interviewee implies, the image of 'gayness' ascribed to and sometimes actively courted by some Goth men owes more to their androgynous style than to their actual or claimed sexual preferences:

> Sometimes I quite like to flirt with this, erm, rather gay streak. Then, don't know, when I turn up in a skirt then, you know, and sometimes I even turned up wearing make-up and, well, emphatically queeny, you know; I can, when I'm feeling good I can really do that quite well. But that's just, it's just rather put on, it's just rather a game. (Kasch, m, 35, Bonn)

Like Veeg and BlackThoughts, Kasch insists that what he calls his 'rather gay streak' does not reflect his true sexuality. For him, flirting with a gay image is nothing serious but just 'a game', just something 'put on'. Apparently, Simpson's (1994, p. 195) thoughts on how some straight Rock musicians appropriate and thus partly neutralise the menacing yet fascinating air of homosexuality also have some currency in the Gothic scene: 'Queerness is accessorized to the heterosexual male in the same way as is femininity – employing its power but removing most of its threat.' While the threatening aspects of male homoeroticism (in particular the threat of actual male-on-male sex) tend to be quite emphatically denied by Goth men, its ample shock value can still be capitalised on. As a statement by a male interviewee about how he reacts to being called 'poof' or 'queen' illustrates, the power of gay male sexuality to shock and rattle ordinary people is sometimes consciously employed to confront the homophobic abuse which androgynous male Goths get outside the subculture:

> Well, 'poof', 'queen' – then I walk up to the people and, I don't know, paw them or something like that, then they'll see it, all right. Well yes, if they, I don't mind if they think I'm a queen, I don't give a shit, absolutely honest. The people who know that I'm not a queen, they also don't think I'm one, after all. ... You know, but if some townie thug comes up to me with like 'queen' or something like that, then I myself go, I'd really like to walk up to him, make eyes at him and say 'well,

don't you wanna come behind that thing there with me' or something like that, *with an affected high voice* 'hey, come on, let's go to the loo together', or just anything along these lines. Cause that's, with that you can usually shock them more than with walking up to them and saying *with an affected deep voice* 'hey, I'm not a queen'. (Ozzy, m, 18, Bonn)

While Ozzy has no qualms about playing 'gay' in front of random people to shock them and confront their homophobic chauvinism, it still seems important to him that people who know him do not think he is a 'queen'. The 'gay' image he projects towards prejudiced people outside the subculture does not grow out of an actual identification with gayness, but reflects a pose of confrontation or rebellion in the face of a general culture which is still deeply phobic about homoeroticism and effeminacy in men. Notably, this pose of rebellion is linked mainly to androgynous style – which triggers the homophobic abuse he reacts against – rather than forming a serious attempt to come across as gay or bisexual.

Although Goth men like Ozzy and Kasch may occasionally choose to adopt a 'gay' image in order to shock or just to play, and although a sizeable minority of them admit to latent bisexual desires, male Goths do not advertise themselves as 'bisexual' to the same extent as Goth women do. As we have seen, they usually insist that they are really straight, or that they would only go to certain limits with other men (e.g. flirting but no snogging). So while projecting bisexuality is a major source of subcultural capital for females, it is not very likely to be used as a means of enhancing status by males. Although bisexual men *can* attain a certain status of desirability among Goth women, male Goths usually do not try to capitalise on bisexuality as a status criterion. For them, subcultural capital in the form of transgression or rebellion obviously resides more in their androgynous style.

Conclusion

This chapter has brought up three main issues which warrant deeper discussion, namely Gothic bisexuality's relation to female subcultural capital, to Gothic androgyny, and to progressive sexual politics.

In a sense, the first two issues are closely linked. Androgyny in popular culture has often been interpreted as a colonising of femininity by men (e.g. Coates, 1997; Simpson, 1994); homoerotic displays, by contrast, seem a chiefly female form of appropriating 'otherness'. Up to the late 1980s, many cultural theorists were convinced that while popular culture had managed to partly colonise certain marginal subject positions – like femininity and blackness – as 'hip' accessories for vacant poses of rebellion, homosexuality remained far too threatening to be colonised in this way (e.g. Moore, 1988). From the 1990s onwards, however, the same process of popular usurpation has begun to colonise the formerly taboo area of homoeroticism as a new trope of transgression. Just like the cool poses of black 'Gangsta' Rap before, poses of same-sex flirtation have become a way to 'signify something radically different' (ibid., p. 186) without having to share the actual struggles and commitments of a marginal cultural position like blackness or gayness. In an attempt to spice up their image, many female stars in particular – a prime example is Madonna, who first popularised this ploy in the early 1990s – have donned their very public and sometimes contrived flirtation with bisexuality as a badge of transgression.

Bearing in mind the close connection Goths themselves draw between the bisexuality (which is mainly claimed by female Goths) and the androgyny (which is almost exclusively reserved to male Goths) pervading their scene, I would suggest a theoretical link between the two phenomena. From the vantage point of gendered subcultural status criteria, the bisexual image which many Goth women project could be posited as a female equivalent to male androgyny in terms of subcultural capital. Goth men's main source of transgression and rebellion vis-à-vis the outside world, and of esteem and heterosexual desirability within their scene, lies in adopting an androgynous style (see chapter 3). For Goth women, an image of bisexuality performs similar functions both outside and within the subcultural sphere. Projecting such an image in spite of their hyperfeminine looks – which still tend to be associated with heterosexuality in general culture – seems a potent way to join in Goth men's pose of rebellious gender-bending, here via the route of sexual instead of strictly gender-related transgression.

In this context, the markedly different relation between bisexuality and androgyny in the Gothic subculture, compared with theories of 'queer' cross-dressing as gender rebellion in the vein of Butler (1990), is worth noting. While theorists of queer drag typically postulate a direct link between queer sexualities and sartorial gender-bending, construing the cross-dressing gender rebels they celebrate as gay, bisexual or transgender, in Goth the relation between these concepts seems rather one of substitution or compensation. Androgynous style is reserved to male Goths, who crucially do not flirt with bisexuality to the extent that Goth women do. To formulate a hypothesis, projecting a bisexual image may partly function as a compensatory move for female Goths, precisely for being largely excluded from gender-bending style practices.

As to Gothic bisexuality's potential for an enlightened politics of gender and sexuality, my conclusions are two-edged. While the general openness of the Gothic subculture towards queer sexualities is one of its main progressive features, the bisexual norm promoted by Goth ideology is a more conflicted phenomenon. Throughout this chapter I have compared Gothic bisexuality to certain academic conceptions of bisexual identity, namely in terms of the affirmative, elitist rhetoric of 'difference as transgression' typically advanced by both types of discourses. However, there is a crucial difference between academic, politically motivated concepts of bisexuality and the subcultural, more image-based and superficial 'bi-ism' of Goth.

As critical bisexual theory (e.g. Baker, 1992; Bennett, 1992) stresses, a culturally progressive and liberating notion of bisexuality must be grounded in an awareness of existing structures of sexual and gender oppression, instead of simply pretending to magically transcend these powerful and pervasive structures. The 'genderless' Utopia promoted by Goth ideology, however, often seems to fall into that very trap – thus unwittingly sustaining a (sub)cultural standard which in effect works to privilege heterosexual and primarily male-defined desire.

8

Goth Music and Media

Autumn 1997, Cologne, a concert venue called the Live Music Hall. US Goth Metal stars Type O Negative are going to play here tonight, and on this sunny afternoon I and a couple of other music writers are already waiting for interviews to be allocated. I am here on behalf of *Sonic Seducer* to do an interview with singer Peter Steele. When the label assistant finally leads me into the backstage area, my earlier feelings of excitement and expectancy suddenly turn into nervousness. After all, I have more than one reason for my nerves playing up. Being a newbie in *Sonic Seducer*'s team, this is my first interview with a professional musician, and Type O Negative are a high-profile band. Moreover, Steele has a reputation for being rude to music journalists – especially female ones – who ask him the 'wrong' questions. I meet Steele sitting backstage with a beautiful Goth girl, who stays there quietly looking up at him throughout the interview. As Steele rises from the sofa and shakes my hand I feel slightly intimidated; he is a veritable hulk of about 6'6" with broad shoulders, long black hair and steel blue eyes. The interview goes better than I thought, though, as Steele comes across as very relaxed and politely answers my questions. So I dare to ask some of the risky questions from the very bottom of my schedule, questions touching on potentially sensitive issues around masculinity and sexuality. To my great surprise, Steele seems delighted rather than taken aback by my unusual quizzing. Much less surprisingly, many of his answers reflect a deep-rooted machismo.

Back home sitting at my desk, I think about what to make of his statements in the final interview article. What about his contention that infidelity in men is a natural fact of human evolution, for example, and what about his male-dominated threesome fantasy of female 'bisexuality'? I am tempted to include some sarcastic commentary in my article, but I know all too well what is expected of me by a magazine which is about to turn from a semi-professional enterprise, having outgrown its fanzine roots, into a full-fledged news-stand title. Convinced that any traces of anti-sexist critique would not survive the subediting process anyway, I instinctively bow to the unwritten rules of Rock music journalism. Little do I know then that years later I will finally get the chance to engage abundantly in critical commentary – concerning not only what musicians say but also the way music journalists write about them.

Mediating Gender

As a music-based subculture, Goth and its gendered meanings call for an analysis of how gender is represented in Gothic music and the subcultural music press. However, there is a crucial difference between the self-representations of individual Goths in interviews or Internet forums, on the one hand, and the mediated, formally published sonic, textual and visual representations in Goth music and media, on the other hand. There exist different cultural fields in or through which the Gothic subculture operates. While the people met and the statements gathered at festivals, clubs or on the Internet express individual – though often collectively shared – viewpoints, marketable media like published music or magazines are a cultural field where the *political economy* aspect of the scene comes into play. In these (semi-)professional media, a cross-cutting of discourses emanating from the Gothic subculture and discourses engineered by the music and media industries with their focus on marketing, advertising and image creation takes place. This small-scale economic aspect has to be considered when analysing such media.

Music and its related media are not simply aesthetic phenomena, but the pleasures and displeasures we experience from them are politically and culturally charged – also with ideologies of gender and the discursive struggles around them. The codes marking gender difference in music partly reflect prevailing cultural discourses. Yet they also actively participate in social formation, as we are socialised into our gendered selves partly through our interactions with cultural forms like music. Music and music writing serve as 'a public forum within which various models of gender organisation (along with many other aspects of social life) are asserted, adopted, contested, and negotiated' (McClary, 1991, p. 8). In this chapter I am going to examine the gender discourses informing the representation and reception of Goth music through an analysis of subcultural music magazines.[1]

The music press plays a crucial role in representing and evaluating musical genres and individual artists. Interview features and record reviews guide consumers towards particular meanings, 'describing and assessing music and musicians in ways that commonly involve reference to well-established gender stereotypes or assumptions' (Sara Cohen, 1997, p. 29). Such stereotypes in the music press can work to reinforce gender bias in the music-based communities it caters to, as they regulate the self-presentation of the bands and musicians featured. To get publicity, 'artists have to legitimate themselves according to the gendered agendas of the music related media' (Negus, 1997, p. 179); they are under constant pressure to present themselves in ways which are in line with these agendas. Consequently, the mise-en-scène of recording Goth musicians is not solely guided by personal or subcultural tastes, but also influenced by commercial concerns and by the deeply entrenched standards of 'Alternative' music promotion and writing. Such factors play a major part in shaping the regulatory gender discourses in Gothic music and magazines.

Davies (2001) argues that the serious Rock music press, while priding itself on its professed liberalism and radicalism, routinely draws on deeply reactionary gender discourses in both journalistic style and content. The mode of address used in this type of music writing creates a 'Boys' Club' atmosphere, where the normative standard is one of male journalists writing for male readers in an idiom echoing that of lads' magazines. Such an idiom has also sneaked into the big German Goth magazines, which have developed from their original fanzine roots into commercially successful news-stand titles and hence have become part of the established music press. In smaller Goth magazines – for example the British titles I analysed but also the non-commercial German fanzines I came across – this tendency is much less pronounced, probably because they are less commercial and their editorial teams tend to be more gender-balanced. However, both non-commercial and profit-making Goth music media are involved in producing and circulating gendered meanings, assumptions and stereotypes, which reflect as well as shape the gender discourses pervading the subculture.

Seductive Divas

Contemporary Goth music covers a wide spectrum of sounds and atmospheres, ranging from gentle, introverted styles inspired by folk or classical music (Neo-classicism, 'Heavenly Voices'), across Rock or Metal styles (Gothic Rock, Gothic Metal), to harsh, martial styles of electronic music (EBM, Electro, Industrial). Much of this music is virtually saturated with gender, to the extent that Goths sometimes spontaneously draw on gendered imagery – or even use the terms 'femininity' and 'masculinity' – when trying to describe it:

> What attracts me to Goth music is its sense of richness and paradox, that femininity and masculinity become blurred. ... So you've got the two extremes in the music, with big drums being more masculine and like nice melodies being more feminine, or low-pitched masculine voice with high-pitched feminine voice. So these are the two extremes that go very well and marry together. (Petit Scarabee, f, 26, Edinburgh)

In speaking of a 'blurring' of femininity and masculinity, Petit Scarabee invokes the familiar Gothic ideal of genderlessness. She experiences the coexistence of gendered 'extremes' of soft and harsh or light and dark in Goth music as displacing fixed gender boundaries, as uniting feminine and masculine elements. However, her metaphor of these extremes 'marrying together' – with its implication of marital male–female roles – is perhaps truer than intended. Both the different subgenres of Goth music and the contrasting elements employed within some of them bear traces of an often rigid and reactionary gendering.

Looking at the softer and harsher ends of the genre spectrum, this gendering becomes very obvious. While the 'Heavenly Voices' subgenre derives its name from its exclusive use of female singers with soft, high, angelic voices, the subgenres of Electro and Industrial with their harsh, distorted vocals and sounds are firmly in male hands. As for mixed genres or genres which combine 'masculine' and 'feminine' elements, there is also a clearly gendered division of labour between male and female artists. A prime example is Gothic Metal, typically featuring a combination of melodic Death Metal guitars with eerie or romantic keyboard sounds and an extreme division of gendered voices in the form of angelic female soprano vocals and deep male growling. This way of sharing vocal duties between male and female lead singers has been adopted by so many bands in this genre that the German Goth music press wearily refers to it by the standard phrase 'the Beauty and the Beast'.

Writing about the similar gendering of male Rappers and female Soul singers in Dance music, Bradby (1993, p. 168) argues that 'this gendering of voices appears as a powerful restatement of traditional gender divisions – the association of men with culture, language and technology, and of women with emotion, the body, sexuality'. In Goth, examples of such a deeply traditional vocal and musical division of labour can be found not only in the Gothic Metal subgenre but also in many of its electronic styles. While purist EBM and Industrial simply exclude female artists, more melodious electronic acts like L'ame Immortelle (Germany), Attrition (UK) and Die Form (France) employ the erotic, sensual charge of female vocals as a contrast to the typically stoic or aggressive male vocals. The way Thomas Rainer, the male vocalist of L'ame Immortelle, describes his and female singer Sonja's side projects – and how their contrasting elements feed into L'ame Immortelle – perfectly captures this rigid gendering:

> While SIECHTUM [his project] is purely electronic, harsh and aggressive, with male 'extrovert' vocals and lyrics, PERSEPHONE [Sonja's project] is acoustic, sombre, melancholic and with female, more 'introvert' vocals. If you add this all up you have a description of L'AME IMMORTELLE... (*Kaleidoscope* 12, Autumn 2002, p. 48)

Here the male is associated with the electronic, technological aspects of the music and with a harsh, direct, aggressive mode of artistic expression, while the female is relegated to the domain of gentle emotionalism and the warmer, more intimate sound of acoustic instruments. Another domain typically delegated to the female is the sphere of sensuality, eroticism and physical beauty. These elements structure the ways many female artists and female-fronted bands present themselves and are represented in subcultural media, as the following descriptions – one from an advertisement for the band Lethargy by their record label, one from a CD review about the artist Computorgirl – illustrate:

> On "Escapa" a seductive diva takes the listener along on a journey through urban Industrial sounds – the ultimate collision of cold machines with the warm, sensuous whispering of a woman. (*Sonic Seducer*, 04/03, p. 89)

If only I still knew who sang the gentle *It's a Fine Day* back then, I could roughly tell you what kind of voice you're dealing with regarding Computorgirl. At any rate, the Electro scene has finally found a talented and, not forgetting, extremely pretty woman for its usually so male-dominated programmers' camp. (Christian Hector; *Orkus*, 07–08/02, p. 48)

The contrast between the sound of 'cold machines' – of course operated by a male musician – and the 'warm, sensuous' voice of a woman invoked in the Lethargy ad, and the description of Computorgirl's voice as 'gentle', again reflect the association of the female with softness, warmth and emotion. Incidentally, the cited contrast between woman and machine is a prime example of the cross-cutting of media or music industry discourses and Goth discourses mentioned above. The political economy of media and music marketing at work beneath the Goth-compatible yet sales-oriented presenta-tion of the music draws on a classic discursive ploy of advertising here. The 'warm, sensuous' aura of woman has traditionally been used to sell 'cold machines' (i.e. technical products like cars, motorbikes or electric tools) to male customers. Obviously, this ploy works just as well for the marketing of certain electronic musical genres to a mainly male audience.

Moreover, Lethargy's singer is characterised as a 'seductive diva', and Computorgirl is described as 'extremely pretty'. Such descriptions mark female artists as gendered and sexualised beings for an implied male audience. As Bayton (1997) points out, female musicians are often subjected to 'sexploita-tive' media coverage, in that their looks and erotic allure are foregrounded at the expense of their talent and artistic expression. Women musicians tend to be 'represented primarily *as* women, rather than as musicians' (Davies, 2001, p. 302),[2] a mode of representation which leads to a constant stress on their appearance and sexuality.

Tough Guys

Masculinist Rock culture defines women in terms of stereotypical representa-tions of female archetypes: as idealised feminine being, sexualised dominatrix, earth mother or submissive sex object (Whiteley, 2000). Such masculinist discourses not only regulate and restrict the roles of women in music, but they also structure the ways male musicians and music fans see and present them-selves. The ideals of masculinity expressed in popular music may reflect not the actual personalities of real-life men but the larger-than-life, sometimes highly contrived performances of music artists. Yet such ideals are still highly potent in that they provide a cultural expression of hegemonic masculinity to which men aspire (Whiteley, 1997b).

In my discussion of how masculinity features in the discourses surrounding Goth music, I focus on the electronic end of the genre spectrum as the main turf on which masculine identity is constructed, defended and affirmed. The British Gothic scene in particular has spawned a brand of Cyber bands (e.g. Goteki, Synthetic) who stand for a softer, more upbeat and melodic version of electronic music. In this type of Electro, masculinity is anything but sacred, and the futuristic, often playful and almost 'camp' styles of dress its protagonists flaunt defy hegemonic masculine values. A fine example is Synara, the singer of Synthetic, whom I have introduced before as one of the few Goth men who sometimes fully cross-dresses. He regularly dons his flamboyant feminine Fetish style for live shows and promo shots.

The German Gothic scene also harbours some popular soft electronic bands (e.g. Deine Lakaien, Wolfsheim), who project a male romanticism and emotionalism strongly at odds with traditional masculinity. However, the predominating styles of electronic music on the German scene are the harsh, martial sounds of EBM/Electro and Industrial. These styles originated in Belgium and Germany and often have a Teutonic feel to them for people from other countries; tellingly, a British review of the German Electro compilation *Septic 3* speaks of 'the distinctively Germanic sounds of crunch and burn ebm' (*Kaleidoscope* 14, Summer 2003, p. 53). Another German-bred, decidedly Teutonic musical style – a crossover between the pounding beats of EBM with Metal guitar riffs and low-pitched, harsh German vocals – is the so-called 'Neue Deutsche Härte'.[3] This style moniker is translated in a British article about the German Gothic scene as 'the New German Hard-men' (*Meltdown* 10, Summer 2002, p. 37).

The popularity of hard, mainly German electronic styles in Goth clubs throughout the world indicates that, despite the substantial differences between national and regional Gothic scenes, musically they share ample common ground. Hence the following discussion of constructions of masculinity in mostly German Electro and Industrial music is also relevant to other national scenes.

The sonic and textual discourses employed by Electro and Industrial music, as well as the discourses filtering its media reception in the Goth music press, brim with a heavily masculine and often militant or militaristic imagery. Testosterone and tough guys are much in evidence here. Many bands in these genres invoke scenarios of battle and war in their lyrics and their choice of sounds and samples, and these preferred motifs are also frequently taken up by music journalists. The one-man Rhythm Industrial act Hypnoskull, for instance, has given two of his albums the prototypical titles *Operation Tough Guy* and *Electronic Music Means War to Us*. In the same vein, a live review of German Rhythm Industrial artist Noisex formulates that he 'assaulted the crowd with an intense form of industrial warfare' (*Meltdown* 11, Autumn 2002, p. 51). A live review of German EBM act Funker Vogt – whose lyrical concept and stage shows are based on an imagery of war and soldierdom – speaks of their 'pure testosterone-fuelled stage presence' (*Kaleidoscope* 13, Winter 2002/3, p. 45). The following record review of Electro-Industrial act

Dioxyde perfectly captures the belligerent and militaristic tone commonly used by journalists writing about the genre:

> Get the clubs out. The Spanish duo sends wonderfully hard rhythms onto the Industrial battlefield torn up by air raids and frontlines [allusion to cult Electro-Industrial acts Feindflug (German for 'air raid') and Frontline Assembly]. Dioxyde club the listener from one electronic steel thunderstorm to the next. Quite obviously they have a soft spot for martial stuff, as the hard, pounding beats are backed up by electronic staccati suggestive of machine gun fire, artillery and gunshots in nearly every song. (Ralf Klossek, review of *Torschlusspanik*; *Orkus*, 11/02, p. 64)

Reynolds and Press (1995, p. 106) point out that hard electronic music and Heavy Metal share certain gender-inflected qualities, especially a fetish for technology and an obsession with volume and speed: 'Heavy metal and techno have a masculine, "hardcore" aesthetic, valorising roughness, speed, and impact, testing the listener's capacity to handle the punishment.' This is all the more true of Rhythm Industrial with its heavily distorted sounds and staccato rhythms resembling machine noise, and its complete absence of harmony and melody. That Industrial fandom is a lot about testing and proving one's capacity to handle its punishing impact is illustrated by a record review of Rhythm Industrial act Mürnau. The male reviewer describes the tracks as 'comparatively (!) tame, but they should still be much more than sufficient for catching one or the other bruise on the next Industrial dance floor' (review of *Recoil*; *Sonic Seducer*, 03/03, p. 107).

In addition, a less visceral, more cerebral mode of masculine affirmation operates in Industrial fandom, in the form of a certain 'nerdism'. True Industrial connoisseurs prove themselves by knowing the most obscure acts and owning the most strictly limited records. In his discussion of record collecting as a male status criterion, Straw (1997, p. 15) views such a veneration of specialist knowledge as 'the successful adaptation of rock music's masculinist impulses to an era of sampling or niche market obscurantism'. While classic EBM bands like Funker Vogt stand for a fairly simple, physical and ostentatious display of masculine aggression and power, Industrial acts like Sonar or Winterkälte go for a more intellectual approach. These bands' mise-en-scène is not gendered that obviously, and their stage shows typically consist of inconspicuous men hiding behind towers of equipment. It almost seems as if the sheer harshness and heaviness of Industrial sound signifies masculinity in such a powerful way that ostentatious macho poses would only distract and detract from its effect. The following male Industrial fan's contrasting of different genres of 'heavy' music substantiates this idea:

> With Heavy Metal and today with the New Metal stuff, it has quite a sort of tough guy image, it's like Wrestling music. Whereas the really heavy stuff, it

doesn't have that sort of an image and, you know, it's just sort of quite skinny guys and they're just playing really heavy music. ... It's like with the Industrial music, that's the really heavy stuff with like noise, and it's totally extreme, but there's no sort of posturing and pretending you're harder than you are, cause that's more about the music. (Deception Boy, m, 24, Edinburgh)

Deception Boy sets the extreme, almost camp caricature of macho masculinity at play in Metal against a more cerebral, supposedly more authentic mode of masculinity inherent in the heavier and purer sound of Industrial. In this connection, Lacan's (1982 [1958], p. 85) dictum that 'in the human being virile display itself appears as feminine' springs to mind. Lacan assumes that precisely an excess of masculine posing can make a man appear feminised – an effect on which the gay camp concept of masculine drag with its ironic display of muscles and cropped hair is based. Conversely, it seems that by avoiding an exaggerated 'tough guy image' some of the heaviest Industrial acts manage to present themselves as purveyors of a more authentic masculinity in music. This type of masculinity does not need ostentatious posturing for its 'really heavy' and 'totally extreme' effect, but can be musically represented and vicariously achieved by ordinary 'skinny guys' through mastery of technology and the creation of a powerful, harsh and punishing sound.

Both modes of affirming masculinity through musical discourses – the more visceral and the more cerebral one – have in common that they must be guarded against the intrusion of allegedly feminine elements. Not only the music as such but also the media discourses surrounding it have to reject 'emasculating' tendencies like pleasant melodies, harmonies or sounds to keep intact 'its mythical Otherness to mainstream culture' (Coates, 1997, p. 60) as an important part of its masculinised cultural power. The intrusion of elements seen as feminine threatens this power, and hence has to be fended off.

Various authors have shown that 'Alternative' music cultures typically associate the commercial and inauthentic with the feminine, and define themselves against a feminised 'mainstream' of mass-produced, commercial pop music (e.g. Davies, 2001; Thornton, 1995). Regarding the microstructures of power within cultural groupings, similar mechanisms of distinction are at play between different factions or elements of a subculture like Goth. Although there are quite a few female Goths with a liking for harsher styles of music, it is commonly held that genres like EBM and Industrial are a male domain, while softer styles with more mass appeal (e.g. Synth Pop) are regarded and sometimes ridiculed as 'music for girls'.

The German Goth music press has even coined the term 'Weiberelectro' – which can roughly be translated as 'Women's Electro', with 'Weib' being an old-fashioned term for woman that is nowadays used as a derogatory label – for a new genre of electronic music that hit the scene a few years ago. This musical style, properly called Future Pop and popularised by mostly all-male acts like VNV Nation and Apoptygma Berzerk, is a mixture of soft EBM and Techno-pop with clear, emotional vocals. Future Pop has become one of the most popular sounds in German, British and many other European Goth clubs; yet it has almost as many opponents as fans, especially in the purist EBM and Industrial camps. Tellingly, a male journalist with a penchant for harsher electronic styles describes the new sound of Imperative Reaction, a former Dark Electro act turned Future Pop, as 'emasculated Pop rubbish with revolting eunuch-like warbling' (review of *Ruined*; *Sonic Seducer*, 10/02, p. 121).

The gendered quality of this formulation with its excessive fear of emasculation – psychoanalysts might even call it castration anxiety – is obvious. Similar sentiments surface in a record review of EBM newcomer Dismantled, whose output is hailed as something like a weapon in an imaginary war against Future Pop, as 'the first serious challenge to the spruced-up softie musicians from the charts and clubs' (review of *Dismantled*; *Sonic Seducer*, 07–08/02, p. 105). The rhetoric of the Goth music press regularly turns the competition between harsher and softer styles of electronic music for supremacy on Gothic dance floors into a discursive struggle between 'masculine' aggression and rebellion versus 'feminine' softness and domesticity. A record review of Electro-Industrial act Velvet Acid Christ illustrates this discursive struggle:

> A brutal response to the developments within the scene in recent years, those that are usually called Weiberelectro, against the softener effect of the housewife music which has brought about incredible phenomena of jolly swaying especially in the course of last year. Here, by contrast, there's fodder for the apocalyptic Noise-Industrial-dens, relentlessly culminating. Here hate and Indie-rebellion are practised, not necessarily hyper-innovative but with dreadful determination. (Kym Gnuch, review of *Hex Angel*; *Sonic Seducer*, 07–08/03, p. 117)

The aggressive, relentless sound of Industrial as a trope of 'Indie-rebellion' is pitted against the soft, undemanding, supposedly mainstream 'housewife music' which so-called Weiberelectro represents. As Davies (2001, p. 312) points out, in the jargon of Rock music writing 'the figure of "the housewife" is used to denote a general category of feminine listener who is working class, not highly educated, and enjoys listening to a conservative type of pop music'. Thus conservatism and commercialism are associated with the feminine once again, more precisely with a type of femininity despised by the hip and young as old-fashioned and reactionary.

Stretching the Boundaries

We have seen how traditional or even reactionary gender roles can be represented in certain styles of Goth music and the media discourses surrounding them. However, the contemporary Goth music scene also fosters various attempts at negotiating and displacing such traditional roles. Through the use of irony, a direct critique of common gender stereotypes, or simply by embodying alternative modes of masculinity and femininity, some styles or individual artists in Goth music rail against the restrictive formulas which govern many of its codes and discourses. Of course such local challenges to subcultural and general social gender norms by publishing musicians or journalists are always embedded in – and hence have to be interpreted against the backdrop of – the political economy of the scene-related music and media industries.

The Gothic subculture – and especially the German scene despite its tough, manly bravado of EBM, 'Neue Deutsche Härte' and Industrial – has spawned quite a few bands and artists who embody a softer, emotional and feminised version of maleness. Male-fronted acts like Lacrimosa, Goethes Erben and Illuminate take inspiration from the Romantic era with its cult of sensitivity, endlessly dwelling on feelings of fear, longing and vulnerability in an intimate, confessional mode which is normally deemed taboo for a man. While such acts may be smiled at by the 'tough guy' camp of Electro and Industrial fans, they have a huge following among Goths of both genders. Moreover, the sensitive, emotional mode of masculinity they embody represents an ideal the Romantic faction of the Gothic subculture values highly. Many male Goths emulate this softer ideal as an alternative way of inhabiting masculine identity, for example by writing very emotional, almost sentimental poetry.

Anna-Varney of popular German Goth act Sopor Aeternus is a more idiosyncratic phenomenon. This artist is an intersexual who does not want to opt for either male or female gender identity, but prefers to be both and neither at the same time. The cover artwork for his/her album *Es Reiten die Toten so Schnell* graphically depicts him/her in the nude with a male torso and implied female genitalia. This artwork, which quite markedly violates normal scopic habits and would probably be met with revulsion rather than appreciation by more conventional audiences, was voted 'Best Album Cover' and 'Best *Orkus* Cover' in the *Orkus* readers' poll of 2002. Moreover, in some Goth magazine interviews Anna-Varney openly criticises the hypocritical treatment of inter- and transsexuals in our society, who are often surgically and psychologically 'forced' into one gender, and pleads for more acceptance and openness.

Another way of challenging traditional conceptions of gender is the use of irony. In postmodern times, pop-cultural movements have become more and more reflexive and tend to cultivate instances of self-parody (Leonard, 1997). Such reflexivity also surfaces in Goth magazines, often in the form of a humorous, ironic take on the subculture's own clichés. For instance, in some cases the hypocrisy inherent in the term 'Weiberelectro' and its negative valuation in subcultural ideology are ironically reflected on by music journalists or musicians from the scene. The following quotes – one from a live review of well-known Future Pop act Apoptygma Berzerk, one from a feature about

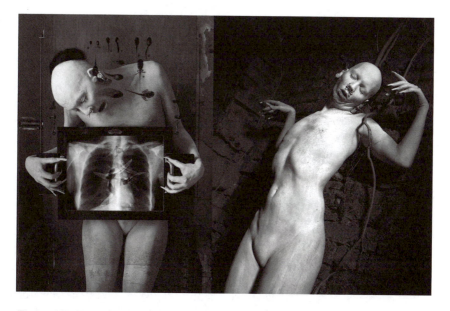

Figure 17 'Both and neither at the same time': Anna-Varney of Sopor Aeternus. Photograph: Image Eye-Luetke Production, www.soporaeternus.de

equally famous Electro-Industrial act Wumpscut – are particularly witty examples of such a critical, ironic engagement with scene clichés:

[about Apoptygma Berzerk's fan merchandise:] It caught my eye that there were more girlie shirts than usual – an indication of their placement in the category "Weiberelectro"? But no, the new catchword is called Future Pop after all, and there the lords of creation are allowed to jiggle along as well again... And I swear I've already seen some guys rushing around in (for example VNV [Nation]) girlie shirts! I bet when buying it they said it was for their girlfriend ;-). (Mildred Guhlke; *Orkus*, 04/02, p. 92)

[About Wumpscut's pop-oriented cover version of Alison Moyet's 'All Cried Out':] I hope that the result won't just be dismissed as Weiberelectro. That's what you people call it, isn't it, if on the one hand you want to distance yourselves from catchy melodies beyond the stuff a hard EBM head is normally only allowed to listen to in order to keep up his image, but on the other hand still stock it in the back of your cupboard, there where one doesn't like see it at first glance. Right! (Rudi Ratzinger, Wumpscut; *Sonic Seducer*, 04/03, p. 14)

In the remark about Apoptygma Berzerk's penchant for so-called girlie shirts (skinny-fit T-shirts usually worn by women), the derogatory and feminising term 'Weiberelectro' – which implies that only women are supposed to listen to this type of music – is juxtaposed with the gender-neutral term 'Future Pop'. The use of this neutral term for the same musical style apparently allows men to enjoy the music as well, without jeopardising their masculinity. That an arbitrary change of genre names is accorded the power to change the gendered connotations of a musical style here highlights the arbitrary nature of these gendered connotations themselves. The jokey idea of male fans trying to deny that they like Future Pop by claiming the girlie shirts they buy for themselves are for their girlfriends further underlines the hypocrisy inherent in gendered value judgements of taste.

Wumpscut's statement about his cover version of a pop song is slightly more complex to evaluate. Doubtless, it contains an element of justification vis-à-vis his hardcore fans, which has a certain promotional interest as well, as it is published in one of the biggest German Goth magazines. By distancing himself from the supposedly hypocritical 'hard', tough underground discourse of pure EBM and Industrial, Wumpscut implicitly justifies the catchy, commercial appeal of the more melodic style of some of his newer tracks. However, his statement also contains a discursive move similar to the one discussed above, revealing the hypocrisy in the Electro-Industrial faction's attitude towards softer styles of music through critical irony. Many dedicated Electro fans would never admit to liking pleasant, pop-oriented tunes simply because listening to this type of music is practically outlawed for a 'hard EBM head'. Yet as Wumpscut suggests, such an EBM head may still keep some pop records – safely tucked away somewhere lest they might ruin his image in the eyes of his peers – because he might want to listen to them secretly if the mood takes him.

As this ironic statement by one of the stars of the hard Electro scene shows, ironic takes on masculinity even occur in the most heavily gendered sections of the Goth music scene. Irony is also employed by Tanzwut, a band mixing the masculinely coded genres of 'Neue Deutsche Härte' and Middle Ages Rock. The promo photographs for their album *Ihr Wolltet Spaß* consciously flirt with an effeminate look resembling gay camp transvestism, rather than presenting the typical 'tough guy' image these genres call for. Their singer Teufel explains this flirtation with gay chic as follows:

> We certainly wanted to point the way to the future a little bit with the photos and to present ourselves in a consciously androgynous fashion mainly through the make-up in order to stand out against all those clichés regarding Neue Deutsche Härte ['New German Toughness']. This whole fuss about manliness, toughness and Germanism really makes us want to puke! (*Sonic Seducer*, 04/03, p. 125)

Of course such a presentation as vanguardist and progressive by commercially successful musicians like Tanzwut is heavily imbued with promotional concerns to create a unique image to stand out against other genre bands. Yet it still offers a poignant critique of a certain reactionary mode of masculinity.

Alongside such critiques and renegotiations of traditional masculinity, the Goth music scene has always harboured some prominent strong women. *Grandes dames* like former Christian Death diva Gitane Demone, performance artist Diamanda Galas and Post-punk heroine Siouxsie Sioux – with their penchant for masterful and menacing female archetypes, like the dominatrix or the witch – are female Goth icons who embody strong, unconventional, sometimes even aggressive modes of femininity. Such female artists often draw on mythological archetypes (e.g. the witch, the madwoman, the moon) as models of female power to renegotiate and reconstruct feminine identity in music. Of course this identification with mysticism and natural powers runs the risk of essentialising 'the notion that woman is innately closer to nature, instinct, intuition, and therefore outside civilisation, reason, language' (Reynolds and Press, 1995, p. 283/284). However, it can still be a strategy for constructing an alternative, powerful and positive female identity precisely by elevating such 'feminine' attributes, which are normally suppressed and denigrated in a rational, masculinist world.

Another strategy for reconstructing femininity in music and its discourses, which is more frequently used by newer female artists in Goth, consists in an opposite move, namely in appropriating and redeploying traditionally 'masculine' qualities. Noise Industrial artist S.I.N.A., also the singer of Electro act Pzychobitch, is a prime example. Affectionately dubbed 'Noise Riot Grrrl' by the German Goth music press and celebrated as one of the leading artists of cult Industrial label Hands Records, her harsh and punishing sound proves that 'loudness and rage are not a question of gender' (review of 'Die Your Life', label special; *Sonic Seducer*, 04/03, p. 50). Moreover, she does not flinch from writing critical lyrics about gender issues. The Pzychobitch song 'Sweet Kiss', for instance, criticises the abundance of sexy, 'perfect' images of women in modern media and advertising, and their negative effects on real-world women and gender relations.

However, female artists who try to break down gender barriers, and who dare to criticise the sexist mechanisms according to which the media industry that they themselves are part of functions, often find themselves in a double-bind. The gendered discourses structuring Western music are so deeply ingrained that women who want to stake out their own niche in this male-defined terrain always 'face the problem of how to participate without unwittingly reproducing the ideologies that inform various levels of those discourses' (McClary, 1991, p. 19). Women musicians in the traditionally male domain of Alternative music have to combat, work around or comply with its hidden patriarchal images and agendas – above all the fact that female performers tend to be seen as sexual commodities regardless of their artistic merits.

Furthermore, women who play music which follows the unwritten rules of 'authenticity' – i.e. no sugary artifice, stripped-down instrumentation and frank, explicit lyrics – throw masculinist categories of 'authentic' versus 'inauthentic' into flux by violating and threatening to expose the artificial gender boundaries of musical expression. Such violations of the invisible yet potent rules of power in serious Alternative music typically 'result in the mobilisation of tropes of "traditional" femininity to keep women firmly in their marginal place' (Coates, 1997, p. 53). This strategy of containment works to stabilise existing gender relations in music, its most typical form being sexualised images of disruptive female artists in promo material and the music press. 'Noise Riot Grrrl' S.I.N.A is no exception here: Pzychobitch issued the cover photograph of their EP *The Day Before*, which shows a scantily clad S.I.N.A. in a lascivious pose, in poster format for the fans – a sadly ironic move in view of her criticism of precisely this type of ubiquitous promotional use of female eroticism in 'Sweet Kiss'.

Woman as Eye Candy

The use of female eroticism to spice up a band's image and to sell products is a marketing ploy the music and media industries readily resort to. Masculinist Rock culture has long established a male-centred agenda, where 'the woman is defined as "other", a sexual commodity whose role is to gratify' (Whiteley, 1997a, p. 73). This mechanism also operates in the – in terms of fans – far more gender-balanced Gothic subculture, whose music scene is still heavily male-dominated. While Goth music features some female artists who represent a self-determined and self-defined eroticism (e.g. Sarn of Synthetic, Diva Destruction, Siouxsie Sioux), the big and relatively commercial German scene in particular displays a growing 'sex sells' mentality. Many of its bands and magazines have obviously realised the promotional value of sexualised images of women in an increasingly lucrative market.

Certain Gothic bands give the impression of reducing the women involved to mere eye candy or sex objects whose main role is to titillate (male) consumers and seduce them into attending a show or buying a product. Prominent examples are some bigger names on the German scene, like Nik Page or Umbra et Imago, whose singer Mozart obviously prioritises the erotic attractiveness of Goth women:

> I think the girls in our scene are just the most attractive, the prettiest, the most rigged-up. I'm not talking of intelligence, but just as far as looks go to start with. (interview in *Orkus*, 11/02, p. 28)

There are also some British and American bands – e.g. Sleep Chamber or Midnight Configuration, with PVC-clad dancing girls on stage – who cultivate a similar exploitative use of female sex appeal.

I have already pointed to the voyeuristic exploitation of lesbian eroticism in the artwork or stage shows of bands like Type O Negative, Umbra et Imago

Figure 18 Woman as prop: erotic stage show of Umbra et Imago. Photograph: Jean Theodorou, www.umbraetimago.de

and Blutengel. Such a use of lesbian poses combines the simple effect of sexual titillation with the transgressive charge of homoeroticism, thus providing a particularly effective promotional tool in a subculture where transgression is cherished. A similar two-in-one effect can be achieved by combining female erotic display with the taboo connotations of S&M and Fetish imagery. This ploy is even more frequently used by Gothic bands and media, often even in combination with lesbian poses. There is a substantial overlap between Goth and the S&M-Fetish scene in terms of style codes and imagery. Many Gothic bands (e.g. Die Form, Umbra et Imago, Blutengel) and magazines (e.g. *Sonic Seducer* with its frequent Fetish specials or calendars) draw on S&M imagery for stage shows, artwork or illustrations, employing the transgressive force of such images for their own artistic and commercial ends.

The cultural effects of sado-masochistic or fetishistic practices and images on women are hotly debated. While early feminists categorically rejected S&M and fetishism as reactionary and abusive, more recent currents in cultural and feminist thought, and especially queer theory, have taken a more differentiating and positive stance towards these marginal forms of eroticism (e.g. Brame et al., 1996; Weinberg, 1995). Here the negotiated and consensual nature of proper S&M is often praised. Goths sympathising with the S&M scene likewise tend to hold that the consensuality of its practices makes it 'respectful and empowering to women' (llew, *uk.people.gothic*, 20/01/03). This view seems to square with Siegel's (2005, p. 63) reading of Goth as 'a celebration of the power of S/M to dissolve conventional sexualities and gender identities'. However, we will see that – apart from the general problems inherent in Siegel's approach of reading off a subculture's politics solely from its artefacts (see Hodkinson, 2007) – the gender-dissolving S&M imagery Siegel deems typical of Goth is anything but representative.

Far more typical of the S&M images taken up by Goth artists or magazines is in fact a markedly skewed gendering. While S&M as advocated by queer theory represents a relative gender balance in male–female roles and prominently features male masochism in its practices and images, submissive males are all but absent in the Gothic S&M imagery I examined. Needless to say, females in submissive poses are much in evidence. The sexy dominatrix is a popular visual trope as well, in different incarnations ranging from the traditional dark sex goddess in forbidding leather gear to the Manga-inspired 'Cyber babe with a laser gun'. Yet if these dominant women get to exert their powers at all in Goth images instead of just posing decoratively, they are typically presented as dominating another female rather than a male – a double trick which renders possible the exscription of both the male as sexual object and male masochism from the erotic imaginary.

In *Male Subjectivity at the Margins*, Silverman (1992) points to the radically transgressive potential of male masochism. While male masochism is a complex phenomenon and not always unproblematically subversive, certain aspects of it can work to shatter received notions of gendered eroticism and subjectivity. Masochism and submission are commonly seen as pathological in men, while at least their milder forms are regarded as 'normal' for women. Consequently, the male masochist 'leaves his social identity completely behind – actually abandons his "self" – and passes over into the "enemy terrain" of femininity' (ibid., p. 190). The open embracing of masochism by a man could call into question his identification with the dominant masculine position, thus opening up scope for the renegotiation of female (submissive) versus male (dominant) roles extending beyond the erotic sphere. So it is easy to see why the representation of submissive men is much more threatening to hegemonic male subjectivity than the representation of dominant women as such, and hence tends to be eschewed in many types of Gothic imagery.

While a few less well-known bands have flirted with male masochism in promo shots or stage shows, and while the US Industrial Metal act Nine Inch Nails – which is very popular among Goths worldwide – has famously taken up this topic in some lyrics and videos, these artists are typically keen to stress the philosophical, seemingly gender-detached dimension of this masochism rather than its sexual, gendered side. For instance, the male protagonist of the German Electro project Call used to employ graphic displays of self-mutilation in his stage shows. In interviews, he explained his performance as a general symbolic struggle with the 'eat or be eaten' mentality of modern human relations. The Scandinavian duo Ordo Equilibrio, who have used promo shots with the male singer in a submissive pose, always emphasise their complex philosophical concept. Far from representing a soft, receptive mode of masculinity, they tend to express an elitist, sometimes militant ideology.

In the countless instances where females are represented in submissive poses, by contrast, the erotic and decidedly gendered aspects of this submission are almost always highlighted. As Silverman (1992, p. 189) points out, masochistic tendencies tend to be regarded as normal and appropriate in the case of women; in psychoanalytical terms, they form 'an accepted – indeed a requisite – element of "normal" female subjectivity, providing a crucial mechanism for eroticizing lack and subordination'. The supposedly transgressive nature of erotic scenarios showing female submission hence frequently amounts to nothing more than a pose, a pose which allows the male artists who employ it to literally stay on top. This dominant position of masculinity is often thinly veiled in a euphemistic rhetoric of reverence for the feminine, especially for the readiness to self-sacrifice which is seen as its main virtue:

[about Rhythm Industrial project Schattenschlag's track 'Unsterbliche Gier':] To briefly summarise, it's about an S&M scenario where the dominant part loses his female lover during a performance and is proud of this self-sacrifice or this courage right into death. (Joachim, Schattenschlag; interview in *Orkus*, 04/02, p. 106)

[from an article about Gothic/Fetish-S&M photographer Magnus Stockhardt:] [The viewer] will inevitably see that the artist reveres the objects of most of his photos, that is women, very much – for them he has even forged verses. But the situations in which he presents the women are extreme in part: in bondage ropes, chains, in mystic rituals or in total submission. (no byline; *Sonic Seducer*, 07–08/03, p. 10)

Davies (2001, p. 315) ironically speaks of 'the "rebellious" rock and roll lifestyle whereby men prove their masculinity and freedom from tedious conventional morality by exploiting and abusing women' as sex objects. Arguably such poses of transgression or rebellion, which actually work to assert male sexual dominance, are deeply reactionary. The male rebel types of the music world, Davies suggests, do not want to admit women to their 'Boys' Club', as this would question the principles on which their pseudo-transgression based on the sexual exploitation of women hinges. Examples of such a 'Boys' Club' atmosphere in the German Goth music scene in particular are plentiful, and they often feature the same usual suspects. For instance, the tour diary of the 'Nosferatour', a joint tour by ASP and Umbra et Imago, sometimes gives the impression that the male musicians involved try to outdo each other with braggart sex banter:

> Full house, copulating couples in the front row, the most beautiful breasts everywhere, there you know why you're a musician! If you think now that we're trying to distinguish ourselves in a cheap fashion, come to Leipzig next time!!! Of course all the naked ones were invited into the backstage area, unfortunately because of the legal protection for young persons we can't go into any detail about the party. (Mozart, Umbra et Imago; *Orkus*, 06/02, p. 108)

Another example is *Sonic Seducer*'s 'Goth>O<Mania' DJ tour, where a couple of well-known Goth DJs tour different German clubs. The advertisement for the 2002 tour is very telling. It presents mugshots of the five male DJs (Mozart, Kramm, Felix, Asp, PeeWee) and a photograph of a nude girl with a coat thrown loosely over her shoulders and a bloody slash across her chest as its centrepiece. An advertising feature for the tour whets the punters' appetite by mentioning 'the obligatory S&M show ... where quite a lot of scantily dressed, nice-to-look-at ladies can be admired' (*Sonic Seducer*, 05/02, p. 20). The feature is illustrated with a photo of a female with a half-opened PVC corset leaning back in a submissive pose, and a fully dressed male grasping her throat from behind with claw-like fingernails.

The message female Goths can draw from such 'Boys' Club' events – where they are all but excluded from the creative sphere of artistic expression yet generously featured as erotic accessories – is pretty clear. Women are implicitly reduced to passive sex objects whose main purpose is to pose for the male gaze, whereas the privileged role of artist and creator remains firmly in male hands. Just like in the masculinist structures of the traditional art world, the greatest honour a woman may hope for in this order of things is to be chosen as a muse or cover model by a male artist. In the Gothic subculture, a key figure in this game of including women as objects rather than subjects in male-created art is the German scene photographer and Silke Bischoff/18 Summers bandleader Felix Flaucher. His bands' earlier record covers were often graced by shots of his current girlfriends. More recently he even started a photo competition where he toured Goth clubs throughout Germany to find a new female cover model, a campaign which was eagerly promoted by the big Goth magazines.

Such an implicit ideology of female sex appeal versus male artistry also surfaces in another 'Boys' Club' type project, namely Nik Page's solo album *Sacrifight*, whose cover aptly features a Fetish model carrying his head on a

Figure 19 Nik Page taming the female flesh. Photograph: Wannsee Records, www.nikpage.de

silver tray. Page is keen to proclaim his respect for women in interviews, even maintaining that 'women are the only thing that really interests and fascinates me besides art' (*Orkus*, 09/02, p. 39). Yet he appears to reduce them to sex, sensuality and beauty in his statements, repeatedly associating them with temptation, lust and eroticism (ibid.). Moreover, the many collaborations with other

Goth artists on his album almost exclusively present male musicians or singers.[4] An excerpt from an interview feature about *Sacrifight* gives the impression that while women may interest and fascinate Page '*besides art*' as erotic turn-ons and accessories, he does not think quite as highly of them *as artists*:

> Given such a lot of male vocal skills, however, the question has to be posed why the fair sex is so underrepresented on Sacrifight? "At the moment there isn't any band with female vocals on the Gothic scene here whose songs I really like", Nik pronounces a hard but not completely unfounded judgement. (Stefan Brunner; *Orkus*, 09/02, p. 39)

An interesting aspect here is the shifting position of the music journalist. While his initial question contains a liminal critique of Sacrifight excluding women artists, he then partly colludes with Page's implied judgement that there are simply no good female vocalists around by declaring it as 'not completely unfounded'. Obviously, the masculinist standards of judging artistic merit are so ingrained in music culture that it is difficult to seriously challenge them.

This is particularly problematic for female musicians in Goth (and other music scenes), who constantly have to negotiate their role between the poles of artist versus sex object. The following interview statement by Alexys of UK Electro band Inertia – about her being voted 'Sexiest Female' in *Meltdown*'s readers' poll of 2001 – shows that some female musicians are acutely aware of their double-bind between these competing roles, and consequently try to minimise the tension between them:

> The less stuff I wear on stage, the more people gather in front of the stage, but I've been holding back a little of late, as I want people to take note of the fact that I've been a musician for 14 years. In the end this doesn't make any difference, though, cause in the male-dominated music biz the most important thing as a woman is how you look. But in addition to the music I also work as a Fetish model, and sexiness is a feature of my personality that I don't ever try to hide but neither use consciously. (*Sonic Seducer*, 04/02, p. 58)

Alexys sees right through the sex sells mechanism of attracting an audience through erotic display towards which female artists are pushed, and actively distances herself from it as she wants to get proper recognition for her musicianship. Yet the fact remains that part of the audience will still look at her primarily as a sex object and only secondarily as an artist. By claiming 'sexiness' as an integral part of her personality rather than refusing it as something forced upon her by the patriarchal structures of the music business, Alexys manages to negotiate the tension between the roles of serious musician versus erotic eye candy – a tension which she, as an attractive female artist, inevitably faces.

'High Art' Meets the Underground

Drawing on Frith's (1996) concept of value discourses which filter the interpretation of music and other art forms, I have demonstrated elsewhere (Brill, 2008) that the discourses surrounding Goth music reception and journalism oscillate between 'high art', 'alternative' and 'commercial'. Frith's concept of music-related value discourses, based on Bourdieu's (1984) notion of different cultural spheres, proposes three types of discursive practice through which music and other cultural texts are evaluated. The *bourgeois* or *high art discourse* (corresponding to Bourdieu's 'dominant culture') revolves around professionalism and hierarchy, valuing formal training and adherence to an elitist tradition. The *folk discourse* (corresponding to Bourdieu's 'popular culture') – which I reframed as *alternative discourse* to include subcultural phenomena – is steeped in notions of authenticity, anti-centrism and non-commercialism. The *commercial discourse* (corresponding to Bourdieu's 'majority culture') centres on routinised patterns, commodification and profit (see Frith, 1996).

Of course these different value discourses also influence how representations of gender are articulated and interpreted in Goth music, art (e.g. photography) and magazines. While the commercial discourse only tends to be expressed in a muted and indirect form in the subcultural sphere, the bourgeois and alternative discourses overtly structure the reception and evaluation of gendered imagery in the Gothic scene. The gendered nature of Gothic imagery is most obvious in erotic representations. Here a striving for artistic merit and formal recognition regularly clashes with a defiant stance of transgression and underground authenticity.

The reception and self-presentation of the Gothic/Fetish-S&M photographer Magnus Stockhardt is a typical example. In an article about his photography in a Fetish Special, the high art value of his work is emphasised by the journalist in the remark that 'he has made a name for himself nationwide with numerous exhibitions, which also took place outside the Gothic and S&M scene' (*Sonic Seducer*, 07–08/03, p. 10). Obviously, a positive reception in the bourgeois art world beyond the Gothic or S&M subculture is seen as a badge of artistic merit. On the other hand, however, Stockhardt is keen to present his art as rebellious and provocative, as compatible only with the tastes and sensibilities of an elect minority who understand its transgressive charge:

> That some viewers, well even convinced Goths, sometimes don't understand my pictures and possibly regard them as a provocation is something I'm absolutely well aware of. ... Often provocation is the essential basis for emerging changes. And these times are in more than dire need of changes. (interview in *Sonic Seducer*, 07–08/03, p. 10)

The rhetoric of 'provocation' and 'change' employed by Stockhardt marks an intersection between the discursive spheres of subcultural underground authenticity and modern high art values, an intersection already prefigured in the works of renowned erotic photographers like Helmut Newton. Myers (1987, p. 60) elaborates the shifting and conflicted position of erotic art photography 'at the intersection of a number of different visual discourses which continually compete for the interpretation of the image' – namely the visual traditions established in fine art, commercial fashion photography and hardcore pornography. The labelling of certain forms of pornographic imagery as 'aesthetic' or 'erotic' is a discursive move which works to exempt such images from legal censorship, thus enabling explicit allusions to sexual violence. This move plays off the discourse of connoisseurist 'high art' – a discourse that can be used to justify degrading depictions of women in sexually provocative and arousing imagery circulated in elitist or subcultural minority markets – against the discourse of lowly 'commercial porn'.

In the work of erotic photographers like Stockhardt, whose pictures often show women in extreme poses of eroticised pain and submission, in effect many of the sensibilities of hardcore pornography are rendered acceptable. In such images, scenes of necrophilia, suffocation, mutilation and sadism appear as condoned, as elevated onto the sphere of high art. This type of erotic image 'trades on a dubious tradition of sexual libertarianism which invests that which is censored with the power to disrupt and liberate' (ibid., p. 61) – a discursive tradition which also shines through Stockhardt's claim that provocation is the 'essential basis' for cultural changes. One caveat to consider in relation to Myers' line of argument drawn on here, however, is that her text represents a fairly orthodox anti-porn position, which has rightly been criticised by newer currents of feminist cultural thought for its restrictive and sometimes erotophobic tendencies.

Yet even from a pro-porn perspective, arguably the reading of the common use of sado-masochistic motifs in what trades under the label of avant-garde erotic photography as 'subversive' is extremely questionable. As we have seen, the way S&M imagery is used in Gothic art – and many other sections of the art world flirting with it – tends to reproduce deeply conventional gender norms by almost always putting the female in the submissive position. Self-evidently, from the vantage point of gender this positioning is anything but radical or progressive, in the sense of disrupting or transcending traditional male–female roles.

Furthermore, as the phenomenon of extreme trash fandoms (e.g. snuff movies, where staged horror is replaced by the filming of real torture) shows, privileging the illicit and extreme for its own sake can result in 'an amorality which valorises transgression irrespective of its content or purpose' (Straw, 1997, p. 12). Despite all the positive aspects of subcultural transgression, this is a reckless intellectual stance. Transgression is not necessarily positive in and of itself regardless of direction or content. In fact the transgressing of cultural norms can even be reactionary, especially if these norms – like anti-racist or anti-sexist taboos – are progressive.

Figure 20 The eroticisation of female torture and submission in Gothic imagery.
Photograph: Arne Jahn, www.arnejahn.net

In a subculture cherishing transgression, anti-censorship and freedom of artistic expression as 'alternative' values which distinguish it from a commercial and conformist 'mainstream', it comes as no surprise that such objections tend to be sidelined in the evaluation of music and other art forms. While direct expressions of crude sexism in mainstream media and culture are usually contested by Goths, such contestation is not so readily happening where sexist representations of women within scene-related bands and media are concerned. Here, purely aesthetic value judgements prevail. This is illustrated by the following Internet forum excerpts comparing the visual erotica employed by experimental Electro act Die Form and Gothic Black Metal band Cradle of Filth.[5] Both statements came in response to a person new to these extreme musical genres asking whether the S&M-influenced imagery the bands use could be seen as demeaning to women.

> Die Form and Cradle of Filth could not be further apart with regard to their image. For me the Cradle of Filth image is just a teenage fantasy from the dark side, engineered to look cool. To me it looks cheap. While Die Form takes a far more mature approach, and take it way beyond just an image. S&M and Dark erotica is their very essence. (llew, *uk.people.gothic*, 20/01/03)

> I've honestly never thought of Cradle of Filth artwork being SM-influenced in any way – I just think of it being pneumatic-chested bimbos dressed up as vampire chicks. ... Die Form have had bondage in some of their artwork; I don't personally think it's demeaning, but it's clearly erotic rather than pornographic because they use black and white film. ;o) (Dave H, *uk.people.gothic*, 16/01/03)

These statements shift the original question – whether the depiction of women as submissive sex objects could be demeaning – onto the sphere of aesthetic judgements, thus eluding the issue of sexism in Gothic art. Juxtaposing Cradle of Filth's 'cheap teenage fantasy' of busty vampire 'bimbos' with the 'mature dark erotica' of Die Form, they evaluate the contrasting modes of aesthetic presentation used by the two bands rather than the similar ideologies of gender they transport. As Berger (1972) has elaborated in *Ways of Seeing*, the presentation of woman as docile sex object for the male gaze pervades all forms of visual representation in our culture, from high art nudes to mundane advertising images. Yet on purely aesthetic grounds Cradle of Filth with their air-brush style pulp images of tortured women are ridiculed or even despised by many Goths. By contrast, Die Form with their erotic art photography celebrating the tortured and mutilated female body, and their arty stage shows drawing on S&M and modern dance theatre, are almost univocally hailed for their artistic merit and their daring transgression of taboos.

The irony in Dave H's claim that Die Form are 'erotic rather than pornographic' simply by virtue of using black-and-white film indicates that some Goths are well aware of the often arbitrary nature of such taste classifications, on which the supposed artistic superiority of their subculture hinges. However, in general this superiority is cultivated by the scene, typically by drawing a rigid line between truly 'Gothic' erotica, accorded 'style' and artistic merit, and 'cheap', undemanding 'mainstream' erotica in the vein of Playboy bunnies and Page-3 girls. The following quotes – one from a *Sonic Seducer* Fetish Special, one from an Internet forum thread about a tabloid's Gothic style guide for women – mark out these aesthetic distinctions:

[about Fetish model Dita von Teese:] She has style. Or rather: She is style. ... Last December the American Playboy even granted her its front cover – although she absolutely doesn't fit into the pattern of the Playboy bunnies: She is pale and represents the grand lady rather than the T-shirt-girl next door ready for mating. (Ramon Estrada; *Sonic Seducer*, 07–08/03, p. 12)

[about a tabloid picture of an ordinary woman styled as a Goth:] Well, basically everything about her look is directly from the lads-mag art-direction book, from the type of model, to the style of makeup, to the hipshot pose. ... It's not meant to be Gothic, it's meant to add an exotic Goth touch without threatening the tiny brains of the readership, who can reassure themselves that underneath it all she's still Mandy from Essex, who likes lads who like football, sportswear, and lager. (dave reckoning, *slashgoth.org*, 03/10/02)

Just like Goths' contempt for a certain type of working-class masculinity, which surfaces again in the second quote, this taste-based distinction between stylish 'grand ladies' and cheap 'girls next door ready for mating' can be taken to reflect a class conflict in Bourdieu's sense. The routine depiction of women as sex objects in lads' magazines and tabloids is rejected, but solely on the grounds of a supposedly more refined, classy sensibility typical of the high art discourse. It is the perceived crude and undemanding character of the aesthetic codes of such images rather than their sexist, objectifying content which is criticised here.

Of course the high art discourse with its air of bourgeois acceptance partly conflicts with subcultural notions of underground authenticity, rebellion and transgression characteristic of the alternative discourse. Aesthetic standards in the Gothic subculture are diverse, as its roots of inspiration range from the high-minded era of literary Romanticism right down to the Punk movement with its provocative crudeness. The discourses Goths invoke in the evaluation of erotic imagery tend to oscillate between these extreme poles, thus eschewing notions of 'mainstream' commercialism which are at odds with both. This oscillating between discursive extremes can lead to the paradox that images deemed 'too crude' by some Goths are found too tame by others. The widely differing judgements Goths pass on Umbra et Imago's stage show – which combines elements of S&M and female bisexual display with Gothic clichés of vampirism – can serve to illustrate these contrasting extremes:

I found it a bit of a show-up somehow. ... If you show something like that you're definitely trying to provoke with it, after all, but probably you're trying to demonstrate an, I'd just say open-mindedness towards eroticism or something like that. But I found that just, that wasn't provocative any more, that was just, that was too – crude! I found that downright crude, that was nothing, I mean like soft-focus eroticism or like what really has artistic merit. I didn't see any merit in that, that was just crude and had nothing to do with eroticism. Simply, just simply naked meat. (Ambra, f, 19, Leipzig)

When I look at Umbra – making a couple of naked birds jump out of a coffin, even I could do that, right. Well, either fuck for real or don't do it at all. As I've already said before, I'm kind of an extreme person, so it's all or nothing. (Muckel, m, 30, Cologne)

Bands like Umbra et Imago and Blutengel (whose show features similar elements) are among the most loved and most hated acts on the German scene at the same time – tellingly, their leaders Mozart and Chris Pohl appear among the top ten 'Most Impressive Personalities of the Year' and the top ten 'Idiots of the Year' in the *Orkus* readers' poll of 2002. While they are very popular among younger Goths, they are scorned by many of the older ones, for whom they embody the increasing sell-out of the Gothic subculture. However, it is almost always the perceived undemanding, tacky character of their music and shows which is being picked at, rather than the reactionary status quo of male–female erotic roles they represent. Only one of my interviewees who talked about Umbra et Imago touched on this issue, pointing out that she found the show 'very conventional actually; it's just, well, Mozart as the all-important guy and the birdies as an addition' (Umbersun, f, 29, Bonn).

Sex Sells

As we have seen, the evaluation of Goth music and its attendant visuals is typically located in the field of tension between the high art and the alternative discourse. The commercial discourse with its focus on mass marketing tends to be eschewed in subcultural rhetoric, which aims to stress the non-commercial, anti-mainstream character of its art. However, over the last decade the by now biggest Gothic scene worldwide in Germany has undergone a notable commercialisation. Hence, it provides an excellent case study to trace the effects which a growing commercial orientation can have on a subculture.

While German Goth still heralds an ideology of underground authenticity, which shrinks from openly acknowledging commercial motives, its media discourses have become imbued with a certain 'sex sells' mentality. This mentality is evident in the way bands like Umbra et Imago and Blutengel use graphic displays of female eroticism to keep their audiences interested. Apparently, many people who attend their concerts are attracted primarily by their sex shows. A review of a festival where both bands had to tone down their shows due to legal censorship mentions that the audience loudly demanded 'more sex', and that 'some people said that without sex the show wasn't worth watching' (*Sonic Seducer*, 05/03, p. 92). Asked what kind of people were likely to buy the Umbra et Imago live DVD *Die Welt Brennt*, singer Mozart – who is normally keen to present his artistic output as avant-garde – readily admits that 'there will certainly be a percentage of peeping Toms who want to watch our ripe girls' (*Sonic Seducer*, 10/02, p. 103).

While Umbra et Imago's and Blutengel's fixation on sex and eroticism is by no means typical of the Goth music scene as a whole, a toying with male-defined representations of female sexuality is quite common in some of its sections. For instance, certain Electro or Gothic Metal acts who enjoy international popularity use samples from porn movies – like female orgasm screams and moans – in their music (e.g. Wumpscut from Germany on the CD *Bunkertor 7* and the track 'Ich Will Dich'; Type O Negative from the US on the CD *Bloody Kisses*). Moreover, some Electro or Industrial acts (e.g. Hocico from Mexico) use film sequences of hardcore porn in their stage shows.

Such elements are often presented as radical and progressive by the artists who employ them. However, the notion that the overt, blunt display of sex typical of hardcore pornography can work as a subversive and liberating force is highly questionable in our current cultural climate. Although early Rock certainly drew much of its transgressive power from flaunting sexuality and unbridled desire, in our liberal late-capitalist culture this 'sexmusic' – which once seemed radical and dangerous – has become an oppressive standard saturating the mainstream media (Reynolds, 1989). Music and other media contents focusing on sex and pleasure are no longer subversive, but have turned into a commercial and cultural norm. This is all the more true in the German mediascape, where big private TV channels have long realised the market value of blatant sex and are capitalising on it with quite graphic late-night programmes.

Another area where the growing 'sex sells' mentality of the commercial end of the German Gothic scene can be traced is the development of its market-leading magazines. Since the late 1990s the use of sexualised images of women in *Orkus* and *Sonic Seducer* has increased markedly.[6] Both magazines appear to seize every opportunity to place even more photographs of semi-nude women on their pages – be it in repeated, extended Fetish Specials and Gothic-Fetish Calendars (*Sonic Seducer*) or in regular erotic photography features and cover artworks for the magazine's CD compilation (*Orkus*). The addition of such specials and illustrations is typically justified by the editors through flowery appeals to a Gothic sensibility which goes beyond mere music, also including the sphere of dark eroticism. While this notion of a Gothic lifestyle embracing many areas of artistic expression is doubtless true, it cannot explain why the sphere of eroticism always has to be represented by women as objects of the gaze. The erotic images gracing the ubiquitous Fetish specials or calendars, nude photography features and CD covers almost exclusively present female nudes, with males only appearing as authors of these images.

In Western culture 'the representation of the female body as the primary site of sexuality and visual pleasure' (De Lauretis, 1987, p. 13) forms a powerful scopic regime. Feminist theory has rendered problematic this gender-biased erotic imagery, as such images – though locating the sexual in or on the woman's body – often work to render this female sexuality the property of an implied male onlooker. As feminist film theory has elaborated, 'many of the pleasures offered by dominant visual culture are connected to the ways in which it addresses a heterosexual *male* spectator' (Betterton, 1987, p. 11, original emphasis). This implied male spectator's enjoyment of woman as sex object is not solely erotic, but also affords him a sense of power and control over the image. While the female body is posed and framed for his pleasure, his own body can remain doubly hidden, because he is the assumed spectator outside of the frame and his eroticised body is not represented within the frame as object of the gaze.[7]

That female sex appeal can be used to sell products is nothing new. Obviously, the fledgling professional media of the German Gothic scene have realised the commercial value of female eroticism – probably well aware of the fact that female nudes are regarded as inoffensive and aesthetic by most young men and women, while a more balanced erotic imagery displaying sexualised male bodies along with female ones might alienate some heterosexual male readers. *Sonic Seducer*'s Gothic-Fetish Calendar 2004 and Felix Flaucher Calendar 2003 are particularly telling cases in point. These calendars solely contain sexualised pictures of women shot by male artists, sometimes in homo-erotic poses so as to create erotic scenarios without having to show the male body.

Moreover, both calendars also include some images of naked or semi-naked women who lack a Goth aesthetic (e.g. blond hair, conventional haircuts and make-up). This makes the appeal to an alleged Gothic sensibility expressed on their pages seem rather threadbare, and reveals the operation of a thinly veiled 'sex sells' mechanism. Obviously, this mechanism works in attracting peripheral male members – and maybe also interested non-Goths – to specific consumables or brands within the subculture. When I was interviewing a male scene newcomer in Berlin, by chance he spotted the Gothic-Fetish Calendar under a stack of magazines in my room. After flicking through it, he spontaneously decided to order this particular back issue of *Sonic Seducer*, and to generally give the magazine (which he had never bought before) a try.

While the *Sonic Seducer* calendars I examined exclusively feature the works of male photographers, the *Orkus* nude photography pages are at least somewhat more gender-balanced in the choice of artists presented. They regularly print erotic images of women by female photographers. Moreover, the motivations for making erotic photographs of women cited by these female artists in the interview section accompanying the images often have a feminist tinge. They typically stress that the aim is to portray women in a respectful, sensitive and individual way, thus refusing the insensitive and male-centred character of most erotic photography:

> At some point it struck me that there aren't many women who make erotic photographs by women and for women. Most of the illustrated books on the market have been published primarily by men. As the models are often portrayed in pornographic and insensitive ways there just to boost sales figures, I wanted to change this state of affairs. As a female photographer I look at women from a totally different angle, that is with a lot of respect and an aesthetic sense. ... My photos differ from those of other photographers insofar as I aim to portray women like they themselves also want to see themselves. (Nina Bendigkeit; *Orkus*, 09/02, p. 91)

Such a recognition of women's role as active (co-)producers and viewers of nude photography – rather than merely as its passive content – is definitely a step towards a more equal coding of erotic images. The narcissistic self-discovery encouraged by images expressing an autonomous female eroticism echoes some aspects of the feminist movement's attempt to empower and politicise female sexuality (Mattelart, 1986). However, while new, strong representations of female sexuality can work to empower and liberate women, they are not necessarily emancipatory as they are often still 'saturated by an ideology of the perpetual sexual availability of women for men' (McNay, 2000, p. 68). This ideology can be commercially exploited by publishers and advertisers. The common depiction of women as romantic and delicate or lusty and seductive objects of desire panders to omnipotent male fantasies of sexual conquest and possession. That these fantasies can be played on as a powerful motive for buying a product or establishing brand loyalty is a basic principle of modern marketing.

The study of women's and fashion magazines, which feature eroticised images of women aimed at female readers, can tell us a lot about the *female gaze* at other women. Typically, the gaze between the perfect models gracing the magazines and their readers 'marks the complicity between women that we see ourselves in the image which a masculine culture has defined' (Winship, 1987a, p. 11), an image that continually exhorts females that they have to be beautiful and desirable to be someone. Erotic representations of women often remain self-limiting for female viewers, as they convey what psychoanalysis calls women's desire to be desired. As Mattelart (1986, p. 40) argues: 'In a masochistic-euphorial tension, flirtatiousness, the desire to be found attractive, the woman-as-prey, are all given modern authority ..., and the relations of woman-world and woman-man which are implied therein are revalidated, confirmed and eternalised.' So images which supposedly liberate female sexuality from received notions of domesticity and passivity can still work to cement traditional gender roles and the underlying dominance system.

Coverage which shows women as primarily sexual fantasy figures influences not only how men see women but also how women see themselves and each other. This logic also applies to the abundant images of women as sex objects in the two market-leading German Goth magazines. I have pointed out before that, on the German scene, the effort Goth men put into their appearance has declined markedly, while Goth women's obsession with looks and styling has probably even increased in certain circles. The following female interviewee – one of the few to comment on the one-sided erotic imagery in the big German Goth magazines – has made the same observation, and sees a link between the two phenomena:

> It's really obvious that these pictures definitely affect how the women in the Gothic scene see themselves, that is always as the looked-at object; I mean, you go to a club and have the feeling you're being looked at as a woman. And the men certainly don't get that in this form, I mean they're the ones that look and are never represented in pictures. Well, there we're again at this point then, erm, that the women get rigged up more and the men don't, you know. (Satyria, f, 25, Berlin)

Satyria's appraisal of the gendered structure of looking in German Goth clubs echoes Berger's (1972, p. 42) dictum that in the patriarchal scopic regime of our culture 'women watch themselves being looked at'. While males are free to gaze at women, females occupy themselves with constantly monitoring their own appearance lest it might not meet the omnipresent, often unreachable standards displayed in erotic images. Without falling back into the stifling erotophobic discourses of radical feminism, there is no easy way out of this scopic dilemma. Winship (1987b, p. 127, original emphasis) cautions that 'we need to be careful that we are not simply outlawing a *sexual* presentation of women'. It will hardly be possible to create new erotic codes without drawing on existing ones. Perhaps the suggestion Satyria made in the further course of our interview could be part of the solution, namely that the ubiquitous erotic presentation of women be matched by an equally sexualised presentation of the male body – crucially not only in dominant but also in submissive poses. This is a move for which Goth with its prizing of male androgyny and vulnerability certainly holds the potential.

Conclusion

While the preceding chapters focused on the individual or collective views of ordinary Goths, this chapter has broadened the perspective by taking the subculture's (semi-)professional music media and their political economy into account.

Crucially, the publishing- and marketing-related aspects of the Gothic scene do have a marked effect on how gender is represented in its media. This effect is most obvious in the venal 'sex sells' and 'Boy's Club' mentality of the big German Goth magazines and some high-profile German bands – especially in comparison with the less corporate British Goth magazines and music scene, which have largely refrained from these exploitative mechanisms so far. The growing commercial success of German Goth has triggered a notable increase in structures as well as images in bands and magazines which replicate the traditional status quo of submissive female versus dominant male erotic and artistic, and by extension also general social, roles.

The question of how the gendered images and ideologies promoted by professional Gothic media relate to the subjective views of individual Goths is compelling, but cannot be answered conclusively here. While it is impossible to prove within the qualitative design of this study, the idea does not seem far fetched that the more rigid, traditional gendering of styles on the German scene – i.e. the decline of male androgyny and the pervasive casting of the female as object of the erotic gaze – is partly inspired by the extremely one-sided gendering of eroticism in German Goth media representations. Such representations may not reflect the actual stylistic and erotic identities of most ordinary Goths; yet they still provide potent models of gendered appearance and eroticism, which likely function as points of reference or guidance especially among younger people new to the scene.

However, there are important differences between the ideal images of Goth in published photography, music and the media discourses surrounding them, on the one hand, and the self-images, styles and attitudes of real-life Goths on the other hand. What is typically represented in – particularly the bigger and more professional – Goth music acts and magazines reflects a normative Gothic ideal rather than the identities of average Goths. Both the gendered archetypes of masculine warrior versus feminine fairy, which are often sonically and textually constructed in Goth music, and the image of the submissive or assertive dark sex goddess pervading the visual aspects of Gothic art stand for an idealised version of Gothic imagery. In fact many of their avid consumers are either unable or unwilling to live up to such stylised clichés, which define Goth identity in an exaggerated and restrictive manner. Instead, they carve out their own subcultural niches and construct more individual interpretations of Gothdom. As in the case of the big girls portrayed in chapter 4, such interpretations sometimes even work to counter the normative pressures of hegemonic definitions of Goth.

9

The Death of Utopia

September 2004, a Goth club in the centre of Berlin near my flat. Tonight I have not come here to observe people or hunt for interviews, but to celebrate having finished the first draft of my thesis. However, ingrained habits are hard to break. I catch myself trying to make out whether the plain, short-haired guy in combats and washed-out Wumpscut T-shirt and the futuristic Fetish princess in a skin-tight black PVC dress dancing opposite each other are a couple, and wondering whether they are aware of their markedly different – and markedly gendered – expressive gestures on the dance floor. Next to them, almost hidden in the fog, I spot a figure with a large mohawk, striding back and forth in powerful movements. A glimpse at the person's face, and I cannot help smiling; the vigorous dancer is actually a girl. Even after more than a decade, the Gothic scene has not entirely lost its capacity to surprise me. One of my friends suddenly interrupts my train of thought, engaging me in a conversation about my thesis: 'So tell me in a few sentences, what is the main finding of your research?' 'Sorry, it's impossible to explain that in a few sentences,' I reply, trying to win some time to come up with a more convincing answer, 'but it surely has a lot to do with the difference between ideal and reality.' Looking a bit bemused, my friend does not seem willing to let me get away that easily. With a tinge of irony in her voice, she asks the seemingly all-important question: 'Hey, what are we then – progressive or reactionary?'

Subversion or Stereotype?

Having traced the construction of gender in Goth across various subcultural practices and representations, in fact it seems slightly off the point to pronounce a clear-cut judgement on the subversive or reactionary nature of Goth gender politics. We have seen, for example, that Gothic male androgyny can function to accrue subcultural capital, and to affirm traditional masculine status criteria like courage and transgression. Yet we have also learned that the androgynous style of Goth men can work to rattle common norms of male appearance and bearing in the world outside the subculture. Likewise, we have looked at the Gothic scene as a heterosexually gendered space, whose courtship norms, status criteria and gender roles display many deeply traditional tendencies. Yet we have also come to see the scene as a space for experimenting with gender and sexuality, where queer orientations like transidentity or same-sex desire are not only tolerated but often even venerated.

So what are we to make of this wealth of competing and sometimes contradictory findings? Are Gothic gender politics in fact deeply reactionary, thinly veiled by a subcultural rhetoric of equality and transgression, as a critical micropolitical analyst like Thornton (1995) might claim? Are they essentially progressive and subversive, with their high-minded intentions just sometimes skewed by a less than perfect translation into action, as an idealistic commentator stressing the subjective meanings the members of subcultures themselves attach to their practices would likely argue (e.g. Pini, 2001)? Or do the practices, images and identities offered by Goth – and other commodity-based subcultures – simply not matter in terms of broader cultural issues like gender, as cultural theorists favouring a macropolitical perspective over the more individualised notion of 'politics' advanced by cultural studies suggest (e.g. Marchart, 2003)?

As so often, the true nature of subcultural practices seems to hide somewhere in between these extreme poles. I think the key to understanding their effects lies in asking precisely *in which contexts* and *from which perspectives* such practices assume progressive or reactionary meanings. A problem with many studies examining the social or political import of subcultural ideologies and practices is that they fail to systematically analyse the micro- *and* macropolitical levels on which this import takes shape. A one-sided focus on either level inevitably entails that some important aspects of subcultural practices are passed over.

For instance, studies in the vein of Thornton (1995), which focus exclusively on the 'microstructures of power' at play within subcultures, do not have much to say about how such practices may impact on broader discursive formations or cultural structures. Arguably, 'this mode of analysis effectively robs youth cultures of any macro-political dimension' (Weinzierl and Muggleton, 2003, p. 13); however 'radical' the practices of a subculture may seem, the analyst reduces them to a quest for subcultural capital at the expense of the 'unhip'. Only through paying attention to both the micro- and the macro-levels of subcultural politics can the different and sometimes conflicting threads making up these politics be highlighted and partly disentangled. From this dual perspective, it becomes clear that practices which work to cement restrictive gender norms inside a subculture (i.e. on the micro-level) may at the same time serve to rattle and disrupt broader cultural gender norms (i.e. on the macro-level), and vice versa.

The ambivalent position of Gothic male androgyny in terms of gender politics is a prime example. On the subcultural micro-level, male androgynous style regularly functions as a source of subcultural capital from which Goth women are excluded, and as an affirmation of traditional masculine status. On the macro-level of general social norms, however, it holds the potential to 'make strange' and throw into flux traditional modes of masculinity through a recasting of male appearance as playful erotic spectacle. Another example is provided by the diverse implications of the hyperfeminine style of female Goths. Viewed from the macroperspective, this highly sexualised style partly conforms to male-defined standards for women in our culture but at the same time transgresses common norms of female propriety by signifying femininity in excess of conventional codes. Viewed from the microperspective of subcultural and subjective meanings, this hyperfemininity on the one hand panders to the erotic gaze of Goth men but on the other hand engenders feelings of empowerment, freedom and protection in the women who don it.

While it is crucial to question and unmask subcultural rhetoric, it is equally important to address the latter aspect mentioned above, namely subjective meanings and experience. As Leonard (1997, p. 252) suggests, the significance of a subcultural movement 'can be measured not in its final "result" but in the effect it has had on individuals'. A one-sided focus on either rhetoric or subjectivity, either internal or broader social effects of subcultural practices, either normative or liberating tendencies runs the risk of only discovering and confirming those 'truths' already known to the researcher. A systematic analysis of all these different facets, by contrast, can help to draw a more nuanced and realistic picture of subcultures, without falling into the trap of portraying their practices as either inherently subversive or reactionary.

A related problem haunting subcultural analysis is the question of how to define precisely what counts as 'progressive' or 'subversive' and what counts as 'reactionary' or 'normative'. Crucially, subcultural practices can be seen as both reactionary and progressive, both fettering and liberating at the same time, depending on the (sub)cultural positions and individual perspectives of the subjects concerned. It is striking how differently members of a subculture like Goth sometimes experience and interpret the practices and images of their scene. For instance, we have seen that most Goth women – despite their expressed liking for femininely styled men – feel that Gothic male androgyny puts pressure on them to embody an even more ornately styled image of femininity, and thus restricts rather than enhances their potential to experiment with gender in style. However, male androgyny can also be viewed quite differently by individual women. My interviewee Petit Scarabee credibly claims that she experiences the androgyny of Goth men as a general relaxing of gender norms and barriers, encouraging her to engage in sartorial practices of gender play herself.

In the case of other central ideologies or practices of Goth – e.g. the veneration of queer sexualities as a trope of transgression – it seems no less tricky to decide whether they have mainly reactionary or progressive effects in the subcultural sphere and beyond. Certainly the co-opting of a marginal cultural position for vacant poses of rebellion is a politically dubious gesture. However, is a valuing of sexual fluidity – or, more generally speaking, an 'ideology of genderlessness' – not a lot more desirable than any ideology of rigid gendering as a matter of principle, regardless of how flawed and deceptive it may sometimes prove in practice? This is a question I will not try to answer conclusively, as there are probably as many sensible arguments for and against the practices or ideologies concerned as there are cultural positions and individual perspectives from which to view them.

Some Situated Conclusions

So does this mean that cultural relativism has won the battle? That researchers cannot really say anything about cultural virtues and vices, that they cannot and should not engage in value judgements? I think they still can, and should! In the postmodern era of late capitalism, it may have become increasingly difficult to analytically separate the good, the bad and the ugly in the nitty-gritty reality of everyday cultural practices and relations. 'In a world where the market structures must be revolutionized to be maintained, the rhetorics of conservatism and radicalism will not be neatly separated.' (Billig, 1997, p. 226) Yet it is still possible to stake out some basic, even if Utopian, desiderata. To revisit the question I posed above: would it not be best if there was a (sub)cultural space where a professed 'ideology of genderlessness' did not remain trapped on the level of fantasy, but was also realised in the actual relations between masculinity, femininity and sexuality?

Such a vision of progressive gender politics, however, may require a level of 'genderless' purity which is unattainable in our current cultural climate. Moving from the high-minded sphere of Utopian desires back to the nitty-gritty everyday with which the ethnographic analyst is faced, I would still hold that certain value judgements – though from a consciously reflexive, historically and locally situated position (Richardson, 1998) – are possible. As something of a necessary evil in academic discourse, they should not be eschewed even in an expressly polyphonic research text with lots of partly conflicting or contradictory original quotations.

From a pro-woman perspective, the artistic and commercial exploitation of female eroticism in some Goth music and media is highly problematic. Here 'the misogynist subtext, the secret complicity in patriarchal values, that often lurks beneath the apparently subversive and libertarian' (Reynolds and Press, 1995, p. xiii) surfaces most clearly. Through an often uncritical toying with the illicit and extreme – as in flirting with hypermasculine tropes of militarism and war in Electro and Industrial music, or in taking up supposedly transgressive yet traditionally gendered images of S&M eroticism in Gothic stage shows and photography – certain prominent currents within Goth indeed replicate deeply conservative gender discourses, thinly veiled by a rhetoric of subversion and transgression.

Crucially, such currents seem strongest in the most corporate spheres of international Goth, namely in the profit-making sections of the big German Goth music scene and its best-selling magazines. The growth of the German Gothic scene into a profitable part of consumer culture proves that a clear-cut distinction between 'underground' subcultures and 'commercial' mainstream is no longer tenable (see McRobbie, 1994, 1999). Yet it also bears ample witness to the notable – and often reactionary – effects on subcultural (gender) politics which the growing commercial success of a subculture can entail. It seems that Goth's progressive tendencies are suppressed and watered down, while its reactionary trends are fostered and capitalised on. For instance, male androgyny has declined and the exploitation of female eroticism has increased markedly with the growing size and corporate character of the German scene, thus party restoring the age-old gendered status quo where the pressure to mind one's appearance is one-sidedly relegated to women.

Apart from such commercial antics, certain Goth norms and practices definitely hold some promise in terms of gender subversion. However, we have to remember that Gothic politics of gender and class are sometimes closely entangled. So could it be that some of the subculture's progressively gendered practices do in fact mainly reflect ideologies of class rather than gender? There is the unwritten law, for example, that sexily styled women are not subjected to unwanted, blunt sexual advances by Goth men. Arguably, this female-friendly norm has more to do with a typically middle-class value discourse of refined, 'arty' appreciation which regulates the general handling of visual eroticism in the Gothic subculture, rather than with genuine respect for women's right to a self-determined sexual expression. After all, certain factions of the scene's male art establishment are far from squeamish about blatantly exploiting female eroticism for their own artistic and commercial ends.

Yet even if the norm of sexily dressed females not being hassled in Gothic spaces is mainly due to a class-based 'snobbism', it still has marked positive consequences for Goth women. Indeed, many of the straight non-Goth venues I visited during the years of my research made me sympathise fully with the feelings voiced by some of my female interviewees about their negative experiences in conventional clubs. On such occasions I found myself wondering whether I was really on the right track in writing such a critical analysis of a subculture whose gender norms suddenly seemed so much more acceptable than what I witnessed in some of those spaces.

After three years of academic engagement with Goth, I finally rest assured that questioning practices and discourses close to one's heart is something of a necessity for a reflexive cultural studies beyond cultural populism. The thin line of a critical yet still respectful treatment of field data is not easy to tread. Yet if researchers are not prepared to walk this tightrope, instead taking a predefined affirmative stance towards supposedly marginal subcultural groups and their productions, what then remains to set their work apart from journalistic cultural commentary? At some point, researchers will always have to take the risk of passing value judgements – no matter how necessarily partial (in both senses of the word: incomplete and biased), fractured and locally or historically specific those judgements may be.

Gender discourses in the Gothic subculture are fragmented and sometimes contradictory, just like in other sections of our increasingly fragmented postmodern culture. Compared with many other sections of society, Goth offers quite a few starting points for a more progressive, more adventurous and more equal renegotiation of masculinity, femininity and sexuality. Its partial blurring of some of the deep-rooted visible gender divisions of our culture through the style practice of male androgyny, its acceptance of queer sexualities and its overarching ideal of genderlessness are all there as potentials to be seized. As we have seen, there are already some individuals – e.g. men like the expressively gender-bending Synara, or women like Petit Scarabee with her variable gender masquerades – who are grasping these potentials and turning them into strategies and resources for their own local challenges to rigid gender stereotypes both outside and within the subculture.

Ideal and Reality

Despite all these potentials, the central finding of this study is probably the glaring gap which often separates ideal from reality in Gothic gender politics. Seduced by the prodigious rhetoric of their subculture, Goths regularly seem to fall into the trap of more or less unwittingly using the trope of a professed 'genderlessness' to mask and thus perpetuate practices and images which are in fact heavily – and sometimes quite perniciously – gendered. A case in point are the discourses sometimes invoked to justify the degrading and sexist depiction of women as docile sex objects in some Gothic art and media. As Goth ideology construes the subculture as a genderless space, that is a space where gender issues simply do not matter, people who criticise sexism in Gothic art run the risk of being dismissed as simply unable to distinguish 'quality' from 'cheap' erotica or, even worse, as unable to understand the supposedly 'subversive' character of such art.

There is a huge discrepancy between the high-minded ideal of genderlessness surrounding all the constitutive practices of Goth – i.e. style, eroticism, music and other art forms – and the often heavily gendered reality of these practices in everyday experience. With its creative and unusual expressive practices, the Gothic scene invokes a palpable sense of the instability and fluidity of gender and sexuality, yet often only to bring it to a fairly normative heterosexual conclusion. While the subculture's practices challenge many common cultural expectations about gender, like the norm of sobriety in male dress or reserve in female sexual behaviour, it leaves untarnished the fundamental gender doctrines of masculine (hetero)sexual dominance and idealised feminine beauty.

Male Goths enjoy an exceptional freedom to experiment with feminine style elements and to thwart traditional images of masculinity, yet still remain largely locked within the discourse of dominant male (hetero)sexuality. Conversely, female Goths are free to experiment with (bi)sexuality – even if acted out mainly on the level of fantasy and flirtation – but stay trapped within the norms of essentially quite standardised and conventional ideals of feminine beauty. Cherishing a version of 'androgyny' which is restricted to the warping of feminine codes by men, and a similarly limited version of 'bisexuality' which often amounts to little more than staged female-on-female poses as a mark of transgression, the subculture is far from realising the genderless Utopia of equality between men and women it claims for itself.

However, maybe the idea of accomplishing such a Utopia within subculture actually misses the point; as already implied, the question of whether the practices of Goth are progressive or reactionary may not be exactly the right thing to ask. What may be more relevant is the question of whether subculture as a social formation embedded in larger cultural structures is really the place to realise Utopian desires of collectively transcending fundamental social constructs like gender and sexuality. Utopia – not in the negative sense of a starry-eyed, escapist delusion but in the positive sense of a purposeful vision of how to create a better future – has long been an important category in philosophical thought. Bloch (1959, p. 5) has postulated the Utopian impulse, understood as 'expectation, hope, intention toward yet unrealised possibility', as a characteristic feature of the human mind. The Utopian impulse is seen here as a necessary, even if not sufficient, condition for cultural progress.

While philosophers like Bloch envisaged the fulfilment of the Utopian impulse through grand political ideologies like Marxism, many young people in our postmodern culture obviously seek to realise this impulse in the small microcosms of subculture. From the early neo-Marxist CCCS studies right through to modern ethnographic analyses like Williamson (2001) or Pini (2001), which focus more on subjectivity than on notions of collective resistance, Utopian desires feature prominently as motors of subcultural alliance. Like my own analysis, both these authors stress the idealistic motives, the Utopian impulse, behind the gendered self-concepts of the subcultures they researched. Yet their studies also directly or indirectly reveal the flawed translation into action of those subcultures' progressive gender concepts in everyday practices.

Subcultures seem to function as preserves for collective Utopian ideals or desires within larger society, providing their members with a shared system of values which partly challenge general cultural norms. In terms of actual practices and lifestyles, however, they tend to remain closely tied to those very norms. After all, young people who join a subculture have already been socialised as gendered beings in our society, and they do not magically shake off this formative influence on entering a scene like Goth. By the same token, subcultures develop partly through definition against, but still firmly embedded in, a larger cultural, political and economic context, which delimits and shapes their potential for transgressing common social norms in subtle yet powerful ways. Contrary to political movements, Goth and other music-based subcultures have never set out to change the world. They aim rather to create a parallel microcosm in which their members can revel, a microcosm subjectively experienced as less normative and restrictive than general society. Yet even within this parallel world, fundamental social structures like binary gender cannot effectively be transcended.

Goth as a subculture is characterised by an inherent tension in its Utopian impulse. The scene works as a repository for collective Utopian desires around gender in which its members believe, but at the same time it does not really work as a space for the collective acting out of such desires. However, on the individual level Goths do produce many local challenges to hegemonic models of gender. In postmodern culture, subcultures seem to be more about an *individual negotiation* of, than a *collective rebellion* against, gender and other structuring principles of society.

On the collective level, Goth – like other subcultures – falls short of realising its professed Utopian ideals, which is one more proof that the time of grand narratives of subcultural resistance is over. In the common practices of Goths, the traditional gender binary is not so much disrupted or transcended as shifted in the direction of femininity. This one-sided shift makes for uneven access to subculturally sanctioned modes of transgressing conventional gender norms. Goth men are encouraged to refuse certain pressures of hegemonic masculinity in their style practices and their means of status attainment. Goth women, by contrast, while cherishing the scene's ideology of genderlessness just as much, remain tied to a fairly restrictive standard of (hyper)femininity for winning approval and status. The genderless Utopia to which the Gothic subculture lays claim would have to manifest itself quite differently. To quote Paoletti and Kidwell (1989, p. 161): 'If and when equality comes, both men and women will be free to express their unique individuality drawing from the broad vocabulary of masculinity and femininity.'

Thoughtful vision or wishful thinking? I will probably have to visit a few more subcultural spaces in the decades to come to see if they will ever evolve into the havens of liberty from restrictive gender norms which Goth already professes to be. Tonight, however, I am content to just sit here in this familiar Goth club and watch people dance as I have done so often over the last few years, musing on the critical difference between ideal and reality – and on the many local challenges which a few imaginative individuals are already posing to restrictive (sub)cultural gender codes here and now, in the face of this seemingly unbridgeable difference.

Notes

Chapter 1 Setting the Scene

1. The terms 'Goth' and 'Gothic' are used by members of the subculture in both Britain and Germany when referring to themselves, their scene and their music. German Goths also use the term 'Schwarz' (Black) to describe the same aspects.
2. The subcultural Internet resource *Jugendszenen.com* gives a rough estimate of 70,000 to 90,000 Goths currently in Germany (source: http://www.hitzler-soziologie.de/jugendszenen/cms/szene-goth).
3. I have not come across any reliable estimates of the number of British Goths; my guess would be about one-fifth of the German Goth population, i.e. around 15,000.
4. See, for example, the *Guardian Weekend Edition Magazine*, 16/12/02, 'Flirting with Hitler' (John Hooper; retrieved 25/11/02 at: http://www.guardian.co.uk/Print/0,3858,4546285,00.html); *Psychologie Heute*, 02/01, 'Schwarze Szene, braun gefärbt [Black scene, stained brown]' (Michael Weisfeld, pp. 48–59).
5. For a detailed account of my methodological framework, see Brill (2006).
6. Sceptics' main objections to using data from Internet sources concern issues of authenticity and research ethics: do the identities presented online correspond to users' offline selves, and is it acceptable to 'harvest' online communities for research purposes? Recent Internet studies, however, conclude that the majority of everyday Internet use displays a high congruence between online and offline self-presentation (e.g. Hine, 2000) and nourishes fairly stable subcultural identities and formations (e.g. Hodkinson, 2003). Moreover, some authors have challenged the blanket adoption of a restrictive human subjects model for all types of online research (e.g. Walther, 2002; White, 2002). Treating Internet materials from open-access forums as published and publicly accessible texts rather than virtual people enables the researcher to engage critically and publicly with their contents, without having to protect anonymity or gain informed consent.
7. I narrate the whole analysis using the so-called 'ethnographic present', as this mode of writing offers the most immediate and vivid account of ethnographic findings.

Chapter 2 Subverting Gender, Gendering Subculture

1. On the relation between dress and gender more generally, see Barnes and Eicher (1993) and Kidwell and Steele (1989).
2. However, these two sites of power should not be conflated. Hegemonic forms of discourse inscribed into the macro-structures of society have a bigger power to

define dominant cultural values, however powerful minority discourses may be in defining specific subcultural values.

3. Earlier conceptions of subculture in the Chicago School tradition (e.g. Merton, 1957) highlighted sociological notions of deviance and focused on delinquent groups.

4. Hodkinson (2002, p. 19–24) discusses such concepts, pointing out that they are often too broadly or narrowly defined to be applied to various kinds of social groupings and also take into account their particularities. The proliferation of newly coined terms in fact does little to solve the complex theoretical and methodological problems which researchers of modern youth culture face.

5. Classic Foucaultian discourse analysis poses people as 'subjectified', i.e. as objects acted upon by ideology and discourse (Foucault, 1977). Critical Discursive Psychology places more emphasis on human agency. Here discourses are seen as less monolithic, more fragmented and open to active negotiation – a view which echoes the notion of (gender) discourse as fragmented and contested that underlies this study.

6. A striking example is that Pini's rose-tinted picture of Rave ignores the repeated mentioning of oppressive heterosexual relationships by some female interviewees (e.g. pp. 73/74, p. 182).

7. I do not discuss Rap/Hip-hop in detail because here issues of racial discrimination cross-cut and shape gender relations in complex ways. On Rap and femininity, see Rose (1994); on masculinity in Rap, see Grimm (1998).

Chapter 3 Style and Status

1. The brackets following Internet quotes give the author's nickname, the respective forum/newsgroup and the date of posting; following interview quotes, they give the gender and age of the interviewee(s) and the place of the interview; following magazine quotes, they give the magazine's name, issue and page number. Please note that Internet quotes are reproduced as they originally appeared, without corrections.

Chapter 4 Female Style and Subjectivity

1. A term coined by Riviere (1986, first published1929).

2. Of course this distancing from a femininity dismissed as unoriginal is not without problems from a feminist perspective.

Chapter 5 Masculinity in Style

1. While this hypermasculine image looks strikingly similar to some versions of gay male 'butch' style, it usually lacks the latter's ironic twist.

Chapter 6 Gender Relations

1. This statement also performs a specific discursive move. By pointing to 'other' predators, Jiad – who has himself had a string of significantly younger girlfriends from the scene – rhetorically produces himself as a 'non-predator', as someone who takes care rather than advantage of vulnerable young women.
2. This mechanism may be even stronger in street-based subcultures like Punk, as the Gothic scene boasts a relatively high proportion of occupationally successful people.

Chapter 7 Queer Sexualities

1. According to my observations, the percentage of non-heterosexual relationships is at most slightly higher in Goth than in other youth cultural groupings.
2. Of course the relation between fascism and gayness or lesbianism is not quite as simple and antithetical as these statements suggest (see Healy, 1996; Jeffreys, 1994; Theweleit, 1978).
3. As in the case of other published statements by musicians I used, Steele's quote reflects a cross-cutting of Goth discourses on sexuality/gender and discourses circulating in the Rock music industry and its media (see also chapter 8). It is probably directed by tactical concerns regarding the mise-en-scène of Steele as a hypermasculine Goth Metal idol as much as by his personal views.
4. One of the most infamous scenes in the band's live performance involved one woman sticking a candle up another's vagina, with the latter woman hanging upside down in a steel construction, and singer Mozart finally lighting the candle in an ostentatious gesture.

Chapter 8 Goth Music and Media

1. Naturally, my analysis focuses mainly on the big German magazines, as they simply yielded more empirical materials. However, the reader should keep in mind that there is no rigid dividing line between German and international Goth in terms of music and its media representation (see chapter 1).
2. As Davies elaborates, this 'sexploitative' mode of representation is not confined to male music journalists but is also used by female ones. This indicates that it is a

discursive system pervading the male-dominated music press rather than an outgrowth of individual journalists' sexism.

3. This musical style has seen the band Rammstein rise to international fame.

4. It should be mentioned that Page's second album *Sinmachine*, released after the time of my research, did prominently feature female vocals.

5. A notorious early artwork used by Cradle of Filth was a T-shirt print showing a tortured, bleeding woman stuck on a post with her vagina; early Die Form also employed graphic displays of tortured and mutilated female bodies.

6. By contrast, the less commercial British magazines *Kaleidoscope* and *Meltdown*, as well as most of the smaller German magazines and fanzines, hardly ever print nude photographs.

7. Of course this conception of the 'male gaze' is simplifying, as it leaves complications like gay and lesbian gazes untheorised.

Bibliography

Amico, S. (2001). 'I Want Muscles': House music, homosexuality and masculine signification. *Popular Music, Vol. 20, No. 3* (pp. 359–378)

Armstrong, G. (1998). *Football Hooligans. Knowing the score.* Oxford: Berg

Arnett, J.J. (1996). *Metalheads. Heavy Metal music and adolescent alienation.* Boulder, CO: Westview Press

Ash, J. (1995). Tarting up men: menswear and gender dynamics. In J. Attfield and P. Kirkham (eds), *A view from the interior. Women and design* (2nd edition) (pp. 29–38). London: The Women's Press

Ault, A. (1999). Ambiguous identity in an unambiguous sex/gender structure: the case of bisexual women. In M. Storr (ed.), *Bisexuality. A critical reader* (pp. 167–185). London: Routledge

Baacke, D. (1993). *Jugend und Jugendkulturen. Darstellung und Deutung* (2nd, revised edition). Weinheim: Juventa

Baddeley, G. (2002). *Goth chic. A connoisseur's guide to dark culture.* London: Plexus

Baker, K. (1992). Bisexual feminist politics: because bisexuality is not enough. In E.R. Weise (ed.), *Closer to home. Bisexuality and feminism* (pp. 255–267). Washington: Seal Press

Barnard, M. (1996). *Fashion as communication.* London: Routledge

Barnes, R. and Eicher, J.B. (eds) (1993). *Dress and gender. Making and meaning.* London: Berg

Barthes, R. (1972). *Mythologies.* London: Paladin

Barthes, R. (1983). *The fashion system.* Berkeley: University of California Press

Bayton, M. (1997). Women and the electric guitar. In S. Whiteley (ed.), *Sexing the groove. Popular music and gender* (pp. 37–49). London: Routledge

Bennett, K. (1992). Feminist bisexuality: a both/and option for an either/or world. In E.R. Weise (ed.), *Closer to home. Bisexuality and feminism* (pp. 205–231). Washington: Seal Press

Berger, J. (1972). *Ways of seeing.* London: Penguin

Betterton, R. (1987). Introduction: feminism, femininity and representation. In R. Betterton (ed.), *Looking on. Images of femininity in the visual arts and media* (pp. 1– 17). London: Pandora

Billig, M. (1997). From codes to utterances: cultural studies, discourse and psychology. In M. Ferguson and P. Golding (eds), *Cultural studies in question* (pp. 205–226). London: Sage

Bloch, E. (1959). *Das Prinzip der Hoffnung (Band 1).* Frankfurt a.M.: Suhrkamp

Blum, A. (2001). Scenes. *Public: Cities/Scenes, Vol. 22–3* (pp. 7–36)

Bohnsack, R. (1997). Adoleszenz, Aktionismus und die Emergenz von Milieus: eine Ethnographie von Hooligangruppen und Rockbands. *Zeitschrift für Sozialisationsforschung und Erziehungssoziologie (Band 1)* (pp. 3–18)

Bourdieu, P. (1984). *Distinction. A social critique of the judgement of taste.* London: Routledge

Bradby, B. (1993). Sampling sexuality: gender, technology and the body in Dance music. *Popular Music, Vol. 12, No. 2* (pp. 155–176)

Braidotti, R. (1989). Organs without bodies. *Differences. A Journal of Feminist Cultural Studies, Vol. 1, No. 1* (pp. 147–161)

Brake, M. (1985). *Comparative youth culture. The sociology of youth cultures and youth subcultures in America, Britain and Canada.* London: Routledge

Brame, G.G., Brame, W.D. and Jacobs, J. (1996). *Different loving. The world of sexual dominance and submission.* New York: Random / Villard Books

Brill, D. (2006). *Subversion or stereotype? The Gothic subculture as a case study of gendered identities and representations.* Gießen: Ulme-Mini-Verlag

Brill, D. (2007). Auf Tod und Teufel? Das 'Böse' in der Gothic-Subkultur. In S. Seybold (ed.), *All about Evil. Das Böse* (pp. 170–177). Mainz: Verlag Philipp von Zabern

Brill, D. (2008). *Subculture for sale? Cultural, content and production values in Goth music journalism.* Berlin: Wissenschaftlicher Verlag Berlin

Butler, J. (1990). *Gender trouble. Feminism and the subversion of identity.* London: Routledge

Butler, J. (1993). *Bodies that matter. On the discursive limits of 'sex'.* London: Routledge

Butler, S. (1987). Revising femininity? Review of *Lady*, photographs of Lisa Lyon by Robert Mapplethorpe. In R. Betterton (ed.), *Looking on. Images of femininity in the visual arts and media* (pp. 120–126). London: Pandora

Case, S.E. (1993). Toward a butch-femme aesthetic. In H. Abelove, M.A. Barale and D.M. Halperin (eds), *The lesbian and gay studies reader* (pp. 294–306). London: Routledge

Chaney, D. (2004). Fragmented culture and subcultures. In A. Bennett and K. Kahn-Harris (eds), *After subculture. Critical studies in contemporary youth culture* (pp. 36–48). Basingstoke: Palgrave Macmillan

Clandinin, D.J. and Connelly, F.M. (1998). Personal experience methods. In N.K. Denzin and Y.S. Lincoln (eds), *Collecting and interpreting qualitative materials* (pp. 150–178). London: Sage

Coates, N. (1997). (R)evolution now? Rock and the political potential of gender. In S. Whiteley (ed.), *Sexing the groove. Popular music and gender* (pp. 50–64). London: Routledge

Cohen, Sara (1991). *Rock culture in Liverpool. Popular music in the making.* Oxford: Oxford University Press

Cohen, Sara (1997). Men making a scene: Rock music and the production of gender. In S. Whiteley (ed.), *Sexing the groove. Popular music and gender* (pp. 17–36). London: Routledge

Cohen, Stanley (1997). Symbols of trouble. In K. Gelder and S. Thornton (eds), *The subcultures reader* (pp. 149–162). London: Routledge

Craft, C. (1989). 'Kiss me with those red lips': gender and inversion in Bram

Stoker's *Dracula*. In E. Showalter (ed.), *Speaking of gender* (pp. 216–242). London: Routledge

Cubitt, S. (1997). Rolling and tumbling: digital erotics and the culture of narcissism. In S. Whiteley (ed.), *Sexing the groove. Popular music and gender* (pp. 295–316). London: Routledge

Davies, H. (2001). All Rock and Roll is homosocial: the representation of women in the British Rock music press. *Popular Music, Vol. 20, No. 3* (pp. 301–319)

Davis, F. (1992). *Fashion, culture, and identity*. London: University of Chicago Press

De Beauvoir, S. (1953). *The second sex*. London: Jonathan Cape

De Lauretis, T. (1987). *Technologies of gender. Essays on theory, film and fiction*. London: Macmillan

DeMello, M. (2000). *Bodies of inscription. A cultural history of the modern tattoo community*. London: Duke University Press

Denski, S. and Sholle, D. (1992). Metal men and glamour boys. Gender performance in Heavy Metal. In S. Craig (ed.), *Men, masculinity and the media* (pp. 41–60). London: Sage

Doane, M.A. (1982). Film and the masquerade: theorising the female spectator. *Screen, Vol. 23, No. 3–4* (pp. 74–87)

Duncombe, S. (1997). *Notes from underground. Zines and the politics of alternative culture*. London: Verso

Eadie, J. (1999). Extracts from *Activating bisexuality: towards a bi/sexual politics*. In M. Storr (ed.), *Bisexuality. A critical reader* (pp. 119–137). London: Routledge

Easthope, A. (1986). *What a man's gotta do. The masculine myth in popular culture*. London: Paladin

Edley, N. (2001). Analysing masculinity: interpretative repertoires, ideological dilemmas and subject positions. In M. Wetherell, S. Taylor and S.J. Yates (eds), *Discourse as data. A guide for analysis* (pp. 189–228). Milton Keynes: The Open University

Ehrenreich, B., Hess, E. and Jacobs, G. (1997). Beatlemania: a sexually defiant consumer subculture? In K. Gelder and S. Thornton (eds), *The subcultures reader* (pp. 523–536). London: Routledge

Eicher, J.B. and Roach-Higgins, N.E. (1993). Definition and classification of dress: implications for analysis of gender roles. In R. Barnes and J.B. Eicher (eds), *Dress and gender. Making and meaning* (pp. 8–28). Oxford: Berg

Emberley, J. (1988). The fashion apparatus and the deconstruction of postmodern subjectivity. In A. Kroker and M. Kroker (eds), *Body invaders. Sexuality and the postmodern condition* (pp. 47–60). London: Macmillan

Evans, C. and Thornton, M. (1989). *Women and fashion. A new look*. London: Quartet Books

Ewen, S. and Ewen, E. (1982). *Channels of desire. Mass images and the shaping of American consciousness*. New York: McGraw-Hill

Farin, K. (2001). *Die Gothics. Interviews, Fotografien.* Berlin: Verlag Thomas Tilsner

Ferrell, J. (1993). *Crimes of style. Urban graffiti and the politics of criminality.* New York: Garland

Fiske, J. (1987). *Television culture.* London: Methuen

Fiske, J. (1989). *Understanding popular culture.* London: Routledge

Flügel, J.C. (1950). *The psychology of clothes* (3rd edition). London: Hogarth Press

Foote, S. (1989). Challenging gender symbols. In C.B. Kidwell and V. Steele (eds), *Men and women. Dressing the part* (pp. 144–157). Washington: Smithonian Institution Press

Foucault, M. (1977). *Discipline and punish. The birth of the prison.* London: Allen Lane

Frith, S. (1996). *Performing rites. Evaluating popular music.* Oxford: Oxford University Press

Gaillot, M. (1998). *Multiple meaning Techno. An artistic and political laboratory of the present.* Paris: Dis Voir Edition

Ganetz, H. (1995). The shop, the home and femininity as a masquerade. In J. Fornäs and G. Bolin (eds), *Youth culture in late modernity* (pp. 72–99). London: Sage

Garber, M. (1992). *Vested interests. Cross-dressing and cultural anxiety.* London: Routledge

Garber, M. (1999). Extracts from *Vice versa: bisexuality and the eroticism of everyday life.* In M. Storr (ed.), *Bisexuality. A critical reader* (pp. 138–143). London: Routledge

Grimm, S. (1998). *Die Repräsentation von Männlichkeit im Punk und Rap.* Tübingen: Stauffenburg Verlag

Gunn, J. (1999). Goth music and the inevitability of genre. *Popular Music and Society, Vol. 23, No. 1* (pp. 31–50)

Gunn, J. (2007). Dark admissions: Gothic subculture and the ambivalence of misogyny and resistance. In L. Goodlad and M. Bibby (eds), *Goth. Undead subculture* (pp. 41–64). London: Duke University Press

Gutterman, D.S. (2001). Postmodernism and the interrogation of masculinity. In S.M. Whitehead and F.J. Barrett (eds), *The masculinities reader* (pp. 56–71). Cambridge: Polity

Hall, S. and Jefferson, T. (eds) (1976). *Resistance through rituals. Youth subcultures in post-war Britain.* London: Hutchinson

Hanna, J.L. (1988). *Dance, sex and gender. Signs of identity, dominance, defiance, and desire.* Chicago: University of Chicago Press

Healy, M. (1996). *Gay skins. Class, masculinity and queer appropriation.* London: Cassell

Hebdige, D. (1979). *Subculture. The meaning of style.* London: Methuen

Hebdige, D. (1988). *Hiding in the light.* London: Routledge

Hebdige, D. (1997). Posing ... threats, striking ... poses: youth, surveillance, and display. In K. Gelder and S. Thornton (eds), *The subcultures reader.* London: Routledge

Bibliography

Helsper, W. (1992). *Okkultismus – die neue Jugendreligion? Die Symbolik des Todes und des Bösen in der Jugendkultur.* Opladen: Leske & Budrich

Hemmings, C. (1999). Extract from *Locating bisexual identities: discourses of bisexuality and contemporary feminist theory.* In M. Storr (ed.), *Bisexuality. A critical reader* (pp. 193–200). London: Routledge

Hine, C. (2000). *Virtual ethnography.* London: Sage

Hodkinson, P. (2002). *Goth. Identity, style and subculture.* Oxford: Berg

Hodkinson, P. (2003). 'Net.Goth': Internet communication and (sub)cultural boundaries. In D. Muggleton and R. Weinzierl (eds), *The post-subcultures reader* (pp. 285–298). Oxford: Berg

Hodkinson, P. (2004). The Goth scene and (sub)cultural substance. In A. Bennett and K. Kahn-Harris (eds), *After subculture. Critical studies in contemporary youth culture* (pp. 135–147). Basingstoke: Palgrave Macmillan

Hodkinson, P. (2007). Gothic music and subculture. In C. Spooner and E. McEvoy (eds), *The Routledge companion to Gothic* (pp. 260–269). London: Routledge

Hollway, W. (2001). Gender difference and the production of subjectivity. In M. Wetherell, S. Taylor and S.J. Yates (eds), *Discourse theory and practice. A reader* (pp. 272–281). Milton Keynes: The Open University

Holmlund, C. (1993). Masculinity as multiple masquerade: the 'mature' Stallone and the Stallone clone. In S. Cohan and J.R. Hark (eds), *Screening the male. Exploring masculinities in Hollywood cinema* (pp. 213–229). London: Routledge

Irigaray, L. (1985). *This sex which is not one.* Ithaca: Cornell University Press

Jeffreys, S. (1994). *The lesbian heresy. A feminist perspective on the lesbian sexual revolution.* London: The Women's Press

Jenkins, H. (1992). *Textual poachers. Television fans and participatory cultures.* London: Routledge

Kaplan, E.A. (1983). Is the gaze male? In A. Snitow, C. Stansell and S. Thompson (eds), *Desire. The politics of sexuality* (pp. 321–338). London: Virago Press

Kaplan, E.A. (1993). Madonna politics: perversion, repression, or subversion? Or masks and/as master-y. In C. Schwichtenberg (ed.), *The Madonna connection. Representational politics, subcultural identities, and cultural theory* (pp. 149–165). Oxford: Westview Press

Kaplan, R. (1992). Compulsory heterosexuality and the bisexual existence: toward a bisexual feminist understanding of heterosexism. In E.R. Weise (ed.), *Closer to home. Bisexuality and feminism* (pp. 269–280). Washington: Seal Press

Kearney, M.C. (1998). 'Don't need you': rethinking identity politics and separatism from a Grrrl perspective. In J. Epstein (ed.), *Youth culture. Identity in a postmodern world* (pp. 148–188). Oxford: Blackwell

Kelly, M. (1996). *Imaging desire.* London: MIT Press

Kidwell, C.B. and Steele, V. (eds) (1989). *Men and women. Dressing the part.* Washington: Smithsonian Institution Press

Kimmel, M. (1987). Rethinking 'masculinity': new directions in research. In M.S.

Kimmel (ed.), *Changing men. New directions in research on men and masculinity* (pp. 9–24). Newbury Park, CA: Sage

Kissling, E.A. (1991). Street harassment: the language of sexual terrorism. *Discourse and Society*, Vol. 2 (pp. 451–460)

Klein, G. (1992). *FrauenKörperTanz. Eine Zivilisationsgeschichte des Tanzes.* Weinheim/Berlin: Quadriga-Verlag

Lacan, J. (1982 [1958]). The meaning of the Phallus. In J. Mitchell and J. Rose (eds), *Feminine sexuality. Jacques Lacan and the Ecole Freudienne* (pp. 74–85). New York: W.W. Norton

Leblanc, L. (1999). *Pretty in Punk. Girls' gender resistance in a boys' subculture.* London: Rutgers University Press

Leblanc, L. (2002). 'The Punk guys will really overpower what the Punk girls have to say': the boys' turf. In C.L. Williams and A. Stein (eds), *Sexuality and gender* (pp. 167–173). Oxford: Blackwell

Leonard, M. (1997). 'Rebel Girl, You are the Queen of my World': feminism, 'subculture' and Grrrl power. In S. Whiteley (ed.), *Sexing the groove. Popular music and gender* (pp. 230–255). London: Routledge

Lincoln, S. (2004). Teenage girls' 'bedroom culture': codes versus zones. In A. Bennett and K. Kahn-Harris (eds), *After subculture. Critical studies in contemporary youth culture* (pp. 94–106). Basingstoke: Palgrave Macmillan

Lurie, A. (1992). *The language of clothes* (2nd, revised edition). London: Bloomsbury

McClary, S. (1991). *Feminine endings. Music, gender, and sexuality.* London: University of Minnesota Press

Macdonald, N. (2001). *The Graffiti subculture. Youth, masculinity and identity in London and New York.* Basingstoke: Palgrave

McDonald, P. (1997). Feeling and fun: romance, dance and the performing male body in Take That videos. In S. Whiteley (ed.), *Sexing the groove. Popular music and gender* (pp. 277–294). London: Routledge

McDowell, C. (1992). *Dressed to kill. Sex power and clothes.* London: Hutchinson

McGuigan, J. (1992). *Cultural populism.* London: Routledge

MacLeod, J. (1995). *Ain't no makin' it. Leveled aspirations in a low-income neighborhood.* Boulder, CO: Westview Press

McNay, L. (2000). *Gender and agency. Reconfiguring the subject in feminist and social theory.* Cambridge: Polity Press

McRobbie, A. (1994). *Postmodernism and popular culture.* London: Routledge

McRobbie, A. (1999). *In the culture society. Art, fashion and popular music.* London: Routledge

McRobbie, A. (2000 [1980]). Settling accounts with subcultures: a feminist critique. In A. McRobbie, *Feminism and youth culture* (2nd edition) (pp. 26–43). London: Macmillan

McRobbie, A. and Garber, J. (2000 [1976]). Girls and subcultures. In A. McRobbie, *Feminism and youth culture* (2nd edition) (pp. 137–158). London: Macmillan

Maffesoli, M. (1996). *The time of the tribes. The decline of individualism in mass society.* London: Sage

Marchart, O. (2003). Bridging the micro–macro gap: is there such a thing as a post-subcultural politics? In D. Muggleton and R. Weinzierl (eds), *The post-subcultures reader* (pp. 83–97). Oxford: Berg

Mattelart, M. (1986). *Women media crisis. Femininity and disorder.* London: Comedia

Matzke, P. and Seeliger, T. (eds) (2000). *Gothic! Die Szene in Deutschland aus der Sicht ihrer Macher* (2nd, revised edition). Berlin: Schwarzkopf & Schwarzkopf

Merton, R.K. (1957). *Social theory and social structure.* London: Collier-Macmillan

Moore, S. (1988). Getting a bit of the Other – the pimps of postmodernism. In R. Chapman and J. Rutherford (eds), *Male order. Unwrapping masculinity* (pp. 165–192). London: Lawrence and Wishart

Mort, F. (1988). Boy's own? Masculinity, style and popular culture. In R. Chapman and J. Rutherford (eds), *Male order. Unwrapping masculinity* (pp. 193–224). London: Lawrence and Wishart

Muggleton, D. (1997). The post-subculturalist. In S. Redhead, D. Wynne and J. O'Connor (eds), *The Clubcultures reader. Readings in popular cultural studies* (pp. 167–185). Oxford: Blackwell

Muggleton, D. (2000). *Inside subculture. The postmodern meaning of style.* Oxford: Berg

Mulvey, L. (1992). Visual pleasure and narrative cinema. In Screen (eds), *The sexual subject. A Screen reader in sexuality* (pp. 22–34). London: Routledge

Myers, K. (1987). Fashion 'n' passion. In R. Betterton (ed.), *Looking on. Images of femininity in the visual arts and media* (pp. 58–65). London: Pandora

Negus, K. (1997). Sinéad O'Connor – musical mother. In S. Whiteley (ed.), *Sexing the groove. Popular music and gender* (pp. 178–190). London: Routledge

O'Flaherty, W.D. (1980). *Women, androgynes, and other mythical beasts.* London: The University of Chicago Press

O'Neal, G. (1999). The power of style: on rejection of the accepted. In K.K.P. Johnson and S.J. Lennon (eds), *Appearance and power* (pp. 127–139). New York: Berg

Paoletti, J.B. and Kidwell, C.B. (1989). Conclusion. In C.B. Kidwell and V. Steele (eds), *Men and women. Dressing the part* (pp. 158–161). Washington: Smithsonian Institution Press

Pini, M. (1997). Women and the early British Rave scene. In A. McRobbie (ed.), *Back to reality? Social experience and Cultural Studies* (pp. 152–169). Manchester: Manchester University Press

Pini, M. (2001). *Club cultures and female subjectivity. The move from home to house.* Basingstoke: Palgrave

Polhemus, T. (1988). *Body styles.* Luton: Lennard Publications

Pollock, G. (1991). Missing women: rethinking early thoughts on images of women. In C. Squiers (ed.), *The critical image. Essays on contemporary photography* (pp. 202–219). London: Lawrence and Wishart

Pollock, G. (1992). What's wrong with 'images of women'? In Screen (eds), *The sexual subject. A Screen reader in sexuality* (pp. 135–145). London: Routledge

Ponse, B. (1998). The social construction of identity and its meanings within the lesbian subculture. In P.M. Nardi and B.E. Schneider (eds), *Social perspectives in lesbian and gay studies. A reader* (pp. 246–260). London: Routledge

Pramaggiore, M. (1996). BI-ntroduction I: epistemologies of the fence. In D.E. Hall and M. Pramaggiore (eds), *RePresenting bisexualities. Subjects and cultures of fluid desire* (pp. 1–7). London: New York University Press

Reynolds, S. (1989). Against health and efficiency: Independent music in the 1980s. In A. McRobbie (ed.), *Zoot suits and second-hand dresses. An anthology of fashion and music* (pp. 245–255). London: Macmillan

Reynolds, S. and Press, J. (1995). *The sex revolts. Gender, rebellion and Rock'n'Roll*. London: Serpent's Tail

Richard, B. (1995). *Todesbilder. Kunst, Subkultur, Medien*. Munich: Beck

Richardson, L. (1998). Writing: a method of inquiry. In N.K. Denzin and Y.S. Lincoln (eds), *Collecting and interpreting qualitative materials* (pp. 345–371). London: Sage

Riviere, J. (1986 [1929]). Womanliness as a masquerade. In V. Burgin, J. Donald and C. Kaplan (eds), *Formations of fantasy* (pp. 35–44). London: Routledge

Rose, T. (1994). *Black noise. Rap music and Black culture in contemporary America*. Hanover, NH: Wesleyan University Press

Rubinstein, R. (1995). *Dress codes. Meanings and messages in American culture*. Oxford: Westview Press

Russo, M. (1988). Female grotesques: carnival and theory. In T. de Lauretis (ed.), *Feminist studies / critical studies* (pp. 213–229). London: Macmillan

Rust, P.C. (1992). Who are we and where do we go from here? Conceptualizing bisexuality. In E.R. Weise (ed.), *Closer to home. Bisexuality and feminism* (pp. 281–310). Washington: Seal Press

Sawchuk, K. (1988). A tale of inscription / fashion statements. In A. Kroker and M. Kroker (eds), *Body invaders. Sexuality and the postmodern condition* (pp. 61–77). London: Macmillan

Schmidt, A. and Neumann-Braun, K. (2004). *Die Welt der Gothics. Spielräume düster konnotierter Transzendenz*. Wiesbaden: VS Verlag für Sozialwissenschaften

Seitz, L. (1998). Heavy Metal und „Böhse Onkelz" – ein Sprachrohr für extreme Gefühle. In A. Schröder und U. Leonhardt (eds), *Jugendkulturen und Adoleszenz. Verstehende Zugänge zu Jugendlichen in ihren Szenen* (pp. 148–159). Neuwied: Luchterhand

Siegel, C. (2005). *Goth's dark empire*. Bloomington: Indiana University Press

Silverman, K. (1986). Fragments of a fashionable discourse. In T. Modleski (ed.), *Studies in entertainment. Critical approaches to mass culture* (pp. 139–152). Bloomington: Indiana University Press

Silverman, K. (1992). *Male subjectivity at the margins.* London: Routledge

Simpson, M. (1994). *Male impersonators. Men performing masculinity.* London: Cassell

Skeggs, B. (1997). *Formations of class and gender. Becoming respectable.* London: Sage

Speit, A. (ed.) (2002). *Ästhetische Mobilmachung. Dark Wave, Neofolk und Industrial im Spannungsfeld rechter Ideologien.* Münster: Unrast Verlag

Spooner, C. (2004). *Fashioning Gothic bodies.* Manchester: Manchester University Press

Spooner, C. (2006). *Contemporary Gothic.* London: Reaktion Books

Stombler, M. (1994). 'Buddies' or 'slutties': the collective sexual reputation of fraternity little sisters. *Gender and Society, Vol. 8* (pp. 293–323)

Straw, W. (1997). Sizing up record collections: gender and connoisseurship in Rock music culture. In S. Whiteley (ed.), *Sexing the groove. Popular music and gender* (pp. 3–16). London: Routledge

Szostak-Pierce, S. (1999). Even Furthur: the power of subcultural style in Techno culture. In K.K.P. Johnson and S.J. Lennon (eds), *Appearance and power* (pp. 141–151). New York: Berg

Theweleit, K. (1978). *Männerphantasien, Band 2. Zur Psychoanalyse des Weißen Terrors.* Frankfurt a. M.: Verlag Roter Stern

Thompson, M. (ed.) (1991). *Leatherfolk.* Boston: Alyson Publications

Thornton, S. (1995). *Club cultures. Music, media and subcultural capital.* Cambridge: Polity Press

Thornton, S. (1997). The social logic of subcultural capital. In K. Gelder and S. Thornton (eds), *The subcultures reader* (pp. 200–209). London: Routledge

Turner, V. (1967). *The forest of symbols. Aspects of Ndembu ritual.* London: Cornell University Press

Tyler, C.A. (1990). The feminine look. In M. Kreiswirth and M.A. Cheetham (eds), *Theory between the disciplines* (pp. 191–212). Ann Arbor, MI: University of Michigan Press

Tyler, C.A. (1991). Boys will be girls: the politics of gay drag. In D. Fuss (ed.), *Inside/out. Lesbian theories, gay theories* (pp. 32–70). London: Routledge

Udis-Kessler, A. (1992). Closer to home: bisexual feminism and the transformation of hetero/sexism. In E.R. Weise (ed.), *Closer to home. Bisexuality and feminism* (pp. 183–201). Washington: Seal Press

Van Zoonen, L. (1994). *Feminist media studies.* London: Sage

Wallraff, K. (2001). *Weiss wie Schnee, rot wie Blut und schwarz wie Ebenholz. Die Gothics, 2. Teil.* Berlin: Verlag Thomas Tilsner

Walser, R. (1993). *Running with the devil. Gender, power and madness in Heavy Metal music.* New England: Wesleyan University Press

Walther, J.B. (2002). Research ethics in Internet-enabled research: human subjects issues and methodological myopia. From *Internet research ethics,* http://www.nyu.edu/projects/nissenbaum/ethics_wal_full.html. Retrieved 19/11/2002

Weeks, J. (1985). *Sexuality and its discontents. Meanings, myths and modern sexualities*. London: Routledge & Kegan Paul

Weil, K. (1992). *Androgyny and the denial of difference*. London: University Press of Virginia

Weinberg, T.S. (ed.) (1995). *S&M. Studies in dominance and submission*. Amhurst, NY: Prometheus Books

Weinstein, D. (1991). *Heavy Metal. A cultural sociology*. Oxford: Lexington Books

Weinstock, J.A. (2007). Gothic fetishism. In L. Goodlad and M. Bibby (eds), *Goth. Undead subculture* (pp. 375–397). London: Duke University Press

Weinzierl, R. and Muggleton, D. (2003). What is 'post-subcultural studies' anyway? In D. Muggleton and R. Weinzierl (eds), *The post-subcultures reader* (pp. 3–23). Oxford: Berg

White, M. (2002). Representations or people? From *Internet research ethics*, http://www.nyu.edu/projects/nissenbaum/ethics_whi_full.html.   Retrieved 19/11/2002

Whiteley, S. (1997a). Little Red Rooster v. the Honky Tonk Woman: Mick Jagger, sexuality, style and image. In S. Whiteley (ed.), *Sexing the groove. Popular music and gender* (pp. 67–99). London: Routledge

Whiteley, S. (1997b). Seduced by the sign: an analysis of the textual links between sound and image in pop videos. In S. Whiteley (ed.), *Sexing the groove. Popular music and gender* (pp. 259–276). London: Routledge

Whiteley, S. (1997c). Introduction. In S. Whiteley (ed.), *Sexing the groove. Popular music and gender* (pp. xiii–xxxvi). London: Routledge

Whiteley, S. (2000). *Women and popular music. Sexuality, identity and subjectivity*. London: Routledge

Widdicombe, S. (1993). Autobiography and change: rhetoric and authenticity of Gothic style. In E. Burham and I. Parker (eds), *Discourse analytical research. Repertoires and readings of texts in action* (pp. 94–113). London: Routledge

Widdicombe, S. and Wooffitt, R. (1995). *The language of youth subcultures. Social identity in action*. Hemel Hempstead: Harvester Wheatsheaf

Williamson, M. (2001). Vampires and Goths: fandom, gender and cult dress. In W.J.F. Keenan (ed.), *Dressed to impress. Looking the part* (pp. 141–157). London: Berg

Williamson, M. (2005). *The lure of the vampire. Gender, fiction and fandom from Bram Stoker to Buffy*. London: Wallflower Press

Willis, P. (1990). *Common culture. Symbolic work at play in the everyday cultures of the young*. Milton Keynes: Open University Press

Willis, P. (2000). *The ethnographic imagination*. Cambridge: Polity Press

Wilson, E. (1985). *Adorned in dreams. Fashion and modernity*. London: Virago Press

Wilson, E. (1992). Fashion and the postmodern body. In J. Ash and E. Wilson (eds), *Chic thrills. A fashion reader* (pp. 3–16). London: Pandora

Winship, J. (1987a). *Inside women's magazines*. London: Pandora

Winship, J. (1987b). 'A girl needs to get street-wise': magazines for the 1980s. In

Bibliography

R. Betterton (ed.), *Looking on. Images of femininity in the visual arts and media* (pp. 127–141). London: Pandora

Woodhouse, A. (1989). *Fantastic women. Sex, gender and transvestism.* London: Macmillan

Wright, L. (1995). Objectifying gender: the stiletto heel. In J. Attfield and P. Kirkham (eds), *A view from the interior. Women and design* (2nd edition) (pp. 7–19). London: The Women's Press

Discography

Computorgirl (2002). *The Computorgirl EP.* EP: Hard Drive
Cradle of Filth (1996). *V Empire.* CD: Cacophonus
Die Form (1997). *Duality.* CD: Trinity
Dioxyde (2002). *Torschlusspanik.* CD: Dying Culture
Dismantled (2002). *Dismantled.* CD: Dependent
Hypnoskull (2001). *Electronic Music Means War to Us.* CD: Ant-Zen
Hypnoskull (2002). *Operation Tough Guy.* CD: Ant-Zen
Imperative Reaction (2002). *Ruined.* CD: Metropolis
Lethargy (2003). *Escapa.* CD: Alfa Matrix
Mürnau (2003). *Recoil.* Single: Deafborn
Nik Page (2002). *Sacrifight.* CD: Hansa
Pzychobitch (2003). *The Day Before.* EP: Minuswelt
Pzychobitch (2004). Sweet Kiss. *The Day After.* CD: Minuswelt
Schattenschlag (2002). Unsterbliche Gier. *Flashback.* CD: Trisol
S.I.N.A. (2002). Die Your Life. *Back in Stereo.* EP: Hands
Sopor Aeternus (2003). *Es Reiten die Toten so Schnell.* CD: Apocalyptic Visions
Tanzwut (2003). *Ihr Wolltet Spass.* CD: EFA
Type O Negative (1993). *Bloody Kisses.* CD: Roadrunner
Type O Negative (1996). My Girlfriend's Girlfriend. *October Rust.* CD: Roadrunner
Type O Negative (2003). I Like Goils. *Life Is Killing Me.* CD: Roadrunner
Umbra et Imago (1998). Viva Lesbian. *Gedanken eines Vampirs.* CD: Indigo
Umbra et Imago (2002). *Die Welt Brennt.* DVD: Oblivion
V.A. (2003). *Septic 3.* CD: Dependent
Velvet Acid Christ (2003). *Hex Angel.* CD: Dependent
Wumpscut (1995). *Bunkertor 7.* CD: Beton Kopf Media
Wumpscut (1999). Ich Will Dich. *Boeses Junges Fleisch.* CD: Beton Kopf Media
Wumpscut (2003). All Cried out. *Preferential Tribe + Bonus.* DCD: Beton Kopf Media

Index